THE CYBER CITIZEN'S GUIDE THROUGH THE LEGAL JUNGLE

Internet Law for Your Professional Online Presence

JOY R. BUTLER

Sashay Communications, LLC

Published by Sashay Communications, LLC
2200 Wilson Boulevard, #102-329, Arlington, VA 22201
www.sashaycommunications.com

ISBN: 978-0-9672940-2-5

Cover and Original Interior Book Design by Shane Felux
Typesetting by JustYourType.biz

Publisher's Cataloging-In-Publication Data
(Prepared by The Donohue Group, Inc.)

Butler, Joy R.
    The cyber citizen's guide through the legal jungle : Internet law for your professional online presence / Joy R. Butler.

    p. ; cm. -- (Guide through the legal jungle)

    Includes bibliographical references and index.
    ISBN: 978-0-9672940-2-5

    1. Internet--Law and legislation--United States--Popular works. 2. Intellectual property--Law and legislation--United States--Popular works. 3. Electronic commerce--Law and legislation--United States--Popular works. I. Title.

KF390.5.C6 B85 2010
343.7309/944

OTHER BOOKS BY JOY R. BUTLER

The Permission Seeker's Guide Through the Legal Jungle:
Clearing Copyrights, Trademarks and Other Rights for
Entertainment and Media Productions

The Musician's Guide Through the Legal Jungle:
Answers to Frequently Asked Questions about Music Law
(Audiobook)

ACKNOWLEDGMENTS

Numerous people helped me in completing this book project.

Thank you to the law school students and recent law school graduates who worked as my research assistants. They are Laura Ball, Yuri Carhill, Cecille H. Chen, Amber Cornish, John DeRusso, Ranjit Doraiswamy, Justin Harris, Miguel P. Harvey, Tamara B. Hudson, Jaylen S. Johnson, Shermineh C. Jones, Fran Mokonogho, Colleen Mulcrone, Courtney Murphy, Jonathan Phillips, Lauren R. Phillips, Jack R. Reed III, La-Vaughnda A. Taylor, Nehanda Wheeler, and Nadia Zaidi. Much success to you in your legal careers.

I also thank and acknowledge my attorney colleagues from the media and intellectual property law bars who generously shared their time and legal expertise by reviewing and offering comments on portions of the book. These attorneys are Barbara I. Berschler, Maureen Cohen Harrington, Kathleen Cooney-Porter, Alan Lewine, M. Melisse Lewis, Leigh Ann Lindquist, John Davis Malloy, Andrew Mirsky, Darrell G. Mottley, Aoi Nawashiro, Laura Possessky, and Diana Michelle Sobo.

Finally, thanks to my mother, Elaine Randall Butler, for her editing and proofreading assistance. With all of her new hobbies since her retirement from a thirty-two year career in English literature and composition, she continues to find time to contribute to my writing projects in a meaningful way.

SUMMARY TABLE OF CONTENTS

TABLE OF CONTENTS

GUIDELINES AND CAUTIONS
FOR THE USE OF THIS BOOK

This book is designed to help you identify legal issues that arise as you develop and maintain your online presence. There are certain guidelines you should keep in mind as you use this book or any other book on legal issues.

The law is complex. To make this book easy to follow, discussions of legal principles have been simplified. Unless otherwise noted, this book covers only principles of United States law. Each principle of law is subject to differing interpretations and may have numerous exceptions. As this book provides a broad overview of the law, it may not cover an interpretation or an exception that applies to your specific legal situation.

The author and the publisher have made their best efforts to ensure that the information presented in this book is as complete and as accurate as possible. However, the internet and the law that governs it are fluid. Industry customs and laws change constantly. Always make sure that you are relying on the most up to date information.

Furthermore, every legal situation is unique. Neither this book nor any book is an adequate substitute for seeking legal advice from an attorney familiar with the circumstances of your particular situation. If you have a specific legal problem, you should consult an attorney.

As a result of the above, the author and the publisher cannot assume any responsibility or liability to any person or entity for any loss or damage caused, or alleged to be caused, by the information presented in this book.

PART ONE
Establishing Your Online Presence

Part One provides an overview of how this book is organized and how it can be useful to you as a cyber citizen. Part One includes a checklist which poses a series of questions about your internet activities and then refers you to subsequent sections of this book for more details on internet law issues relevant to your professional online presence.

Chapters in Part One:

INTRODUCTION 1

1.1. Are You a Cyber Citizen?

Yes, you are a cyber citizen—if you actively participate in cyberspace and the online community offered through the internet. Active cyberspace participation includes operating a website, blogging, podcasting, or contributing to a social networking site.

Before delving into what it means to be a good cyber citizen on the internet, we should define cyberspace and the internet. Although cyberspace and the internet are often used interchangeably, I view cyberspace as an amorphous term while the internet has a more solid, concrete definition.

1.1.1. What Is Cyberspace?

Cyberspace is the imaginary space in which you travel while on the internet. It is the non-physical space or virtual world that you access through your computer and in which you interact with other people.

1.1.2. What Is the Internet?

We talk about "the internet." However, the internet is not one centralized system nor is there a single person or organization that operates and controls the internet. Instead, the internet consists of tens of thousands of independently operated computer network systems around the world. A computer network is simply two or more computers connected in a manner that allows messages to be sent from one computer to another. Operators of computer networks hooked into the internet can be almost any person or any organization including an individual hobbyist, university, municipality, small businesses, Fortune 500 company, or government agency.

Several services are offered through the internet. The best known internet services are probably email and the world wide web. Email stands for electronic mail and is a message sent via the internet from one person to another. The world wide web is a collection of interconnected documents. The websites we visit are on the world wide web.

1.2. Who Should Read This Book?

If you actively use or want to use the internet to advance your business and professional endeavors, this book is for you. More companies and individuals have established online presences in conjunction with their business and professional endeavors. They produce and distribute their own online content through websites, blogs, podcasts, social networking sites, email newsletters, and other cyber communities.

As a good cyber citizen, you want to stay legal online and protect your online interests. This book addresses legal issues that arise during the process of establishing and maintaining your online presence.

1.3. How to Use This Book

Use this book as a reference tool for establishing and maintaining your online presence. You can read the book from cover to cover for a grounding in the internet laws that affect your professional online presence. Alternatively, you can go directly to the section that addresses your question of the moment. This reference book includes three parts:

Part One. Establishing Your Online Presence

Part Two. Knowing Your Online Rights and Responsibilities

Part Three. Engaging in Specific Online Activities

Part One, Establishing Your Online Presence, provides an overview of the internet and cyber law issues that impact you as a cyber citizen with a professional online presence. It includes a detailed checklist to help you spot issues and then refers you to subsequent sections of this book for greater explanation.

Part Two, Knowing Your Online Rights and Responsibilities, provides a detailed discussion of how you can protect your online presence including protecting original content, your domain name, and proprietary technology. Relevant laws discussed include copyright, trademark, patent, and trade secret laws. Part Two also includes a discussion of how and when you may use other people's materials, images, and names online and a discussion of your legal obligations to your online visitors and the greater online community.

Part Three, Engaging in Specific Online Activities, builds on Part Two. Many of the concepts and procedures discussed in this reference book apply to all internet activities. However, there are special considerations for certain types of online activities. Part Three offers a discussion of legal issues related to specific online activities such as fan sites, blogs, podcasts and social networking sites; explains some of these special considerations; and provides examples of how the concepts explained in Part Two apply to specific types of internet activities.

The book also includes an Appendix with resources and sample forms. The Appendix contains instructions for registering the copyrights and trademarks for your website, blog, and other online materials.

This book provides examples from real-life situations and legal battles to illustrate the results generated by particular sets of circumstances. While the real-life examples offered throughout this book provide insight into how your own situation might play out, they do not provide definitive answers. For attorneys and others who may want to read the entire court opinion from the real-life examples, I do include legal citations for most of the cases discussed. The legal citations provided typically do not include complete prior and subsequent case histories.

CHECKLIST OF LEGAL ISSUES FOR THE CYBER CITIZEN

The following checklist can help you spot legal issues relevant to your activities as a cyber citizen. By necessity, the discussion within the checklist is cryptic. The checklist refers you to subsequent sections of this book for greater explanation. The checklist is not an exhaustive list of every issue relevant to your online activities. Each question may not be relevant to you.

Protection and Ownership of Online Content

Have you created original online content you would like to protect? You can use copyright law as well as other laws to protect your online content. (Chapter 3) While copyright registration is not required for a valid copyright, copyright registration maximizes your ability to protect your content. (Chapter 4)

Is someone using your online content without your permission? If someone uses your online content without your permission, your options include sending a cease and desist letter, submitting a takedown notice, and filing a lawsuit. (Section 3.8)

Did someone else construct your site for you? If your employee created a portion of your website or other online work within the scope of his employment, you own the copyright in the online work as a work made for hire. If you retained a freelancer, the freelancer owns the copyright unless the freelancer signed a written agreement indicating otherwise. (Section 3.4)

Have you created an online work in collaboration with others? All collaborators have a right to claim joint copyright ownership of the resulting work—unless you have a written agreement that specifies otherwise. (Section 3.4)

Do you have a blog or other online work to which visitors contribute comments, articles, images, and other materials? You do not own the rights in the contributed material unless the contributor assigns you those rights. You likely have an implied license to post or otherwise use contributed material directly in connection with your blog or website. If you want to use the contributed material more broadly, you should include the right to do so in your terms of service. (Sections 11.2 and 15.2)

Does your online work incorporate technology that you want to protect? You may be able to protect it as a patent or as a trade secret. (Chapter 7)

Selection and Protection of Domain Names

Do you need to obtain a domain name? Domain name registrars issue domain names on a first-come, first-served basis. (Section 5.3) However, there can be legal consequences if you select a domain name that violates someone else's trademark rights. (Chapter 6)

Is the domain name you want unavailable? If your preferred domain name is unavailable, your options include selecting another domain name or attempting to purchase the domain name from its current holder. If someone else's use of the domain name violates your trademark, an additional option includes initiating a domain name dispute. (Section 5.3.1)

Is someone using a domain name that includes your trademark or your personal name? Not every unauthorized use of your trademark or personal name is an impermissible use. In those cases when an unauthorized use does violate the law, your options potentially include initiating an action under the Uniform Domain Name Dispute

Resolution Policy, the Anticybersquatting Consumer Protection Act, or traditional trademark laws. (Chapter 6)

Are you using a company name, trademark, or celebrity name as part of the domain name for your fan site, gripe site or criticism site? This is permissible if you use the domain name with a non-commercial site or in a manner that does not confuse consumers. (Section 6.8) Non-commercial websites include websites offering parody, criticism, or commentary. (Chapter 13)

Have you been accused of using a domain name that violates a trademark? If a trademark owner initiates a legal proceeding over your domain name, to be able to keep the domain name, you must demonstrate that one of the necessary elements for the trademark owner's successful claim is not true. Depending on how the trademark owner pursues the claim, your successful rebuttal may be that your domain name is not confusingly similar to the trademark, that your use of the domain name has not been in bad faith, or that your use of the domain name is non-commercial. (Sections 6.4, 6.5, and 6.6)

Is someone impersonating you online? Sometimes impersonation is a crime. (Section 9.4) Even when the impersonation does not amount to a crime, you can sometimes successfully challenge a domain name that uses your personal name in an improper manner. (Sections 6.9)

Using Third Party Materials

Do you want to incorporate someone else's content into your online work? As a general rule, you should obtain permission before using someone else's content. There are exceptions to this general rule. The First Amendment, copyright fair use, and other laws sometimes allow you to use other's material without permission. (Chapter 8)

Do you see elements on another website that would be perfect for your website? It is permissible to use ideas and facts from another website. (Section 3.3) It is not permissible to make a verbatim copy of another website or duplicate the website's look and feel. (Section 3.6.2)

Do you use music on your site? Normally, unless the music is in the public domain or your use qualifies as a fair use, you must obtain a license to use the music. (Sections 8.3, 8.5, and 8.6) The license required to use music on the internet depends on whether you use the song, the sound recording or both and how you use them. (Section 8.10)

Do you allow visitors to post material on your site? The Digital Millennium Copyright Act includes safe harbor protections that insulate online sites from claims of copyright infringement for material posted by their customers and online visitors. (Sections 3.8.2 and 12.5) Under the Communications Decency Act, if someone else posts a defamatory statement on your site, you are not legally responsible. (Section 8.9.3)

Privacy Concerns

Do you mention people by name or discuss actual events in your online work? You may use a person's name in non-commercial contexts such as news reporting and commentary sites. (Section 8.2 and Chapter 13) When focusing on real people, you should consider privacy, publicity, and defamation laws. (Section 8.9)

Have you posted an online privacy policy? Federal law does not require you to post a privacy policy unless your website collects personal information from children. However, some state laws may require posting of a privacy policy. (Sections 9.1 and 9.2)

Is your site targeted to children? If yes, you must comply with the provisions of the Children's Online Privacy Protection Act (COPPA). COPPA compliance includes posting a privacy policy, providing parental notice and getting parental consent before collecting personal information from children. (Section 9.2)

Do you send email announcements to existing and potential customers? You must comply with a federal law known as Controlling the Assault of Non-Solicited Pornography and Marketing Act (CAN-SPAM Act). The CAN-SPAM Act does not prohibit sending an initial email. Instead, it requires you to use honest business practices and to offer an opt-out mechanism. (Section 9.3)

Specific Online Activities

Do you report news online? If you offer news or public affairs information through a blog or other online forum, you may qualify as a journalist and have the same benefits and concerns as print and broadcast journalists. Specific laws of interest to online journalists include reporter's shield laws, fee waivers for Freedom of Information Act requests, and campaign finance laws. (Section 11.5)

Do you exchange files online? There are legal uses of peer-to-peer file sharing networks. Exchanging copyright-protected materials without permission is not a legal use of peer-to-peer file sharing. (Chapter 14)

Do you talk about your job on your blog or on other social network sites? An employer may legitimately fire an employee whose blog or internet activities include disclosing the employer's confidential information, making defamatory comments about the employer, threatening people in the work place, or violating the employer's social networking policies. An employer may not fire an employee for her online activities if the firing is motivated by an illegal reason. (Section 11.4)

Do you have a fan site or gripe site? The First Amendment protects your right to offer a non-commercial fan site, gripe site or other website through which you offer commentary. Commentary sites can lose their First Amendment protection if they become commercial, defamatory, or confusing to consumers. (Chapter 13)

Do you write and post online product reviews? If you receive the products for free or any other compensation for posting the reviews, federal guidelines indicate that you should disclose that fact. Federal guidelines also include the expectation that you provide truthful and substantiated descriptions of the products you review. (Section 11.5.3)

Do you post original content on social networking sites? While in most cases, you retain the copyright in your original content, most social networking sites take a non-exclusive license to use your content. (Chapter 10) If you incorporate other people's material into you social networking postings, there are some best practices you should consider following. (Sections 12.3 and 13.2)

PART TWO
Knowing Your Online Rights and Responsibilities

Part Two provides a discussion of your online rights including how you can protect your original content, domain name, and proprietary technology. Relevant laws discussed include copyright, trademark, patent, and trade secret laws. Part Two also includes a discussion of how and when you may use other people's materials, images, and names online and your legal obligations to your online visitors and the greater online community.

Chapters in Part Two:

PROTECTING YOUR ONLINE CONTENT 3

When you think of protection for the content you post online, copyright law is likely the first thing that comes to mind. Indeed, copyright law is the workhorse for the online protection of content and thus the focus of much of this chapter.

However, there are other laws that protect online content. They include the laws of contract, trade dress protection, trade secret protection, idea misappropriation, and other laws specifically targeted to online activities. This chapter also includes a discussion of how these laws can protect your online content.

3.1. Copyright Law Basics

The Copyright Act of 1976 governs current copyright law in the United States. Under current law, you have a valid copyright as soon as your work is *fixed in a tangible medium of expression*. That language comes directly from the Copyright Act and means that your work is copyrighted as soon as you write it down or record it. For example, as soon as you type the appropriate html code at your computer keyboard and your webpage appears on the screen of your monitor, your webpage is fixed in a tangible medium of expression and you have a valid copyright.

Producing a tangible form of your original, creative work is the sole requirement for copyright protection. Registration with the Copyright Office is not required; however, registration does provide a number of benefits. I discuss those benefits and the procedure for copyright registration in Chapter 4.

Copyright law protects original creative works such as books, poems, magazine articles, artwork, songs, sound recordings, designs and, of course, websites and other online materials. It takes very little to meet the originality threshold for copyright protection. Your work is original as long as you do not copy it from another source.

The Copyright Act has its own jargon. All creations are works regardless of whether they are sculptures, songs or online newsletters. The creators of those works are authors.

3.2. Your Exclusive Rights in Your Copyrighted Work

As the owner of a copyright, you have certain exclusive rights in your work. With some limited exceptions, this exclusivity makes you the sole person who may use your copyrighted work or authorize others to use it. The Copyright Act provides six exclusive rights:

Exclusive Right to Reproduce the Copyrighted Work. When you print, download, or stream an online work, you are reproducing that work. Although I am not aware of any court rulings on this point, most legal commenters believe that a visitor to a publicly accessible online work may legally print one copy of the work for his personal and non-commercial use. The visitor's right to make one copy comes pursuant to an implied license or as a fair use exception to copyright law.

Exclusive Right to Distribute Copies or Phonorecords of the Copyrighted Work to the Public. When you forward or give a copy of a work to someone else, you are distributing the work. There are outstanding questions concerning whether putting up a webpage or making other online materials available to the public qualifies as distributing the work. This question has become especially relevant in the music industry in the context of peer-to-peer file sharing. See Section 14.2.1 for further discussion of the making available argument in the music and entertainment industries.

Exclusive Right to Prepare Derivative Works Based on the Copyrighted Work. A derivative work is a new work based on or derived from another pre-existing work. For example, if you write new lyrics for an existing song, your song with the new lyrics is a derivative work of the existing song.

Here is an example more relevant to the internet. Julie Powell was an aspiring actress sidelined to a job as an administrative temp. Powell worked through her professional frustrations by challenging herself to cook every recipe in Julia Child's *Mastering the Art of French Cooking* within a one-year period. Powell blogged about her cooking project throughout the year. After Powell's blog became wildly popular, she turned the blog postings into a memoir titled *Julie & Julia: 365 Days, 524 Recipes, 1 Tiny Apartment Kitchen*. Powell's book, *Julie & Julia*, is a derivative work of her blog. Subsequently, the movie, *Julie & Julia*, was produced and released. The movie is a derivative work of the book and blog.

Exclusive Right to Perform the Copyrighted Work Publicly. The exclusive right of public performance applies only to works that can be performed. Such works include songs, plays, and films. As the copyright owner, you do not have an exclusive right to control private performances of your work. You control only public performances.

Disagreements on what constitutes a *public performance* versus what constitutes a *private performance* have sparked many lawsuits. According to the Copyright Act, a performance is public if the performance takes place before a number of people substantially larger than the number of people within a family circle. Court opinions tell us that a performance can qualify as public even if:

- The people viewing or hearing the performance are geographically dispersed as in the case of a radio broadcast received in numerous private homes.

- The people see or hear the performance at different times as in the case of a performance rendered through a website.

- Only a small number of people hear or view the performance if a larger number of people had access to the performance.

Hence, there can be a public performance even if an online work is streamed on-demand to one person at a time.

Exclusive Right to Display the Copyrighted Work Publicly. The applicability of the display right depends on the type of work. You can publicly display a painting or a sculpture or publicly display a song if, for example, you display the song lyrics. In contrast, it is not possible to publicly display other types of works such as a sound recording.

For Sound Recordings, the Exclusive Right to Perform the Copyrighted Work Publicly by Means of a Digital Audio Transmission. This exclusive right is applicable only to sound recordings that are digitally transmitted. A digital transmission conveys information in a format that a computer understands using a stream of 0's and 1's. Hence, this performance right applies to performances of sound recordings on the internet, on satellite radio, and cable television. For further discussion on what a sound recording is and how a sound recording differs from a song, see Section 8.10.1.

3.3. What Is Not Protected by Copyright?

Certain elements are not eligible for copyright protection. These elements include ideas, procedures, processes, systems, methods of operation, principles, discoveries, titles, short phrases, and facts.

3.3.1. Ideas

Ideas are not protected by copyright but the expression of the idea is. Separating the "idea" from the "expression of the idea" is often subjective and not necessarily intuitive.

For example, suppose you own a women's clothing store. A local competitor operates a website on which it offers coupons, discusses upcoming sales and special events, and provides fashion advice. You decide to develop a website that highlights your inventory, upcoming special events, and special sales. Like your local competitor, you offer fashion advice on your website. Building a website featuring your business activities is a relatively raw idea and you are free to implement it even if you got the idea from observing your competitor. However, if you duplicate actual text, photographs, design and layout from your competitor's website, you have crossed the line from using the raw idea to using the manner in which your competitor expresses the idea. Such verbatim duplication is copyright infringement.

3.3.2. Procedures

Procedures, processes, systems, methods of operations, principles, and discoveries are not copyrightable. While such elements cannot be protected by copyright, they may be eligible for trade secret or patent protection which I briefly discuss in Section 3.7.4 and Chapter 7.

One example of a procedure or process related to the internet is a patent held by Audible. Audible, a company that provides downloadable audiobooks, holds a patent in a method and apparatus for the secure streaming of digital audio and visual content.

3.3.3. Names, Titles, and Short Phrases

Names, titles, and short phrases lack the originality and creativity required for copyright protection. Your domain name is among those names and short phrases that do not qualify for copyright protection. Although they have no protection under copyright law, under certain conditions, names, titles, short phrases, including domain names, may be protected by trademark law. See the discussion of trademark basics in Section 5.5.

3.3.4. Facts

Facts are not copyrightable. Copyright protection requires at least a minimal level of originality. If you research and write down facts, the result of your efforts is not original. You did not independently create the facts. Hence, the facts by themselves are not subject to copyright protection regardless of the research time and effort you spent gathering them.

For example, one sunless tanning product manufacturer sued a competitor claiming that the competitor had infringed its online Frequently Asked Questions webpage. The manufacturer lost the lawsuit. It was true that both webpages used common words such as "can," "is," "what" and "will" at the beginning of each question. However, none of the competitor's questions was worded identically. The sequence, webpage layouts, and the number of questions also differed. The only similarities between the two webpages were factual similarities. Both companies provided a similar product made from similar ingredients. It was therefore inevitable that their Frequently Asked Questions webpages would cover similar information. (*Miston-Systems v. Gilley's European Tan Spa*, 303 F. Supp. 2d 974 (W.D. Wis. 2002)).

While raw facts and data are not copyrightable on their own, a compilation of facts may be eligible for copyright protection. I discuss copyright ownership for compilations in Section 3.6.3

3.4. Who Owns the Copyright in an Online Work?

The same rules that apply to the copyright ownership of hard copy works apply to online works. In most cases, the creator of the online work owns the copyright in that work. Ownership questions can become complicated when collaborators, freelancers, and employees participate in creating the work.

Created by You. If you are the sole creator of the work, you are the sole copyright owner.

Created by You and Collaborator. You might have assistance in creating your online work. A collaborator might be a co-writer, co-producer, illustrator, or editor. If you do not intend for the work to be a joint work and for your collaborators to share copyright ownership of the online work, you should confirm those intentions in writing.

Joint Work by Accident. You do not need a contract for the creation of a joint work. It is possible to take on a joint author without the explicit intention of doing so. Anyone who contributes material to your project has a potentially valid claim as a joint author, and thus, joint owner. To qualify as a joint author, the contributor must make more than a minimal contribution to the work and the material contributed must be copyrightable on its own merit. As discussed in Section 3.3, certain elements are not copyrightable. These elements include ideas, names, titles, and facts. A contributor who contributes only such elements has not contributed independently copyrightable material and, thus, does not have a claim of joint authorship.

Rights of Joint Authors. Unless the authors agree otherwise, each joint author is an equal owner of the copyrighted work. Each joint author may exercise the exclusive rights in the work. As a joint author, you may grant non-exclusive licenses for use of the work without permission from your co-authors. The only requirement is that you give your co-authors a proportionate share of any licensing revenue. All authors must agree to an outright sale of the work or to the grant of an exclusive license in the work.

Created by an Employee/Work Made For Hire. When an employee creates a work as part of his job, the resulting work is a work made for hire and copyright law views the employer as the author of the work. As the recognized author, the employer—and not the person who actually created the work—has the authority to exercise all the exclusive rights I discuss in Section 3.2.

There is sometimes disagreement about whether a person is an employee. Just because you call the person your employee, does not necessarily mean that the law will agree. How the parties act within the relationship carries much more weight than the label the parties give to the relationship. A court evaluates whether the relationship has elements that are more like an employer-employee relationship or more like a client-freelancer relationship. Elements that distinguish the two relationships include the amount of supervision provided, control over schedule and work site, supply of tools and materials, and whether the person in the employer role acts like a typical employer by doing things such as withholding taxes and providing employee benefits.

Created by a Freelancer or Other Third Party. You might retain a freelancer or outsource the work to another company. A copyrighted work created by a freelancer is owned by the freelancer unless the freelancer indicates otherwise in writing. Your agreement with the freelancer might convey the entire copyright to you, or the freelancer may retain copyright and simply license certain uses to you.

If there is no written agreement, you have, at most, a license to use the online work for the purposes for which you ordered it. Failure to put your agreement in writing can lead to a copyright dispute between you and the freelancer regarding who owns the online work and what rights you have to use it.

For example, in one such case, a computer consultant hired to update and host two websites filed a copyright infringement action after the client moved the websites to another server. While the computer consultant and client had no formal written agreement, the consultant had confirmed the arrangement in a letter to the client. Although the letter did not address ownership or licensing issues, the court decided that the client had an implied, irrevocable, nonexclusive license in the website. (*Attig v. DRG, Inc.*, 74 U.S.P.Q.2d 1614 (E.D. Pa. 2005)).

In this case, the situation ultimately resolved itself in favor of the client. While you may ultimately win the right to continue using an online work you have commissioned without a proper written agreement, achieving that result can be an expensive proposition.

3.5. Copyright Law Formalities

Under current law, there are no formal actions required to obtain and maintain a copyright. However, such formalities existed under previous versions of United States copyright law. While compliance with most formalities is no longer required, the formalities still have some impact on maximizing your rights and determining the copyright duration of older works. Formalities include copyright registration, copyright notice, and copyright renewal.

3.5.1. Copyright Registration

While you do not need to register your copyright with the Copyright Office in order to have valid copyright protection, registration does offer several benefits. I discuss the benefits of and the procedures for copyright registration in Chapter 4.

3.5.2. Copyright Notice

Prior to March 1989, publishing a work without a proper notice could result in the loss of copyright protection. Copyrighted works published on or after March 1, 1989, are not required to have a copyright notice. The change occurred when the United States joined the Berne Convention, an international copyright treaty, and modified certain provisions of United States copyright law to bring them into compliance with the treaty.

Even though you are no longer required to use a copyright notice, it is still a good idea to include a notice on all your work for a number of reasons:

- to inform the public that the work is protected by copyright
- to identify yourself as the owner and make it easier for people to find you if they want to license your work
- to show the year of first publication

Including notice carries another benefit in the event your published work is infringed. If your work contains a proper copyright notice, an infringer can not claim he did not realize that the work was protected by copyright and that his unauthorized use was accidental or innocent. This is important because the amount of money damages a court awards you against an innocent infringer may be much less than the amount to which you would otherwise be entitled.

A proper copyright notice contains three elements:

- the word "Copyright", the abbreviation "Copr.", or the symbol for Copyright which is ©
- the year of first publication
- the name of the copyright owner

These three elements should appear together. Here are examples of proper copyright notices:

Copyright 2010 Karla Webmaster

Copr. 2008 William Writer

If you release subsequent editions of your work, the notice can include the year of first publication and the year of each subsequent edition. For example, if you first launched your website in 2009 and make revisions in 2011, your copyright notice might read as follows:

Copyright 2009, 2011 by Tonya Finnegan

3.5.3. Copyright Renewal

Copyright renewal is relevant to works governed by the previous copyright statute, the 1909 Copyright Act. It is not relevant to works created in or after 1978 which are works governed by the current copyright statute, the Copyright Act of 1976. Nevertheless, renewal does impact the copyright duration of contemporary works.

Under the 1909 Copyright Act, copyright lasted for an initial term of twenty-eight years. After the initial twenty-eight-year term, copyright owners could renew the term for an additional number of years.

If the work was published prior to 1964, the copyright owner had to file a renewal application with the Copyright Office in order to receive the additional term. If the copyright owner failed to file the renewal application, the work fell into the public domain after expiration of the initial twenty-eight-year term. Filing a renewal application is not a requirement for maximizing the copyright term of works published in or after 1964.

For more information on renewal requirements and the copyright duration of specific works, see Sections 8.6.1 and 8.6.2.

3.5.4. Publication

While not technically a copyright formality, I discuss publication of your copyright work in this section because the publication date can impact your copyright. First, the publication date impacts the duration of copyright and public domain status for certain works. I discuss this concept further in Section 8.6.1. Second, the publication date determines whether or not your copyright registration is timely which in turn determines whether you are eligible to receive statutory damages in a copyright infringement lawsuit. I discuss the interrelationships among timely registration, publication, and statutory damages further in Section 4.1.

Effective Publication. When is a work published? In order for a work to be considered published, multiple copies of the work must be available to the public with the authorization of the copyright owner. The public display of a work or the distribution to a few friends does not necessarily qualify as a publication.

While the deceptively simple question of "When is a work published?" has not always had a straight-forward answer, issues surrounding publication have grown more complicated with the increase of internet activity. Posting music files, software or photographs on a webpage has been held in numerous instances to constitute publication. When a website goes live and becomes accessible to the public, multiple copies of the work are then available to the public. Whether publishing and making copies available constitutes the exclusive right of distributing the copies is a hotly debated issue in peer-to-peer file sharing cases. I discuss the making available argument further in Section 14.2.1.

3.6. Specific Online Content Protected by Copyright

Some categories of content and works entitled to copyright protection are obvious. They include books, magazines, newspapers, poems, songs, plays, photographs, paintings, sculptures, films, and designs. Other categories of content and works entitled to copyright protection are less obvious. Below I discuss a few of the less obvious categories most relevant to cyber citizens.

3.6.1. Computer Code and HTML

Copyright law protects computer programs. The Copyright Act defines a computer program as a set of statements or instructions to be used directly or indirectly in a computer in order to bring about a certain result.

Hypertext markup language, or html, is one of the computer programs used to create webpages. In comparison with most computer programs, html is relatively simple. Html consists of tags that "tell" a webpage how to format itself. For example, <p> is the html tag to tell the webpage to begin a new paragraph; <b> is the html tag to tell the webpage to put text in bold print; and <ul> is the html tag to tell the webpage to begin a bulleted list of items.

Suppose you visit a webpage on the website of a company called Al's Auto Repair. You might see the following text:

This Week's Specials at Al's Auto Repair

- Oil Change, $29.95
- Tire Rotation, $69.95
- Brake Pad and Rotor Replacement (front or rear), $225

Call us at 555-1212 to schedule an appointment.

You can view the html of any webpage you access through your web browser. For example, if you use the Internet Explorer web browser to view websites, to view the html code of any webpage you are viewing, you select "Source" from the "View" pull-down menu. If you did that while at the Al's Auto Repair webpage above, the html you would see might look like this:

```
<b>This Week's Specials at Al's Auto Repair</b>

<p>
<ul><li> Oil Change, $29.95
<li> Tire Rotation, $69.95
<li>Brake Pad and Rotor Replacement (front <u>or</u> rear), $225</ul>

<p>Call us at 555-1212 to schedule an appointment.
```

It is copyright infringement to copy someone's html code verbatim or in large quantities and simply paste it into your own webpage.

On the other hand, the html behind two webpages may share similarities due to the fact the two resulting webpages offer similar information or serve similar functions. This is fine provided that the two webpages were in fact independently created and one html programmer did not deliberately copy the html code of another programmer.

3.6.2. Look and Feel

Look and feel refers to the overall appearance of a copyrighted work. You may not deliberately duplicate the look and feel of another copyrighted work.

For example, the Elliot Institute for Social Sciences Research, a Missouri-based advocacy group that opposes stem cell research, built a website that used the exact same pictures in the exact same layout on each webpage as used on the website of the Missouri Coalition for Lifesaving Cures, a Missouri-based advocacy group that supports stem cell research. The Missouri Coalition argued that by using the same pictures and the same layout, the Elliot Institute had copied the look and feel of the Missouri Coalition website and, thus, infringed the Missouri Coalition's copyright.

A court agreed with the Missouri Coalition and ruled that the Elliot Institute had committed copyright infringement by duplicating the Missouri Coalition's website's look and feel. (*Peri Hall & Associates, Inc. v. Elliot Institute for Social Sciences Research*, 78 U.S.P.Q.2d 1414 (W.D. Mo. 2006)).

You must distinguish look and feel from elements that are not protectable by copyright. One lawsuit involved two competing websites: yachtbroker.com and yachtworld.com. The websites offered listings of yachts available for sale. Yachtbroker copied certain content from Yachtworld. The copied content included pictures and descriptions of yachts for sale. The copyrights in the pictures and descriptions were owned by the brokers offering the yachts for sale and not by either of the website companies. Hence, Yachtworld had no copyright interests in those pictures and descriptions. Yachtbroker did not copy the html of Yachtworld's webpage so Yachtbroker was not guilty of infringing the copyright in Yachtworld's html. While Yachtworld alleged infringement of the look and feel of its website, the court found that Yachtbroker displayed and arranged the copied content in a substantially different manner. For example, Yachtbroker presented descriptions in a table while Yachtworld presented descriptions in a bulleted list; Yachtbroker placed the pictures to the right of the text while Yachtworld placed pictures to the left of text; and Yachtbroker used a different color scheme and logo than used by Yachtworld.

The court said any similarities between the two websites resulted from the common use of elements Yachtworld could not protect such as factual headings and descriptions and pictures owned by others. The Yachtbroker website had not infringed the look and feel of the Yachtworld website. (*Nautical Solutions Mktg., Inc. v. Boats.com*, Copyright Law Reporter P28,815 (M.D. Fla., April 1, 2004)).

3.6.3. Compilations and Databases

A compilation is a collection of pre-existing materials or data. A database is a type of compilation. If you present the compilation in a manner that is original, you can claim a copyright in the compilation.

Copyright in Compilation Versus Copyright in Compiled Material. The copyright in the compilation is distinct from the copyright in the material you have compiled. Even when you can claim copyright ownership in the compilation, you may not always be able to claim copyright ownership in the underlying material. The underlying material may not be eligible for copyright protection or it might not be copyrighted material in which you own the rights. For example, if you compile raw facts, the underlying material of the compilation is not copyrightable since, as discussed in Section 3.3.4, facts are not subject to copyright protection. In contrast, if you compile your original photographs, the underlying material within the compilation is your copyrighted work. If you compile photographs that were taken by others, the underlying material within your compilation is copyrighted material but it is not your copyrighted material.

Compilations That Qualify for Copyright Protection. For copyright law to protect your compilation, you must use some originality in its creation. Copyright law does not care how much time, money, or resources you devote to the compilation. The good news for compilers is that the originality threshold is very low. Hence, many compilations pass the originality test. For a compilation, originality is based on the selection, arrangement, and coordination of the material. For copyright protection to apply, there must be originality in at least one of these elements.

Selection is the exercise of judgment in choosing which materials to include in the compilation.

Arrangement is the ordering or grouping of material into lists or categories. Arrangement must go beyond the mere mechanical grouping of data. If you arrange the material in alphabetical, chronological, or sequential order, it is unlikely your arrangement will meet the originality threshold to qualify for copyright protection.

Coordination is often used interchangeably with the concept of arrangement. Although case law does not clearly define the term, courts seem to view coordination as an organizational activity that goes beyond arrangement and affects how one element of the compilation complements another.

Real-Life Examples of Compilation Copyrightability from the Phone Book Industry. A progeny of cases involving phone books illustrates the cut-off point at which a compilation is deemed sufficiently original for copyright protection.

Where the producer of a white pages phone book selected basic information such as name, town and telephone number of each person applying for phone service and arranged the information in alphabetical order by surname, there was no creativity in and therefore no copyright protection for the phone book. (_Feist Publications v. Rural Telephone_, 499 U.S. 340 (1991)).

In contrast, a telephone book of New York City's Chinese-American community did qualify for a compilation copyright. The creator showed originality in selection by exercising judgment to find those businesses of interest to the target audience. The creator also arranged the businesses in a manner that would appeal to the Chinese-American community and included some categories not common to yellow pages. (_Key Publications v. Chinatown Today Publishing_, 945 F.2d 509 (2d Cir. 1991)).

Databases. A database is a type of compilation. The traditional definition for a database is a collection of information or data that can be used with a computer or an electronic format.

Typically, a database contains fields and records. A field is a category of information or one item of data. A record consists of all the fields for one entry. For example, envision a database of employee information at a company. The collected information for each employee is a record. Each item of information in the record is a field. In this example, the fields within each record might list the name, social security number, title, home address, and home phone number for that employee.

When a database consists of raw information or data, the data is not copyrightable. However, the database as a whole may qualify for copyright as a compilation. Like any other compilation seeking copyright protection, the database must exhibit some originality in its arrangement, selection, or coordination.

A sample case in which a database of raw data was deemed a copyrightable compilation involved property tax assessment data. In this case, the compilation was quite complicated. The tax assessment data was automatically allocated into 456 fields. Those 456 fields were in turn grouped into thirty-four master categories referred to as tables. The database would not have been viewed as a copyrightable compilation had the tax assessment data been organized in an obvious manner such as an alphabetical listing by name or a numerical listing by taxpayer id number. (*Assessment Technologies of Wisconsin v. WIREdata*, 350 F.3d 640 (7th Cir. 2003)).

Infringement of Your Compilation or Database Copyright. Even when protected by copyright, the level of protection for a compilation is often low. Works with a low threshold of copyright protection are often referred to as having a weak or thin copyright. The less copyright protection a work receives, the more similarity between the original work and potentially infringing work is required for a finding of copyright infringement.

One issue for a database on the internet is spidering. A spider is a program that visits websites, reads their information, and catalogs the information for various applications. For example, Google builds up its search engine of website pages in part through the use of spiders. Spiders are also referred to as bots or crawlers. If you have a database of raw data, anyone may spider or copy the raw data without violating copyright law although other laws, discussed in Section 3.7, may be violated by the unauthorized access and copying of your online database. In contrast, duplication of any original arrangement, selection, or coordination in your online database is an infringement. Here are some real-life examples illustrating these points about infringement of databases:

Significant Copying Required for Database with Thin Copyright. There was potential infringement of the online compilation created by Benbargains.net, a website that posts daily lists of the best internet deals for various products. BensBargains' owner used his individual judgment to select and arrange the deals. Thus, the compilations were original and entitled to copyright protection. When a competitor began copying BensBargains' deals, the court concluded that while there was no copying of the arrangement, there was sufficient similarity in the selection of deals to allow a lawsuit to continue.

Since the database carried a thin copyright, the court allowed BensBargains' lawsuit to continue only for those compilations from which the competitor had copied seventy percent or more of the listed deals. The court did not allow the lawsuit to continue for those compilations from which the competitor had copied less than seventy percent of the listed deals. (*BensBargains v. XPBargains*, No. 06cv1445 BTM (S.D. Cal., Aug. 16, 2007)).

Internet Spiders Aren't All Bad. In a case involving information about yachts, one compiler of yacht information spidered a competitor's website, copied the information, and indexed those facts in a searchable database. The spider made only a momentary copy while it extracted the descriptions and pictures. It did not copy the html or the entire webpage. Individual yacht owners owned the copyright to the pictures and descriptions. The court held that the spidering of the website and extraction of its raw data was a fair use. Also, since the compiler displayed the copied content in a substantially different arrangement from its competitor, there was no infringement of any compilation copyright. (*Nautical Solutions v. Boats.com*, Copyright Law Reporter P28,815 (M.D. Fla. April 1, 2004)).

3.7. Other Laws that Protect Your Online Content

While copyright is the workhorse for protecting online content, it is not the only law useful for this purpose. In this section, I discuss laws other than copyright available to cyber citizens who want to protect their online content. The laws covered in this section is not an exhaustive list of federal and state claims that may be useful in protecting content.

3.7.1. Contracts and Terms of Service

The purpose of a written contract is to document that two or more people have reached a mutual understanding. The terms of service in which you outline the guidelines and rules for accessing your on-line work can form a binding contract with visitors to your website. Terms of service are also sometimes referred to as terms and conditions or terms of use.

Terms of service frequently come in the form of a click-wrap agreement. A click-wrap agreement is a contract for the purchase, use or license of products or services offered online. The visitor or purchaser agrees to the terms by clicking on an icon which is typically a button that says "I Agree." Since the online visitor or purchaser has little input into what the terms provide, courts verify that the contract is reasonable before they will enforce it.

Reasonable Terms. Your terms of service must be reasonable. If the terms appear to be too one-sided or overreaching, a court may declare the terms to be unenforceable.

Reasonable Notice. In order for the terms of service to be enforceable, the customer must have reasonable notice of the agreement and an opportunity to opt out of the agreement. If you do not require clicking of an "I Agree" or similar button, you should at least prominently feature a link to the terms. Most owners of online works place a link to their terms of service on each webpage. Prominence of the terms may make the difference between being able to enforce your terms and not being able to enforce them.

Ability to Review and Save. Your online visitors must have an opportunity to review the terms in their entirety before agreeing to them. Online visitors should also have the ability to save a copy of the terms for future reference.

3.7.2. Hot News/Misappropriation

Hot news is information that is valuable due to its timeliness and freshness. Hot news typically has a short lifespan because it quickly becomes old news that is known to everyone.

Here is an example of information that might qualify as hot news. Imagine your business compiles and analyzes the daily performance of the stock and capital markets and you release such information for each trading day immediately after the close of business on the trading day. While the information you provide is valuable to financial professionals as they plan out their strategies for the next trading day, the information is valuable only if they receive it within a short-time frame. The information for the market's performance on May 4 is very valuable on the morning of May 5 but much less valuable a month later on June 5.

If your online work focuses on providing hot news and someone is usurping that hot news, you may be able to make a hot news or misappropriation claim. Such claims are usually based on state unfair competition and other laws. In general, to win a hot news claim, you must show the following:

- You generate or collect information at some cost or expense.
- The value of the information you collect is highly time-sensitive.
- Someone else uses the information in direct competition with your product or service and that person's use constitutes free-riding on your efforts.

- The other person's free-riding is a disincentive to your continuing to collect the information and offer your product or service.

3.7.3. Trade Dress Protection

Trade dress laws protect the appearance of a product. Stated simply, trade dress protects the packaging and manner in which a product is presented. This may include features such as size, shape, color, color combinations, texture, graphics, and even particular sales techniques. For example, trade dress has been used to protect the appearance of a video game console, the overall look of greeting cards, the layout and appearance of a mail order catalogue, and the overall look of sales brochures.

Trade dress is a component of trademark law and is governed by provisions of the federal Trademark Act of 1946, often referred to as the Lanham Act, as well as by provisions of parallel state trademark and unfair competition laws. To prevail in a federal trade dress infringement claim, you must show that:

- Your trade dress is inherently distinctive or has acquired secondary meaning.

- Your trade dress is primarily non-functional. The test for functionality is whether the feature is essential to the product's purpose, use, cost, or quality. The intent of the non-functional requirement is that no one be able to monopolize useful designs and product features by claiming them as trade dress.

- The defendant's trade dress is confusingly similar to the trade dress of your product.

I discuss the trademark law concepts of distinctiveness, secondary meaning, and confusing similarity further in Section 5.5.

It is still debatable as to whether trade dress protection extends to online works. While academics support the theory that trade dress protection should protect the look and feel of a website, I am not aware of any court cases that have conclusively made this determination.

3.7.4. Trade Secret Protection

A trade secret is confidential information of a particular company that gives the company a competitive advantage over other businesses. The primary benefit comes from the fact that other companies do not have the same information. Specifically, a trade secret can consist of a practice, a method, a design, computer software, a customer list, a database, a compilation of information, or other know-how.

Trade secret protection is based primarily on state law and can theoretically last forever. To prevail on a trade secret claim, you must show the following:

- the misappropriated information constitutes a trade secret,
- the defendant used the trade secret, and
- you were actually damaged by the misappropriation or the defendant was unjustly enriched by such misappropriation and use.

For example, it was possible for a user name and pass code required for access to an online medical database to qualify as a trade secret under California law. In this case, the medical database owner sued a customer which purchased a single-user subscription and then shared the access information with numerous employees. (*Therapeutic Research Facility v. NBTY*, 488 F. Supp. 2d 991 (E.D. Cal. 2007)).

I discuss using trade secrets to protect technology in Section 7.5.

3.7.5. Idea Misappropriation

As discussed in Section 3.3.1, copyright law does not protect ideas. It protects only the expression of the idea. While it is often difficult to protect a raw idea, some states do have misappropriation laws that cover ideas. Success under these idea misappropriation laws requires proof that you submitted the idea with the intention of selling it and proof that the person to whom you submitted the idea actually used the idea.

Idea misappropriation cases are difficult to win—and even more difficult to win in a meaningful manner. One must prove the monetary value of the idea and, thus, the monetary damage award that one should receive from the person who misappropriated the idea. That can be difficult.

3.7.6. Computer Fraud and Abuse Act

The Computer Fraud and Abuse Act (CFAA) is a federal law designed to reduce the hacking of computer systems. The CFAA prohibits accessing a protected computer without permission or in a way that exceeds authorization. While the CFAA is a primarily criminal statute, it does allow individuals and companies to file civil lawsuits under certain conditions. A few conditions apply for use of the CFAA as a claim in a civil lawsuit:

- The computer must be a protected computer. A protected computer is a computer used by or for a financial institution or the federal government or that is used in interstate or foreign commerce or communication.
- The transmission or access must be unauthorized.
- The transmission or access must cause damage. The damage can be a loss of money.

For example, the owner of an online database had a legitimate CFAA claim against a customer that gave access to multiple employees when the customer had purchased a license for only one user. (*Therapeutic Research Faculty v. NBTY* 488 F. Supp.2d 991 (E.D.Ca. 2007)).

3.7.7. Stored Communications Act

The Stored Wire and Electronic Communications and Transactional Records Access law is part of the federal Electronic Communications Privacy Act. It is referred to as the Stored Communications Act for short.

Under the Stored Communications Act, "a person or entity providing an electronic communication service to the public shall not knowingly divulge to any person or entity the contents of a communication while in electronic storage by that service . . . ." In other words, your internet service provider can not hand over your email communications to a third party who asks for them. There are exceptions to this prohibition including permissible disclosures related to child abuse and permissible disclosures related to authorized wiretaps.

The exceptions do not include discovery requests and subpoenas issued as part of a civil lawsuit. For example, if you were sued, the person suing you could subpoena email communications that are in your possession. However, the person suing you cannot force a third party provider like AOL to hand over your personal communications as such action would violate the Stored Communications Act.

In a case involving Apple Computer, the Stored Communications Act protected the content of private messages stored by an email host provider. Apple wanted the content of private messages stored by an email host provider to learn the Apple insiders who had divulged confidential information about a product in development. Apple's attempts were blocked due to the Stored Communications Act. (*O'Grady v. Superior Court*, 44 Cal. Rptr. 3d 72 (2006)).

3.8. Options if Your Online Content Is Used without Your Permission

What should you do if someone uses your work without your permission? First, you should evaluate whether the use is one that does not require your permission such as a use that qualifies under the Copyright Act's fair use doctrine. Sections 8.2 through 8.5 include a discussion of uses that do not require permission. If you determine that someone has used your online work in a manner that infringes your rights, there are a few options open to you.

3.8.1. Cease and Desist Letter

You can send a cease and desist letter. A cease and desist letter is a letter that a rights owner or her attorney sends to someone who is allegedly violating her rights. In the letter, you explain how the other party is violating your rights and demand that the party cease those activities. There are right ways and wrong ways to send cease and desist letters.

Cease and desist letters usually carry the threat of additional legal action, usually a lawsuit, if the other party does not stop the infringing activity. In some cases, the sender means business and has the intention and the resources to follow through with a lawsuit if the other party fails to comply.

In other cases, the cease and desist letter is the equivalent of huffing and puffing with insufficient power to blow the house down. In effect, the rights owner is just bluffing, has no valid legal argument against the other party's activities, and simply hopes that the cease and desist letter will scare the other party into compliance. Sometimes the other party calls the bluff. A cease and desist letter too strongly worded can backfire as bad publicity for the sender.

A Mild-Mannered Cease and Desist Letter. Cease and Desist letters do not have to be mean and nasty. As a blogger, my blog postings sometimes get copied. Here is an example of my mild-mannered cease and desist letter to one person who took my content without providing any attribution:

Dear Blogger,

I noticed your March 11 blog entry entitled "Key Legal Issues for Bloggers." Your entire posting is a verbatim duplicate of my blog posting located at www.GuideThroughtheLegalJungleBlog.com. As you probably know, your action is an infringement of my copyrighted material.

If you want to keep my entry up on your blog, please include an attribution to me by adding to the posting "Written by Joy Butler, attorney and blogger. Please send me a reply email by Friday, February 1 to confirm that you have taken this action.

In the future if you see any postings on my blog that you like, consider submitting a comment on my blog or posting an "original" commentary on your blog with a link to the posting you like.

Sincerely,
Joy Butler

3.8.2. DMCA Takedown Notice

If the infringement is online and the infringer is based in the United States, you can submit a takedown notice to the social networking site or to the web host pursuant to the Digital Millennium Copyright Act (DMCA). The DMCA includes safe harbor protections that insulate online sites from claims of copyright infringement for material posted by their customers and online visitors. To qualify for the DMCA safe harbor, online sites must comply with several requirements which include removing infringing material upon the request of the copyright owner.

The DMCA refers to the request as a takedown notice. The takedown notice must identify the copyrighted work, describe the infringing activity, indicate the online location of the infringing material, and provide other specific information. If the site hopes to enjoy DMCA protection, it will have instructions online regarding to whom and how to submit such a takedown notice. The Appendix includes examples of DMCA takedown notices.

Abuse of the DMCA Takedown Provision. While the DMCA offers remedies for the improper removal of material and a mechanism for customers to submit a counter notice requesting reposting of improperly removed material, there have been many complaints of copyright owners abusing the DMCA takedown notice provisions.

Sometimes, the situation turns into a dance of takedown notices and counter notices.

Brian Kopp is the author of *The Ultimate World of Warcraft Leveling & Gold Guide*, an instructional book for the video game, *World of Warcraft*. While Kopp's book does not contain any of the game's copyrighted text or storyline, it does contain screen shots of the game. Vivendi Universal Games, the parent company of the game maker, objected to Kopp's book, sent takedown letters to eBay, and got Kopp's eBay store shut-down several times.

Kopp decided to fight back and filed a suit asking for a court ruling that his book's use of the screen shot qualifies as a fair use. Before the lawsuit advanced very far, the parties settled. As part of the settlement, Vivendi agreed to stop objecting to Kopp's sale of the instructional book. (*Kopp v. Vivendi Universal Games*, No. 2:2006cv01767, (C.D. Cal. 2006, *dismissed* June 14, 2006)).

3.8.3. Lawsuit

If a cease and desist letter or DMCA takedown notice does not resolve the issue, a lawsuit alleging copyright infringement or other violation may be the only remaining alternative. Unfortunately, a lawsuit is an elusive alternative for many because the cost of a lawsuit may exceed the damages that can be recovered from the infringer. An estimate of $5,000 to initiate a copyright infringement lawsuit is on the low side. Taking a simple copyright infringement lawsuit through trial costs tens of thousands of dollars. Legal fees for a complex case that goes to trial can easily cost each party a six-figure amount.

Prior to filing the lawsuit, you have to evaluate your potential damages. If you are eligible for attorneys' fees and you have a good claim against a defendant with ample financial resources, you might sometimes be able to persuade an attorney to handle your copyright lawsuit on a contingency basis.

Copyright Registration as Requirement for Lawsuit and for Statutory Damages. Copyright registration is required before you may file a copyright infringement lawsuit against someone who has used your work without your permission. If you win a copyright infringement lawsuit—and you have filed a timely registration, you will be eligible to receive statutory damages and to have your attorneys' fees paid by the losing party. As the name implies, statutory damages are set by legal statutes—in this case by the Copyright Act. Statutory damages for copyright infringement normally range from $750 to $30,000, but they can go up to $150,000 if a court finds that someone deliberately infringed your copyright.

If you are not eligible for statutory damages, money damages you can receive are your actual damages plus any additional profits the infringer garnered as a result of the infringement. Requesting actual damages requires you to prove how much money you lost due to the infringement. That is not always easy to do. It may seem like a minor point but your eligibility for statutory damages can sometimes determine whether it is worthwhile to pursue a copyright infringement claim.

Litigation Costs Out of Control. Here is an example of a copyright infringement lawsuit that probably should have never been filed. Webloyalty and Consumer Innovations operate similar membership discount program businesses that they advertise online. Consumer Innovations (CI) used a promotional sell page and an online banner that were clearly copied from Webloyalty. In fact, one of CI's drafts of the sell sheet still had Webloyalty's phone number in the text. However, CI refused to come clean and instead lied about using the Webloyalty material in depositions and at trial.

Judges are not fond of liars in their courtrooms. For that reason, CI not only lost the case but was also ordered to pay statutory damages as well as Webloyalty's attorneys' fees and costs. Despite the win, Webloyalty still ended up in the hole financially. Here is why: Courts have discretion in setting statutory damages which range from $750 to $150,000. The court normally wants the damages to bear some relationship to the profits earned by the infringer and the revenue lost by the copyright owner. The court was not convinced that Webloyalty lost significant revenue as a direct result of the infringement.

CI generated only $1,000 from its use of the sell sheet and banner. The court set statutory damages at $50,000.

A $50,000 statutory damage award for Webloyalty would be okay except for the fact that Webloyalty spent over $300,000 in attorneys' fees to win the lawsuit. While Webloyalty was eligible for CI to pay its attorney fees, the law restricts the payment to reasonable attorneys' fees. The court decided that only seventy-five percent of Webloyalty's attorneys' fees was reasonable. As a result, CI had to reimburse Webloyalty for $226,611 in attorneys' fees plus $42,727 in other legal costs.

In the end, by my calculation, Webloyalty spent over $344,876 to recover $319,338 from CI in total damages. That is a deficit of more than $25,000 to pursue a copyright violation that resulted in a loss of about $1,000. (*Webloyalty.com. v. Consumer Innovations*, 388 F. Supp. 2d 435 (D. De. 2005)).

A Happier Litigation Story. Although I do not recommend that non-lawyers represent themselves in copyright infringement lawsuits, here is one such situation with a positive outcome.

Stock photographer, Chris Gregerson represented himself in a copyright infringement lawsuit after discovering that Vilana Financial, Inc. had used his photo of the Minneapolis skyline in multiple internet and print advertisements.

Vilana claimed it had validly licensed the photos from a photographer whom the company owner met at a gym. Yet, neither Vilana nor its owner could produce contact information for the photographer. The court rejected Vilana's version of events as non-credible and awarded Gregerson close to $20,000 in damages. (*Gregerson v. Vilana Financial*, 446 F. Supp. 2d 1053 (D. MN. 2006)).

3.8.4. International Infringers

Cyberspace is global. As a result, people who infringe and take your online material without authorization may be located outside of the United States. Combating infringement of your online work by individuals located outside of the United States can be a challenge. It is questionable whether you can successfully sue a foreign infringer in a United States court. For a court to preside over a lawsuit involving a defendant from out-of-state or outside of the country, the defendant must have minimum contacts or some relationship with the state of the court seeking to hear the lawsuit.

If no United States court has jurisdiction, your option may be filing suit against the infringer in the infringer's country. That is an option used by major record and film companies. Obviously, there must be money at stake to make this costly option worthwhile.

REGISTERING THE COPYRIGHT IN YOUR ONLINE WORK

4.1. Benefits of Copyright Registration

As noted in Section 3.1, registration is not required to have a valid copyright in your work. However, registration does bestow a number of benefits:

Public Record. Registration establishes a public record of your claim as the valid copyright owner of the work.

Lawsuit. Registration is required before you may file a copyright infringement lawsuit against someone who has used your work without your permission.

Statutory Damages. If you win a copyright infringement lawsuit and you have filed a timely registration, you will be eligible to receive statutory damages and to have your attorneys' fees paid by the losing party. I discuss statutory damages further in Section 3.8.3.

What Is a Timely Registration? You are eligible for statutory damages and attorneys' fees only if you file a timely copyright registration for the infringed work. The timeliness of your copyright registration is tied to the publication status of your work.

For a published work, you have a three-month grace period after the publication date in which to file a copyright registration application and have that application treated as timely. For example, if you publish your work in January, your work is infringed in February, and you file a copyright registration application in March, your registration is timely for purposes of your eligibility for statutory damages and attorneys' fees.

For unpublished works, you must register the work prior to any act of infringement in order to be eligible for statutory damages and attorneys' fees. There is no three-month grace period for unpublished works. If your unpublished work is infringed in February and you file a copyright registration application in March, your registration is not timely and you are not eligible for statutory damages and attorneys' fees.

I discuss the concept of publication further in Section 3.5.4.

4.2. Necessity of Registering Your Online Work

You are not required to register the copyright in your online work. That begs the question of whether you should register the copyright in your online work. The answer is it depends.

If most of the content in your online work is based on another work and that work is already registered, registration of your online work may not be necessary. For example, if you have written, published, and registered the copyright in a printed book and then develop a blog or website comprised of excerpts from your book, it may not be necessary to register the copyright in the blog or website.

As another example, your online work may consist of marketing information for your product or service and it may not be possible or worthwhile to register if the online work consists primarily of material that is not qualified for copyright protection. See Section 3.3 for a discussion of elements that are not eligible for copyright protection.

4.3. Copyright Registration Basics

4.3.1. Copyright Registration Application

To register your copyright, you must submit three items to the Copyright Office: a completed application, a deposit, and a filing fee.

Completed Application. The Copyright Office's website provides free instructional circulars that provide guidance on completing copyright applications. The Appendix of this book includes examples of completed copyright registration applications as well as contact information for the Copyright Office.

Q **Deposit.** A deposit is a copy of the work you are registering. If your work is published both online and in the form of physical copies offline, you must follow the deposit rules applicable to the physical version. While the number of copies to be submitted can vary, the deposit requirement is usually one copy for unpublished works and two copies for published works.

3 **Filing Fee.** Filing fees change periodically and you should verify current fees at the website of the Copyright Office prior to filing. You can pay via check made out to the Register of Copyrights or you can open a Copyright Office deposit account. When filing electronically, payment by credit card is an option.

4.3.2. Processing Time

The Copyright Office will process your application and send you a certificate of registration. Processing time varies depending on the Copyright Office's backlog of applications. Even though processing time may take several months and sometimes up to or over a year, your registration is effective as of the date on which the Copyright Office receives all components required for your complete registration. The Copyright Office's website provides estimates of current processing times.

If you file online, the Copyright Office will send you an email confirming receipt of your application. If you send your registration application via mail and want confirmation of receipt, send it by registered or certified mail and request a return receipt from the post office. Another option for confirmation of receipt of your hard copy application is using a private carrier such as Federal Express or United Parcel Service.

4.3.3. What Registration Covers

Normally, registration covers your work in the form it exists on the registration date as reflected in the deposit. For basic filings, registration does not cover revisions. Registration for revisions requires an additional application with an additional registration fee. This is a disadvantage for online works with frequently changing or rotating content.

For example, suppose you create a website featuring your photography on January 15. You rotate the photos featured on the website every thirty days so you rotate content on February 15 and March 15. You register the copyright in the website on February 15. The registration covers the website as it exists on February 15. The registration does not cover the website as it exists on January 15 or March 15.

A potential solution to this problem is the group registration methods discussed in the following sections. Under certain circumstances, you can register your online work as an automated database or as a serial. The group registration methods can minimize the number of applications you must file and the filing fees you must pay.

4.4. Online Registration

4.4.1. Online Registration, Generally

The Copyright Office encourages copyright owners to use online registration for all filings for which online registration is available. To register online, you first create a free account on the Copyright Office's website. The Copyright Office refers to the section of its website devoted to online registration as the electronic Copyright Office.

Advantages to online registration include a lower filing fee, faster processing time, the ability to track the status of your application online, and fewer opportunities to make errors on your application.

As of the writing of this book, online registration is available only for basic claims. Basic claims include registrations for the following:

- a single work
- multiple unpublished works by the same author and owned by the same person
- multiple published works published together on the same date and owned by the same person

An application for most online works can qualify as a basic claim. That means you can use a basic claim online copyright registration application for your website, blog, podcast, social networking site, email newsletter or other online work. Even when registration as a basic claim is available for your online work, you may be able to save money and time by using one of the group registration methods discussed in Sections 4.7 and 4.8.

As of the writing of this book, online registration is not available for group registrations. Currently, you must file your group registration application in hard copy form via mail. This situation may rapidly change as the Copyright Office expands its online registration capabilities.

Online Registration Compared to Paper Application Form. If you filed registration applications with the Copyright Office prior to its adoption of online registration, you may have used one of the following paper application forms:

- Form TX for literary material
- Form VA for pictorial and graphic works
- Form PA for audiovisual material
- Form SE for single serials
- Form SR for sound recordings

Online registration is designed to replace these paper forms. Most of the information required for online registration is identical to the information required on the old paper forms. Online registration does include new optional categories of information such as an ISBN number for books and permission data to make it easier to track down a copyright owner.

Also, since you must complete the application by selecting responses from a limited number of options, online registration offers fewer opportunities to make some of the common copyright registration errors made by applicants using paper application forms on which applicants can write free-form answers. For example, the application asks for the nature of authorship where you briefly describe the material in which you claim copyright. Although you might be tempted to claim material such as concept or story idea, these elements do not qualify for protection and such a response will delay processing of your application. In contrast, when preparing an online registration for your literary work, your choices for describing the material in which you claim copyright are limited to text, editing, photographs, artwork, translation, compilation, and computer program.

At the time of this writing, the Copyright Office still accepts paper application forms; however, online registration and Fill-In Form CO will gradually phase out the paper forms. It is also more difficult to obtain Forms PA, SE, SR, TX, and VA. The Copyright Office does not freely offer these paper forms through its website but will mail you copies upon your request.

4.4.2. Deposits for Online Registration

The deposit options for online registration include uploading the deposit electronically or sending in a hard copy of the deposit by mail.

Electronic Deposit. You may submit the deposit electronically if the work being registered is one of the following:

• an unpublished work

- a work published only electronically, or
- a work for which the Copyright Office requires only identifying material as a deposit.

If the work requires only identifying material, you may submit as your deposit a representational portion of the work rather than a copy of the entire work.

Hard Copy Deposit. If you plan to mail a hard copy of your deposit, as part of the online registration process, you generate and print out a shipping slip. You include the shipping slip when you mail in your deposit so that your deposit can be matched with the application you submit online.

For certain works, you must mail in a physical copy as your deposit. If your work is published both as an online publication and as physical copies, you must submit the physical copy as your deposit. For example, if you offer your novel as a digital electronic book available online and as a physical book, you must use a copy of the physical book as the deposit of your copyright application.

4.5. Online Fill-In Form

Fill-In Form CO is an alternative to online registration and is the Copyright Office's next preferred method of registration for basic claims if you are not going to file electronically. You access Form CO online through the Copyright Office's website, complete it on your computer, print it out, and mail it to the Copyright Office along with the filing fee and your deposit.

As you complete the information, the form generates a unique two-dimensional barcode incorporating the information you provide. The Copyright Office can then process these forms more quickly and efficiently than paper forms completed manually. Like online registration, Fill-In Form CO gives you limited options for your responses. Hence, there are fewer opportunities to make some of the common copyright registration errors made by applicants using paper application forms.

Fill-In Form CO has the same limitations in terms of what registration covers as does online registration for basic claims. I discuss those limitations in Section 4.3.3.

4.6. Group Registration, Generally

Group registration is a single registration covering multiple works, multiple versions of a work, or multiple issues of a series. You file group registrations on one application and pay one filing fee.

In Sections 4.7 and 4.8, I discuss those group registration procedures most likely to be useful to cyber citizens. I discuss group registration for updates or revisions to an online work that qualifies as an automated database; group registration for a group of serials; and group registration for daily newsletters and daily newspapers. Group registration procedures I do not discuss here at length include group registration of published photographs and registration of a group of contributions to a periodical. Cyber citizens who want additional information on either of those group registration methods can find information at the Copyright Office's website.

If your online work qualifies as an automated database or as a serial, you may be able to use one of the group registration methods. The options and requirements for group registration depend in part on the ownership structure of the work. To evaluate those options and requirements, you need to understand the ownership concepts discussed below.

4.6.1. Collective Work

A collective work includes a number of independent contributions. Most newspapers, magazines, and periodicals qualify as collective works because they contain numerous articles and materials from multiple authors. For example, if many writers contribute to your online newsletter, you can consider it a collective work. Anthologies and encyclopedias may also be collective works.

When you claim copyright ownership in the collective work, you are claiming the whole. In other words, you are claiming copyright ownership in the newsletter as a whole, in the magazine as a whole, or in the encyclopedia as a whole. You are not necessarily claiming ownership in each of the individual articles, photographs, or other elements that comprise the whole newsletter, magazine, or encyclopedia. You may or may not have copyright ownership in these individual components.

All components of your work must be published at the same time to be considered one collective work. If, for example, you publish one article per day in your online publication, the Copyright Office will not consider your online periodical to be a collective work.

4.6.2. Work Made for Hire

When a work qualifies as a work made for hire, copyright law views the employer or person who commissioned the work as the author of the work. As the recognized author, the employer or the client—and not the person who actually created the work—has the authority to exercise all the exclusive rights in the work. See Section 3.2 for a discussion of the exclusive rights in a copyrighted work. There are only two ways in which a copyrighted work becomes a work made for hire:

Work Created by an Employee. A copyrighted work created by an employee within the scope of his employment is a work made for hire. There are sometimes disputes concerning whether or not an individual is an employee or whether an employee's creation of a particular work was within the scope of his employment. I discuss these work made for hire concepts further in Section 3.4.

Work Created by a Freelancer. If a freelancer creates the work, the work is a work made for hire only if two conditions are met. First, the freelancer must sign a written agreement stating that the resulting work will be a work made for hire. Second, the copyrighted work must fall into one of the categories of commissioned works listed in the Copyright Act as eligible to be a work made for hire. Those categories include the following:

- a collective work
- any work created specifically for an audio-visual production
- a translation
- a supplementary work which includes maps, editorial notes, illustrations, a musical arrangement, and an index
- a work created as part of a compilation

The remaining categories, which are less relevant for many cyber citizens, are works created as an instructional text, as a test, as answer material for a test, or as an atlas.

4.6.3. Author and Claimant

Every copyright application asks you to list the author and the claimant. The author is the creator of the copyrighted work. The claimant is the person or entity who owns the copyright. While the author and claimant can be the same person, it is not always the case that the person who created the work is also the person who owns the copyright. After creating the work, the author may have transferred the copyright to another person. If the work was done as a work made for hire, the law views the employer or the commissioning party as the author.

To use some group registration methods, the author and the claimant must be the same person. For example, group registration of multiple issues of a serial requires that the author and claimant be the same. Suppose Jack authors three issues of an online magazine and then transfers copyright ownership of the issues to Jill so that Jill is the claimant of those three issues. As a result, group registration is not available. To register the online work as a group of serial issues, either Jack must be both the author and claimant or Jill must be both the author and claimant. In this case, Jack is the author and Jill is the claimant.

Let's change the scenario so that Jack is Jill's employee and creates the online magazine issues within the scope of his employment. In that case, the copyright in the issues belongs to Jill as a work made for hire. Since the issues are a work made for hire, copyright law views Jill as the author. Hence, Jill is both the author and the claimant. As a result, in this scenario, the online work can be registered as a group of serial issues.

4.7. Group Registration of Your Online Work as an Automated Database

If you update your online work frequently, it may qualify as an automated database. The Copyright Office defines an automated database as a body of facts, data, or other information assembled into an organized format suitable for use with a computer and comprising one or more files. In this discussion, I deal only with registering the copyright in the content of the database. I do not discuss the software or computer code that may accompany the database and may also be a copyrightable element.

If your online work qualifies as an automated database, you may file all updates from a three-month period on a single application for one filing fee. This differs from registering the copyright in your online work as a basic filing which would cover the online work only as it exists on the date of filing. See discussion in Section 4.3.3 on what is covered by copyright registration.

Another advantage to registering your online work as an automated database is that the registration extends to the entire copyrightable content of the work, even though the entire content is not required in the deposit.

4.7.1. Your Online Work as a Published or Unpublished Database

The Copyright Office distinguishes between a published database and an unpublished database. The distinction determines the registration procedure you must follow. Unfortunately, the Copyright Office provides little guidance on when a database should be considered published. The decision is left to the copyright holder. As a general rule, you can consider your online work as published if the public can access it. For the remainder of this discussion about automated databases, I assume that your online work is a published automated database.

4.7.2. Requirements for Registration of an Online Work as an Automated Database

A group registration of an automated database must include updates or revisions. If the database is published, you may file a group registration for just the updates and revisions published during a period of up to three months. It does not matter if a prior registration for the initial database was ever made. You may also file the first registration as a group registration to cover the database as first published plus its updates and revisions. In this case, all the material must have been published within the same three-month period and within the same calendar year.

You may do a group registration of your online work as an automated database only if the following conditions apply. All the updates or revisions must:

- be published only in machine-readable format;
- have been first published within a three-month period and within the same calendar year;
- be owned by the same person or entity;
- have the same general title;
- be similar in their general content, including their subject; and
- be organized in a similar manner.

For example, suppose you have a website featuring photographs. Your website goes live on February 15 in its original format. You revise the website on March 15, April 15, and September 15. You cannot do a group registration with the February 15 version because it is the initial database. It contains no updates or revisions. You may do a group registration for the March 15 and April 15 versions. You may not include the September 15 version in a group registration with any of the earlier versions because the September 15 material was not published in the same three-month period as the materials published on February 15, March 15, and April 15.

4.7.3. Deposit for Group Registration of an Online Work as an Automated Database

Normally, you do not need to submit the entire automated database as your deposit. Instead, you submit identifying material. The identifying material must consist of fifty records unless the fifty records runs more than fifty pages, in which case you submit only the fifty pages. For example, if you register a website featuring photographs as an automated database, you might consider each separate photo a record and submit copies of fifty photos as the deposit.

4.7.4. Registration Process for an Automated Database

As of this writing, a group registration for an automated database cannot be filed via online registration and is still to be filed on Form TX. This situation may change soon. The Copyright Office is considering making group registration available only via online registration.

4.8. Group Registration of Your Online Work as a Serial

Group registration is available for serials including serials published online. Serials include periodicals, newspapers, magazines, bulletins, newsletters, annuals, journals, and similar works. I have seen copyright registration applications in which blogs or newsletters distributed via online posting have been accepted as serials.

4.8.1. Registration of Your Online Work as a Group of Serials

Requirements. All the following conditions must be met to take advantage of group registration for serials:

Collective Work. The claim to copyright must be in a new collective work. For example, if many writers contribute to your newsletter, you can consider it a collective work. See Section 4.6.1 for further discussion about collective works.

Work Made for Hire. Each issue must be a work made for hire. Section 4.6.2 provides more details about work made for hire status. It is the issue in its entirety that must be a work made for hire. The individual articles and other contributions need not be works made for hire.

Author and Claimant. The author and claimant must be the same for all the issues. See Section 4.6.3 for further discussion on authors and claimants.

Timing of Publication. The serial must be published at intervals of one week or longer. If it is a serial published more than once per week, you may be able to register as a daily newsletter. All issues in the group must be published within a three-month period and within the same calendar year. Each issue must have been created no more than one year prior to the date of publication of that issue.

Group. It must be registration of a group. That means at least two issues must be included in the group application.

Deposit for Group Registration of Serials. Your deposit should consist of one copy of each issue listed on the application. Typically, prior to any submission for copyright group registration, you must provide two complimentary subscriptions of the serial to the Library of Congress. However, if the serial is distributed in an electronic online version only, this requirement does not apply.

4.8.2. Registration of Your Online Work as a Daily Newsletter

If your online work qualifies as a daily newsletter, you may register the copyright as a group of newsletter issues.

Advantages. For each issue in the group, registration includes all the material in which the claimant owns the copyright. This includes the authorship of compiling and editing the work as a whole as well as the content of any contributions done by employees of the claimant as works made for hire. In addition, it includes any independent contributions authored by non-employees and subsequently transferred to the claimant. These other contributions are included even though the individual contributors are not named on the application. The registration does not include any independently authored contributions in which all rights have **not** been transferred to the claimant.

For example, suppose you offer a daily newsletter. Three employees, Larry, Curly, and Moe, contribute articles to your newsletter. Two freelancers named Jack and Jill contribute photographs to the newsletter. Jack assigns to your company the entire copyright ownership interest in the photographs. Jill licenses you the right to use the photographs in one issue of your newsletter but retains all other rights in her photographs. Your copyright registration of the newsletter includes the newsletter as a compilation, the articles written by Larry, Curly, and Moe, and the photographs assigned by Jack. It does not include Jill's photographs because Jill's photographs are independently authored contributions in which all rights have not been transferred to you.

Requirements. To register your online work as a group of daily newsletters, each of the following conditions must apply:

The Online Work Is a Daily Newsletter. The Copyright Office defines a daily newsletter as a serial that has information of interest chiefly to a special group and is published and distributed by mail or online. For example, Digital Music News publishes and sends via email every weekday morning the *Daily Snapshot* featuring several short articles on the music industry. The founder and a news analyst write the articles. The *Daily Snapshot* would qualify as a daily newsletter and would be a good candidate for group registration as a daily newsletter.

Collective Work. Each issue must be an essentially all-new collective work or all-new issue that has not been previously published. See Section 4.6.1 for further discussion about collective works.

Work Made For Hire. The online work must be a work made for hire. Section 4.6.2 provides more details about work made for hire status. It is the newsletter issue in its entirety that must be a work made for hire. The individual articles and other contributions need not be works made for hire.

Author and Claimant. The author and claimant must be the same person or organization. See Section 4.6.3 for further discussion on authors and claimants.

Group. The claim must include two or more issues. All issues must have been published within the same calendar month.

Timing of Publication and Registration. You must publish issues of the publication at least twice per week. If your newsletter is published only weekly or monthly, you may be able to register it as a group of serials. You must file the application within three months after the last publication date included in the group.

Deposit for Group Registration of Newsletters. The deposit should include one complete copy of each issue included in the group of newsletters. If the newsletter is published only online, your deposit must include either one complete printout of each issue, or a computer disk containing all the issues along with a print-out of the first and last issues included in the group registration.

4.8.3. Registration of Your Online Work as a Daily Newspaper

If your online work qualifies as a daily newspaper, you may register the copyright as a group registration for daily newspapers.

Advantages to Registering Your Online Work as a Daily Newspaper. Registering your online work as a daily newspaper offers the same advantages discussed in Section 4.8.2 for registering your online work as a daily newsletter.

Requirements. Your online work may be registered as a group of daily newspaper issues if the following conditions apply:

The Online Work Is Actually a Daily Newspaper. The Copyright Office defines a daily newspaper as a serial designed mainly to be a primary source of written information on current events. Newspapers contain a broad range of news on all subjects and activities and are not limited to any specific subject matter. Today, many newspapers are distributed online only.

Collective Work. Each issue must be a new collective work or an essentially all-new issue that has not been published before. See Section 4.6.1 for further discussion about collective works.

Work Made For Hire. The work must be a work made for hire. Section 4.6.2 provides more details about work made for hire status.

Author and Claimant. The author and claimant must be the same person or organization. See Section 4.6.3 for further discussion on authors and claimants.

Timing of Publication and Registration. The registration must include all issue dates within one calendar month and the registration must be filed within three months of the last publication date included in the group. For example, suppose you publish an edition of the newspaper each day in May. For a group registration, your registration should include all thirty-one issues and the application must be filed by the last day of August.

Deposit for Group Registration of Newspaper. As of this writing, the Copyright Office rule requires that a deposit of positive 35 mm silver-halide microfilm of all issues within the calendar month accompany the application. The Copyright Office, which realizes that many newspapers are now published only online, is re-evaluating the deposit requirement for newspapers. In the meantime, it may be possible for copyright holders to receive an exemption to the microfilm requirement and instead deposit one of the following:

- complete print copies of the first and last issues of the month
- print copies of the first section of the first and last issues of the month
- print copies of the first page of the first and last issues of the month

4.9. Preregistration

Preregistration is available for works that have a history of infringement prior to authorized commercial distribution. For example, it is not uncommon for the CD recording of popular recording artists to be leaked to the public prior to the official street date set by the record label. The purpose of preregistration is to allow copyright owners whose work has been leaked to file a copyright infringement lawsuit before full registration, and to still be eligible to receive statutory damages and attorneys' fees.

As discussed in Section 4.1, a copyright owner is entitled to statutory damages and attorneys' fees in a lawsuit only if the copyright owner has filed a timely registration. For unpublished works, a registration is considered timely if the registration is filed prior to the act of infringement. While one may register a work as an unpublished work prior to authorized commercial distribution, most registration filings require submitting a copy of the work which becomes available to the public. Hence, such a submission would frustrate the goals of copyright owners of popular movies, books, and albums whose marketing plans depend in part on building excitement by keeping the work from public view until the authorized release date. For example, imagine J.K. Rowling registering the copyright in the unpublished manuscript of one of the Harry Potter books prior to the book's official release date and making the unpublished manuscript part of the public record. In contrast, J.K. Rowling could preregister a Harry Potter book without submitting a deposit or copy of the work.

Preregistration is not a substitute for registration. If you do preregister your work, you are still required to register it when it is published. To preserve eligibility for attorneys' fees, statutory damages, and other legal benefits of preregistration, you must register your work within one month of becoming aware of infringement and no later than three months after first publication. Although first publication is a technical concept as explained in Section 3.5.4, the date of first publication is likely to be the commercial release date.

You may preregister your work only if your work is a motion picture, musical work, sound recording, computer program, book, or advertising photograph and the following conditions apply:

- The work is unpublished at the time of preregistration.
- Creation of your work has begun.
- Your work is being prepared for commercial distribution.

You must submit your preregistration application electronically. Preregistration requires a completed application and payment of the preregistration fee. No deposit is required. Instead, you must include a description of the work on the application.

4.10. Available Copyright Registration Methods for Specific Online Works

As discussed in this chapter, the cyber citizen frequently has options in the manner in which to register the copyright in an online work. Frequently, the registration of your online work can be formatted as a basic claim or as a group registration claim. This section discusses which of the registration methods are appropriate for particular online works.

I discuss the methods that are most likely to apply in most circumstances. However, your situation may have unique characteristics not highlighted in this discussion.

4.10.1. Registration of the Copyright in Your Website

You can register the copyright in your website as a basic claim using online registration or Fill-In Form CO. See Sections 4.4 and 4.5 for more details. If your website qualifies as an automated database, you can consider a group registration as an automated database. See Section 4.7 for more details.

4.10.2. Registration of the Copyright in Your Blog

You can register the copyright in your blog as a basic claim using online registration or Fill-In Form CO. See Sections 4.4 and 4.5 for more details. If your blog qualifies as an automated database, you can consider a group registration of your blog as an automated database. See Section 4.7 for more details.

4.10.3. Registration of the Copyright in Your Podcast

I am using the term podcast; however, this discussion applies to any original audio recording you produce. You can register the copyright in your podcast as a basic claim using online registration or Fill-In Form CO. See Sections 4.4 and 4.5 for more details.

Your podcast consists of two separate copyrightable elements. There is a copyright in the recording and a copyright in the underlying material. For example, suppose you write and develop a seminar on woodworking and then record a podcast featuring that seminar. There is a copyright in the seminar content you developed. There is also a separate copyright in the podcast recording of the seminar. See Section 8.10.1 for an explanation of how this dual copyright concept applies to songs and sound recordings in recorded music.

If you are the producer of the podcast, claim ownership only in the sound recording. If you are also the owner of the underlying material, you may claim ownership in both the sound recording and the underlying material. By registering the underlying work and sound recording together in one application, you pay one filing fee instead of two.

If a guest participates in your podcast, your guest maintains copyright ownership of his spoken comments unless your guest transfers to you ownership in the content of his interview. This assumes your guest's comments are eligible for copyright protection. If, for example, your guest's comments consist of brief impromptu answers to interview questions, those comments may not qualify for copyright protection.

4.10.4. Registration of the Copyright in Your Electronic or Online Newsletter or Newspaper

You may be able to register multiple issues of your online publication as a group registration. Your options depend in part on the frequency of publication:

- If you publish your online publication at intervals of one week or longer, you may be able to register multiple issues as a group of serial issues. See Section 4.8.1 for more details.

- If you publish two or more issues per week of your online publication, you may be able to register multiple issues as a group of newsletters. See Section 4.8.2 for more details.

- If your online publication is a daily newspaper, you may be able to register multiple issues as a group of daily newspaper issues. See Section 4.8.3 for more details.

There are several conditions for use of these group registration methods as discussed in Section 4.8. If you do not meet all the requirements, you likely will have to file each issue of your online publication separately as a basic claim for which you can use online registration or Fill-In Form CO. See Sections 4.4 and 4.5 for more details.

4.10.5. Registration of the Copyright in Your Social Networking Site

You can register the copyright in original content you add to your social networking site as a basic claim using online registration or Fill-In Form CO. See Sections 4.4 and 4.5 for more details. If your social networking site qualifies as an automated database, you can consider a group registration of your social networking site as an automated database. See Section 4.7 for more details.

SELECTING YOUR DOMAIN NAME 5

5.1. What Is a Domain Name?

Domain names are a focal point for online communications. Each domain name is a routing address for locating a website or delivering email on the internet. Website addresses are also often referred to as url's which is an acronym for uniform resource locator.

Computers communicate through numbers. You get routed to a website because there is a unique series of numbers associated with each website. The series of numbers is called an internet protocol address, or ip address for short, and is expressed as four groups of numbers separated by periods—such as 123.45.78.90.

To avoid having to remember a series of numbers for each website we want to visit, we use the domain name system. A domain name is a mnemonic corresponding to an internet protocol address. For example, www.yahoo.com is a domain name mnemonic. One of the internet protocol addresses for www.yahoo.com is 69.147.76.15.

Each domain name must be unique. Domain names are usually comprised of a second level domain name followed by a dot followed by a top level domain name. For example, sashaycommunications. com is a domain name consisting of com, the top level domain name, and sashaycommunications, the second level domain name. Most domain name disputes focus on second level domain names.

5.1.1. Top Level Domains

Top level domains (TLDs) include generic top level domains (gTLDs) and country code top level domains (ccTLDs). Here are the most commonly used gTLDs:

gTLDs	Intended User
com	commercial, for profit organizations
edu	colleges and universities
gov	United States federal government agencies
int	international organizations
mil	United States military organizations
net	network infrastructure machines and organizations
org	non-profit organizations and individuals

There are over 250 country code top level domains in use. Each corresponds to a country, territory, or other geographic location. Country code top level domains include ca for Canada, uk for the United Kingdom, and au for Australia.

The country code top level domains are administered by a country code manager within each specific country. Each country determines who may use its country code. Some countries require that users of their country code be citizens or have some association with the country. Other countries allow wider use of their ccTLDs. If you are interested in using a specific ccTLD, you can check with the registrar offering ccTLD registration services regarding the specific terms and conditions for registration. The Appendix includes contact information for locating ccTLD registrars in the Domain Name Resources section.

5.1.2. Domain Name Hierarchy

There is a hierarchy of domain names. The domains at the top level of the hierarchy maintain lists and addresses of the domains just beneath them. At the top level, the list is small. This very small database is called the root. The root list provides the comprehensive inventory of both generic top level domains and country code top level domains.

Each top level domain has many second level domains. These subordinate domains in turn maintain lists and addresses of the domains beneath them, and so on. For example, the url for Sashay

Communications is www.sashaycommunications.com. "com" is a generic top level domain and is listed in the root directory. "Sashay-Communications" is a second level domain name and is listed in the top level domain, "com".

This concept is easier to grasp with a more complex url. For example, we have all seen urls such as classes.med.StateUniversity.edu. Starting at the top of the hierarchy, "edu" is the top level domain and is listed in the root directory. "StateUniversity" is the second level domain and is listed in the top level domain "edu". "med" is a third level domain and appears on the list for the second level domain "StateUniversity". "classes" appears on the list for the third level domain "med". Most likely, State University has its own web server and decides whether to have a .med on the State University list. State University might also include third level domains in addition to .med such as .law, .economics, and .math.

5.1.3. Email Addresses

Email addresses also use domain names. For example, info@sashay-communications.com is an email address. "info", the first part of the email address found to the left of the @ sign, is the user name. The user name identifies the person to whom you are sending the email.

The domain name immediately follows the @ sign. The domain name consists of two parts: "sashaycommunications" which is the second level domain name and "com" which is the top level domain. The second level domain name identifies the computer system on which the user has an email account. It may be the name of a company as in my example where the domain name is Sashay Communications. Alternatively, if the user has a personal email account rather than an account at his company, the domain name may be the name of the user's internet service provider, or ISP for short. For example, America Online and the Microsoft Network are ISP's used by individuals. AOL and MSN are the respective domain names for these ISP's. JoanComputerUser@aol.com may be the email address for an individual with a personal account on America Online.

5.2. *Your Relationship with Domain Name Registries, Registrars, and ICANN*

The players in the domain name system include registrants, registries, registrars, and ICANN. As a cyber citizen, you will likely never interact directly with a registry or ICANN. However, you should understand the roles these organizations play in the domain name system.

Registrant. This is you. Individuals and companies who register domain names are sometimes referred to as registrants. Most of your interaction for domain name issues will be with the registrar you select for registration of your domain name.

Registries. A domain name registry operates one or more top level domains. The term registry is also used to describe the actual listing of all the domain names that are registered and included within a top level domain.

ICANN assigns management and administration responsibility for each top level domain to a single registry. One registry may administer more than one top level domain. For example, Verisign Global Registry Services is the registry that operates the .com and .net top level domains. The registry that operates the .org top level domain is the Public Interest Registry. Registries affiliate with registrars and registrars ultimately issue second level domain names to individuals and companies.

Registrars. Registrars are the intermediaries between the registries and you. Registrars have direct access to the registry. In addition to distributing domain names to registrants, registrars also maintain WHOIS information and make changes to the registry on behalf of the registrants. The WHOIS database is a central database that tracks domain name and ip registrations. The database, which is open to the public, includes the name of the registrant as well as the administrative, billing and technical contacts for the registrant.

Popular registrars for the .com top level domain include Go-Daddy and Network Solutions. Most registrars can register domain names in more than one top level domain. For example, the generic top level domains in which Network Solutions can register domain names include .com, .org, .info, .mobi, .net, .biz, .pro, and .name. Network Solutions is also a registrar for over sixty-five country code top level domains.

Registrar Resellers. Some accredited registrars allow third parties to resell their services. These third parties are called resellers. Resellers do not have direct access to the registry, and must process registrations and renewals through the registrar with which they have a relationship. If you register your domain name through a reseller, the accredited registrar will still be your registration contact and will be responsible for maintaining your contact information in the WHOIS database.

ICANN. The Internet Corporation for Assigned Names and Numbers (ICANN) is a non-profit corporation that has oversight responsibility for the administration of domain names. ICANN sets the principle relationship structure between the registrars and registrants. However, each registrar can build additional, non-conflicting terms into its contracts with domain name registrants.

5.3. How to Select a Domain Name

To establish a website, you first need some internet virtual real estate to call your own. You can register your own domain name and be www.mycompany.com. To register your own domain name, you select a second level domain name such as "mycompany". Normally, this second level domain name is simply referred to as the domain name.

Once you have selected a desired domain name, you register it with one of the registrars. Registrars register domain names on a first-come, first-served basis. If no one else has registered the domain name, the registrar will accept your registration. However, as discussed more fully in Chapter 6, there can be legal consequences if you select a domain name that violates someone else's trademark rights.

Using a Sub Domain. Instead of registering your own domain name, you can piggy-back on someone else's domain name and construct your online presence as a sub domain. For example, if you blog and use a sub domain of your blog host provider, the address of your blog location may be mycompanyblog.typepad.com. typepad.com is the domain name of the blog hosting service. Mycompanyblog is a sub-division on the typepad.com domain.

Social Network User Names. If you use social networking sites such as YouTube, Twitter, and LinkedIn, your presence on the social networking site is often a sub-division under your selected user name. For example, if you choose the user name JaneSmith for your Twitter account, people will find you on Twitter by visiting www.twitter.com/JaneSmith. Typically, the user name must be unique within the particular social network. This means there can be only one JaneSmith on Twitter. Hence, if your name is also Jane Smith, you will need to select a different user name for your Twitter account. However, you could still be Jane Smith on another social networking site if you are the first to register that user name.

5.3.1. Your Options If Someone Is Already Using the Domain Name You Want to Use

If someone has already registered the domain name you want to use, you have a few choices:

Choose Another Domain Name. Select another domain name that is available. You can creatively vary the domain name or use the same second level domain name with another generic top level domain such as .biz or .info. For example, if you desired the domain name www.AutoRental.com and discovered it was registered to another party, you might choose instead www.AutoRentals.com, www.IndianaAutoRentals.com, or www.AutoRental.info as appropriate for your purposes. However, you must be careful that your variation does not infringe any trademark rights of the earlier domain name registrant. See Section 5.5.3 for further discussion on this issue.

Buy the Domain Name. You can attempt to purchase the domain name from the person or organization that has registered it. Domain name purchase prices vary widely and are completely dependent on what the buyer and seller negotiate.

Selling domain names has become big business. You may want to handle the purchase by approaching the owner directly or using a domain name broker.

Assert Your Rights in the Domain Name. If the other party's use of the domain name is trademark infringement or cybersquatting, you can attempt to force a transfer of the domain name. See Chapter 6 for a discussion of domain name disputes.

5.3.2. Who Owns the Domain Name?

Once you register a domain name, it is yours to use as long as you maintain your registration and do not use it in a manner that violates another's trademark rights. If you allow your domain name registration to lapse, you can lose your domain name if someone else registers it. If that happens, your opportunities to retrieve it include purchasing the domain name back or initiating a domain name dispute if the subsequent owner is using it in bad faith or in a manner that violates your trademark. See Chapter 6 for more information on domain name disputes.

Sometimes cyber citizens enlist a third party such as a hosting service or website developer to register the domain name. If you take this route, make sure that the domain name is registered in your name or your company's name. Otherwise, there can be issues involving ownership of the domain name.

Loss of Domain Name Due to Fraud. Courts have acknowledged that domain names constitute property at least sufficient to support a claim for conversion. Conversion is the wrongful exercise of dominion over the property of another. In other words, you can fight back and sue if someone wrongly takes your domain name from you.

This happened in a case involving the domain name express.com, a domain name estimated to be worth at least one million dollars. After fraudulently changing the contact information for the domain name, an unidentified person sold the express.com domain name to domainer Gregory Ricks for $150,000. Ricks had no phone or in-person contact with the seller. Instead, the transaction was negotiated and completed through email and through escrow.com, a third-party website for secure online transactions. Nevertheless, by filing a lawsuit against Ricks, the rightful owner was able to reclaim the domain name express.com. (*Express Media Group v. Express Corporation*, No. C06-03504 WHA (N.D. Cal., May 10, 2007)).

5.4. Qualifying a Domain Name as a Trademark

Domain names potentially interact with trademark law in two ways. First, domain names can be trademarks and, thus, protected by trademark law. Second, domain names used improperly may infringe an existing trademark and violate trademark law.

Every domain name is not a trademark. A domain name is protectable as a trademark only if it in fact functions as a trademark. As discussed further in Section 5.5, the principle purpose of a trademark is identifying the source of a good or service. To qualify as a trademark, your domain name must identify the source of a good or service that you sell, market or promote. The domain name must also be distinctive and be used in commerce.

Lack of distinctiveness is often the factor that disqualifies domain names as trademarks. For example, coffee.com as the domain name for a website selling coffee and drugstore.com as the domain name for a website offering pharmaceutical drugs are fantastic marketing tools. Every consumer who wants to purchase coffee or fill a prescription, respectively, will find them. However, they are poor trademarks. On the trademark scale of distinctiveness discussed in Section 5.5.1, coffee.com and drugstore.com in these contexts are at best merely descriptive and therefore, do not qualify as protectable trademarks.

5.5. Trademark Basics

The federal statute that governs trademark law is the Trademark Act of 1946. It is often referred to as the Lanham Act. Most states have parallel laws that mirror the Lanham Act.

Trademarks identify the source of specific goods and services. Trademarks apply to goods and service marks apply to services. The legal process for acquiring and protecting trademarks is virtually identical to the process for acquiring and protecting service marks.

Often, the terms mark or trademark are used interchangeably as a reference to both trademarks and service marks. For the purposes of this book, I treat trademarks and service marks as functionally identical. Unless I indicate otherwise, I use the terms mark and trademark interchangeably to refer to both trademarks and service marks.

Trademarks can be words or phrases. They can also be logos, graphic symbols, designs, sounds, shapes, colors and even smells. Trademarks consisting of words are most relevant to our discussion of domain names.

To qualify for trademark protection, the word or phrase must meet the following conditions:

- It must be distinctive.
- It must be used in commerce.
- It must not infringe or cause a likelihood of confusion with a pre-existing trademark.

5.5.1. Trademarks Must Be Distinctive

Trademark law only protects names that are distinctive. Trademark jargon includes a scale that measures distinctiveness. The distinctiveness scale consists of five categories. Going from most distinctive to least distinctive, the categories are fanciful, arbitrary, suggestive, merely descriptive, and generic.

Fanciful. Fanciful trademarks are made-up words such as KODAK or EXXON.

Arbitrary. Arbitrary trademarks are ordinary words used completely out of context such as APPLE for the name of a computer or CAMEL for a brand of cigarettes.

Suggestive trademarks hint at but do not directly name the good or service. They require some use of your imagination to come up with the nature of the actual good or service. Examples include the trademark, SURFVIVOR, used in connection with beach-themed products and the trademark, CHICKEN OF THE SEA, used in connection with tuna fish.

Merely Descriptive. A merely descriptive trademark indicates a characteristic, function, use or other attribute of the good or service. Trademarks primarily based on a geographic location or a surname also fall into the category of merely descriptive. Descriptive trademarks receive little or no trademark protection. There is an exception for a descriptive trademark that has acquired secondary meaning. Secondary meaning exists if the public clearly associates the trademark with the good or service. CHAP STICK for lip balm and AMERICAN AIRLINES for air transport of passengers and freight are protectable trademarks which began as descriptive and over time developed secondary meaning.

Generic. A generic term is the common name of the good or service itself such as soap or hairspray. Generic terms never receive trademark protection. For example, if you use the term "java" to sell your brand of coffee beans, that is a generic use of "java" and you will receive no trademark protection for that use. However, note that "java" becomes an arbitrary trademark when used to describe a product completely unrelated to coffee—such as a computer programming application.

Determining where a particular trademark falls on the scale of distinctiveness is often subjective. What one person sees as suggestive, another person may call merely descriptive.

5.5.2. Trademarks Must Be Used in Commerce

You obtain rights in a trademark by being the first person to use the trademark in commerce in a particular geographic region. Use in commerce means you have used the trademark in connection with offering a good or service for sale. This can mean that the trademark appears on the good or its packaging or that the trademark is used or displayed in the sale or advertising of the good or service.

You are eligible for federal registration of your trademark if you have used the trademark in connection with a good or service you offer in interstate commerce. Interstate commerce means you have offered the good or service across state or national lines. Offering a good or service via a website normally qualifies as offering it in interstate commerce.

5.5.3. Trademarks Must Not Infringe or Cause a Likelihood of Confusion with a Pre-Existing Trademark

Domain names can infringe trademarks. Trademark infringement exists when there is a likelihood of confusion between two similar or identical trademarks. A likelihood of confusion exists when a consumer might confuse your proposed trademark with an existing trademark already being used to identify the source of a similar good or service.

Identical or similar trademarks can co-exist if the trademarks are used in connection with different goods or services. For example, HERTZ is the trademark owned by Hertz Systems, Inc. and is used in connection with the automobile rental and sale business. It might be okay for you to develop a salad dressing called Hertz salad dressing. Consumers would not likely believe that the car rental company manufactures salad dressing so there would be no likelihood of confusion between the Hertz Car Rental service and your Hertz Salad Dressing. However, you might be in trouble if you name your limousine service the Hertz Limousine Service.

Likelihood of Confusion Factors. Determining the likelihood of confusion is another subjective area of trademark law. Case law has developed a number of factors to consider when making the determination; however, no one factor is determinative.

There are eight questions a court frequently asks in a likelihood of confusion case. These questions are often referred to as the Polaroid factors after the legal case, *Polaroid Corp. v. Polarad Electronics Corp.*, 287 F.2d 492 (2d Cir. 1961), that first used them:

- How distinctive is the pre-existing trademark?
- How similar are the trademarks?
- How similar are the goods or services identified by each trademark?
- Are the goods or services marketed in the same marketing channels?
- If the goods or services are not similar, what is the chance that one trademark owner will eventually expand into the business of the other trademark owner?
- Have consumers actually been confused by the similarity in the trademarks?
- Was the accused trademark infringer acting in good faith when he selected the similar trademark or was he attempting to benefit from the good will associated with the pre-existing trademark?

- How much attention do customers pay to the trademark in this good or service category when making a purchase? In trademark jargon, this question is posed as what is the level of consumer care.

Likelihood of Confusion Factors for the Internet. In the context of the internet, a court may place additional focus on three of these eight questions: the similarity of the trademarks, the similarity of the goods and services, and the parties' use of the internet as a marketing channel. Courts view use of a similar trademark on the internet as particularly susceptible to a likelihood of confusion since internet use allows competing trademarks to be encountered at the same time and on the same screen.

Real-Life Application of the Likelihood of Confusion Test for the Internet. eBay is an online auction and shopping website on which people and businesses buy and sell goods and services worldwide. PerfumeBay.com is an online retailer of perfumes. eBay objected to the use of the domain name, PerfumeBay.com.

The court held that conjoined forms of "perfumebay" created a likelihood of confusion with eBay and prohibited PerfumeBay from using PerfumeBay or Perfume-Bay in advertisements and from using the domain name www.perfumebay.com. However, the court allowed the perfume company to continue using non-conjoined forms of "Perfume Bay" since these non-conjoined forms did not create a likelihood of confusion.

The court focused its analysis on the three internet factors:

- Similarity of the Trademarks. Perfumebay incorporated the eBay trademark in its entirety.

- Similarity of the Goods. Perfumebay and eBay both sold perfume on the internet. In fact, eBay's annual transactions for perfume during the relevant period of 2002 to 2004 averaged approximately two million dollars.

• Use of the Internet as a Marketing Tool. Both companies utilized search engines extensively for attracting customers.

Because the three primary factors for trademark use on the internet weighed against Perfumebay, the remaining factors— distinctiveness of the senior trademark, likelihood of expansion into other markets, actual confusion, Perfumebay's intent, and degree of consumer care—would need to weigh strongly against a likelihood of confusion to avoid the finding of infringement. The court decided that the remaining factors did not weigh sufficiently heavily against a likelihood of confusion. (*Perfumebay.com v. eBay*, 506 F.3d 1165 (9th Cir. 2007)).

5.5.4. How Domain Names and Trademarks Differ

While some domain names double as protectable trademarks, there are many domain names which do not qualify as trademarks. This dichotomy exists because there are a number of distinctions between domain names and trademarks:

Co-Existence. Identical trademarks can co-exist if they are in separate markets. In contrast, every domain name must be unique. Two parties cannot use the exact same domain name. For example, OUT-BACK is the trademark for a model of an automobile and for a restaurant. However, there can be only one www.outback.com.

Flexible Appearance. Trademarks can be varied with fonts and designs. Domain names are text-based only and lack this flexibility. Visualize the Nike swoosh and the McDonald's golden arches, both of which function as trademarks. A domain name cannot accommodate such design elements.

Use in Commerce. In order to qualify for protection, a trademark must be used in commerce. Domain names are used in both commercial and non-commercial contexts.

Search Prior to Selection. Selection and registration of a trademark requires a search to confirm that there are no conflicting pre-existing trademarks. The Patent and Trademark Office will not accept a trademark for registration if the proposed trademark causes a likelihood of confusion with a trademark that is already registered or pending for registration.

Domain name registrars register domain names on a first-come, first-served basis. As long as no one else has registered a particular domain name, the domain name registrar will accept your registration. A domain name accepted for registration by a registrar can generate claims of trademark infringement. Hence, it is advisable to conduct a trademark search prior to registering a domain name.

5.5.5. Trademark Registration Process

Federal registration with the United States Patent and Trademark Office (PTO) is not required to develop valid trademark rights. You obtain rights in a trademark simply by being the first to make legitimate use of the trademark in commerce. When you earn rights in a trademark you have not registered, you have common law rights in the trademark.

Benefits of Federal Trademark Registration. Even though registration is not required, federal registration of your trademark carries several benefits:

Nationwide Exclusivity. In most circumstances, federal registration with the PTO gives you the exclusive right to use the trademark nationwide. Without federal registration, you have trademark rights only in the geographic region in which you actually use the trademark.

Public Notice. A federal trademark registration places others on notice that you claim ownership of the trademark.

Increased Damage Awards. With federal registration, you are eligible to collect attorneys' fees and increased monetary damages from an infringer if you file and win a trademark infringement lawsuit.

Incontestability. After five years your federal registration qualifies for incontestability which makes it difficult for anyone to claim that your trademark is not valid.

International Trademark Protection. You are eligible to use the easier, streamlined application process for international trademark protection. Registration with the PTO protects your trademark within the United States. PTO registration does not provide any international protection for a trademark. In general, a trademark must be registered on a country-by-country basis. However, the Madrid Protocol, an international treaty to which the United States belongs, allows a trademark owner to seek registration in any of the countries that have joined the Madrid Protocol by filing a single application.

Steps for Federal Trademark Registration. Here is a simplified outline of the federal trademark registration process:

Submission of Application. You submit a completed application to the United States Patent and Trademark Office (PTO). You can submit your application in hardcopy form or in electronic form. The PTO encourages electronic filings.

Examiner's Review. A trademark examiner verifies that your application is complete and that your trademark qualifies for federal registration. The PTO will refuse to register a trademark that is not distinctive. As discussed in Section 5.5.1, distinctiveness means the trademark fits into the category of fanciful, arbitrary, or suggestive. If the PTO classifies the proposed trademark as merely descriptive, the trademark must have secondary meaning in order to qualify for registration. The PTO will also refuse to register the proposed trademark if it is likely to cause confusion with another trademark that is already registered or pending for registration.

Office Action. If the trademark examiner finds a distinctiveness, likelihood of confusion, or other problem with your application, she sends you a letter explaining the problem. The letter is called an Office Action. You have six months in which to respond to the Office Action.

Publication. Once the examiner is satisfied with your application and responses to any Office Action issued, your trademark is published in the PTO's *Official Gazette.* Third parties have thirty days to object to the registration.

Registration or Third Party Objection. If no one objects, the PTO registers your trademark. If someone does object, there is a proceeding before the PTO to resolve the dispute. The PTO proceeding is similar to a lawsuit in federal court so having representation by a trademark attorney is highly recommended.

Even if everything goes smoothly, it can take a year or more for your trademark to be accepted for registration. The Appendix includes an example of a completed trademark application for a domain name.

In Use Versus Intent to Use. Federal trademark registration requires use of the trademark in interstate commerce. However, if you are not currently using your trademark in interstate commerce and you have a bona fide intention of doing so, you can reserve a trademark by filing an intent to use application with the PTO. An intent to use application goes through almost the same federal trademark registration procedure described above. However, there is an additional step. After determining that there are no third party objections or resolving any third party objections, the PTO does not register your trademark. Instead, the PTO issues a notice of allowance. Your trademark is not registered until you file an additional document stating that you have begun to use the trademark in commerce. This supplemental document is called a statement of use.

You have six months from the date of the issuance of allowance to begin using the trademark in commerce and to file the statement of use. You can extend this deadline for five additional periods of six months each provided you have a legitimate reason for the delay in your use of the trademark.

Preparing the Trademark Registration Application for Your Domain Name. Cyber citizens registering their domain names as trademarks may wonder whether they should include the "www" and the top level domain as part of the trademark to be registered. As discussed in Section 5.1.1, the top level domain is the .com portion of the domain name. Other common top level domains include .org, .net, and .biz.

You often have a choice of including or excluding the top level domain from your trademark application. Many choose to register only the second level domain name since in some circumstances, that option may provide more flexibility and ease in both the trademark registration process and subsequent use of the trademark.

Matching the Specimen with the Trademark as Registered. When deciding whether to include the "www" and the top level domain in your registration, you must be careful that the specimen submitted with your application matches your trademark application. Specimens are the samples of how you use the trademark and are a required part of your trademark registration application.

The trademark as it appears on the specimen must match the trademark as you register it. However, the PTO views the second level domain as the portion of the domain name indicating source. The PTO generally views the top level domain and the www as less significant. As a result, you can register just the second level domain name even if the specimens show a use of the trademark that includes the top level domain or the "www". For example, a specimen showing the trademark as www.xyz.com is acceptable for a trademark registered as XYZ. The adverse is not true. If you register the trademark as www.xyz.com, specimens of use must show the trademark being used as www.xyz.com as the PTO will not accept specimens that show only XYZ.

The Specimen Must Show Use as a Trademark and Not Just Use as an Address. The specimen must show that you are using the domain name as a trademark and not just as an internet address. For example, a specimen that shows your domain name as part of your contact information or in the web browser box or as part of language such as "visit us on the web at www.xyz.com" does not demonstrate trademark use of the domain name.

PROTECTING YOUR DOMAIN NAME AND PERSONAL NAME

CHAPTER

6

6.1. How Domain Name Disputes Arise

A domain name can infringe an existing trademark resulting in a domain name dispute.

Domain name disputes arise in several ways

Identical Names from Different Industries. Identical trademarks from different industries can co-exist. However, only one company can use the name or trademark as a domain name within the same top level domain. Even though both Delta Air Lines and the Delta Faucet Company have trademark rights in the word Delta, www.delta.com belongs to Delta Air Lines.

Cybersquatting. Cybersquatting is the registration of a domain name identical or very similar to a well-known trademark with the intention of selling the domain name to the trademark owner or to someone else at a significant profit. During the move of companies to the internet, there were several high-profile cybersquatting cases.

Commentary Site. Commentary sites include gripe sites, criticism sites, and fan sites. An operator of a commentary site may have a First Amendment right to use a trademark in the website's domain name. However, the First Amendment protections do not always mean the trademark owner will not make an objection. I discuss commentary sites in Chapter 13.

Traditional Trademark Dispute. Companies may honestly disagree as to the likelihood of confusion between a domain name and a pre-existing trademark. The likelihood of confusion, discussed further in Section 5.5.3, is at the heart of trademark infringement claims.

6.2. *How to Avoid Domain Name Disputes*

The best way to avoid selecting a domain name that infringes a trademark is to conduct a trademark search. The best approach to a trademark search is retaining a professional search bureau to conduct a search of the proposed trademark and then having a trademark attorney review the results of the search. In a full trademark search, the search bureau verifies whether your proposed name is registered or pending for registration with the Patent and Trademark Office, or with any of the states. The search bureau also uses public and proprietary directories and other resources to determine whether anyone is using the proposed name or a similar name without having registered it.

Trademark Search Resources. There are online and offline resources you can use to conduct a trademark search yourself.

Directories. You can start by checking some of the directories that list similar goods or services. Your local library may have copies of these directories that are useful for your trademark search.

PTO Database. The Patent and Trademark Office makes its federal trademark database of pending and registered trademarks available for free through its website.

Search Engines. Plugging your proposed domain name into one or more of the several available internet search engines is a good way to find trademarks that are in use but have not been federally registered.

State Registrations. You can contact one or more state secretaries to determine whether there has been a state registration of the trademark. Many states offer online searchable databases that allow you to search for company names and registered state trademarks.

6.3. Resolving Domain Name Disputes through the UDRP, ACPA and Traditional Trademark Lawsuits

A trademark owner has a few courses of action if a domain name infringes her trademark. The options include the following:

- initiating an action under the Uniform Domain Name Dispute Resolution Policy (UDRP)
- filing a lawsuit under the Anticybersquatting Consumer Protection Act (ACPA)
- filing a traditional trademark lawsuit under federal or state trademark laws and related statutes

The options are not necessarily mutually exclusive. A trademark owner that loses a UDRP proceeding may later file a lawsuit. Many trademark lawsuits include a combination of ACPA claims and more traditional trademark law claims.

6.3.1. Similarities among Domain Name Dispute Options

Actions under the UDRP, the ACPA, and traditional trademark laws share some common elements. In all such actions, the person challenging the domain name must demonstrate the following:

Valid Trademark. The person challenging the domain name must have valid trademark rights in a trademark. The UDRP panel or the court will accept that you have rights in the trademark if you have registered your trademark with the PTO. While an advantage, federal registration is not absolutely necessary to win a domain name dispute. Trademark owners have won UDRP proceedings and lawsuits by showing they have common law trademark rights.

The exception to the requirement of holding a valid trademark is an action under the provision of the ACPA that protects personal names. I discuss the personal name ACPA provision in Section 6.9.1.

Similarity of Trademark and Domain Name. The contested domain name must be the same as or confusingly similar to the trademark in which the person has rights.

6.3.2. Differences among Domain Name Dispute Options

There are also some marked differences in the requirements for actions under the UDRP, the ACPA, and traditional trademark laws:

Bad Faith. When initiating an UDRP or ACPA action, the trademark owner must show that the domain name registrant acted in bad faith. There is no bad faith requirement in traditional trademark litigation. I discuss the bad faith requirement for UDRP or ACPA domain name disputes in Section 6.7.

Use in Commerce. To win most traditional trademark lawsuits, the trademark owner must show that the domain name owner is using the domain name in commerce. As discussed in Section 5.5.2, use in commerce means use of the trademark in connection with offering a good or service.

There is no use in commerce requirement for UDRP and ACPA actions. If you are registering domain names and simply warehousing them, you cannot be sued in a traditional trademark lawsuit; however, you can still lose the domain name in an ACPA or UDRP proceeding.

While neither the ACPA nor the UDRP has an in commerce requirement, they both make an inquiry into commercial use. An ACPA inquiry includes whether you are attempting to profit from the trademark. Bad faith under both UDRP and ACPA may investigate whether you attempt to use the domain name for profit.

Precedent. Courts in ACPA and traditional lawsuit proceedings adhere to precedent meaning that they will review and often apply the rationale followed by previous courts adjudicating similar cases. Even when a particular court is not obligated to follow the decisions and interpretations of previous courts, it is at least often persuaded by prior court opinions. In contrast, the UDRP does not operate on a strict doctrine of precedent meaning that one UDRP panel need not be bound by the decisions of a previous UDRP panel. However panels consider it desirable that their decisions are consistent with prior panel decisions dealing with similar fact situations.

Likelihood of Confusion. I discuss the concept of likelihood of confusion in Section 5.5.3. Trademark owners using most traditional trademark laws do need to show a likelihood of confusion. UDRP and ACPA proceedings do not require a likelihood of confusion between the goods and services offered by the domain name registrant and the trademark owner. Nevertheless, trademark owners initiating UDRP and ACPA proceedings do need to demonstrate that the disputed domain name is identical to or confusingly similar with the trademark.

Remedies. If you win a UDRP proceeding, the only available remedies are transfer of the domain name to you or cancellation of the domain name. You cannot collect any money from the losing party in a UDRP proceeding. Remedies in both traditional trademark lawsuits and ACPA proceedings include injunctions and money damages.

The following chart summarizes some of the similarities and differences among UDRP, ACPA and a traditional trademark lawsuit under the Lanham Act:

Feature	UDRP	ACPA	Lanham Act
Person disputing domain name must have trademark rights	Yes	Yes	Yes

UDRP, ACPA, Traditional Trademark Comparison Chart (continued)

Feature	UDRP	ACPA	Lanham Act
Domain name must be the same or confusingly similar to trademark	Yes	Yes	Yes
Domain name registrant must use domain name in commerce	No	No	Yes
Money damages are available	No	Yes	Yes
Domain name can be transferred	Yes	Yes	Yes
Domain name registrant must act in bad faith	Yes	Yes	No

6.4. Uniform Domain Name Dispute Resolution Policy (UDRP)

The Uniform Domain Name Dispute Resolution Policy (UDRP) is an administrative procedure designed for the quick resolution of domain name disputes. The Internet Corporation for Assigned Names and Numbers (ICANN) developed the policy and all ICANN-accredited registrars must use it. While domain name registrants must go through the UDRP proceeding if a trademark owner initiates it, the UDRP does not prevent either the trademark owner or the domain name registrant from pursuing a more traditional lawsuit.

The UDRP proceedings are designed to last fewer than sixty days. Proceedings do not take place in person. They are completely on paper. The trademark owner who believes that a domain name violates rights in his trademark initiates the UDRP proceeding by filing a complaint. A panel consisting of one or three arbitrators decide the matter based upon their review of the documents submitted by each party. The only remedies available are cancellation of the domain name or transfer of the domain name to the trademark owner. To obtain money damages for a domain name dispute, the trademark owner must file an ACPA or traditional trademark infringement lawsuit.

6.4.1. Winning a UDRP Proceeding

A trademark owner who believes a domain name infringes his trademark may initiate a UDRP proceeding. In order to be successful in a UDRP proceeding, the trademark owner must prove the following:

Valid Trademark Rights. The trademark owner has rights in the trademark.

Similarity of Trademark and Domain Name. The disputed domain name is identical or confusingly similar to the trademark.

No Legitimate Interest by Domain Name Registrant. The domain name registrant has no rights or legitimate interests in the disputed domain name.

Bad Faith. The domain name registrant registered and is using the disputed domain name in bad faith. I discuss the bad faith requirement further in Section 6.7.

For the domain name registrant to be successful in a UDRP proceeding and to be able to keep the domain name, at least one of the prongs must be false. The prong is viewed as false if the trademark owner fails to provide adequate arguments to convince the panel or if the domain name registrant successfully rebuts the trademark owner's arguments.

6.4.2. Steps in a UDRP Proceeding

Here is a simplified outline of the steps in a UDRP Proceeding:

Trademark Owner's Complaint. Only the trademark owner—and not the domain name registrant—can initiate a UDRP proceeding. The trademark owner initiates the procedure by filing a complaint with the approved administrative-dispute-resolution service provider of its choice. An adequate complaint explains how the dispute satisfies each of the requirements discussed in Section 6.4.1. The trademark owner must also send a copy of the complaint to the domain name registrant.

Currently, there are four providers who administer UDRP Proceedings: the Asian Domain Name Dispute Resolution Center, the Czech Arbitration Court, the National Arbitration Forum (NAF), and the World Intellectual Property Organization (WIPO). NAF and WIPO administer most UDRP proceedings among United States trademark owners and domain name registrants. While each provider follows the UDRP policy and rules established by ICANN, each provider also has supplemental rules.

Domain Name Registrant's Response. The domain name registrant, called the respondent, has twenty calendar days to respond to the complaint. If the domain name registrant fails to respond, the domain name registrant defaults. While defaulting is a factor that counts against the domain name registrant, in the event of a default, the panel still evaluates the merits of whether the domain name should be cancelled or transferred.

Appointment of Panel. After receipt of the domain name registrant's response, the provider has five days to appoint a panel. A panel can consist of one member or of three members.

For a single-member panel, the provider chooses the panelist. For a three-member panel, the trademark owner and domain name registrant each nominate three candidates to serve as one of the three panelists. The provider chooses the third panelist. The trademark owner and domain name registrant can express a preference for which panelist the provider should choose.

The trademark owner pays all panel fees if the parties use a single-member panel. The trademark owner also pays all fees for the three-member panel unless the trademark owner selected a single-member panel in its complaint and the domain name registrant expressed a preference for a three-member panel. In cases in which the domain name registrant elects a three-member panel over the trademark owner's election of a single-member panel, the domain name registrant must pay half of the fees for the three-member panel.

Decision. The panel has fourteen days from its appointment in which to render a decision. The rules require that the panel's decision be in writing, provide the reasons on which the decision is based, indicate the date on which it was rendered, and identify the names of the panelists. If the panel decides that the trademark owner should win the proceeding, the only remedies are cancellation of the domain name or transfer of the domain name to the trademark owner. Most trademark owners request transfer.

Options for Losing Registrant or Trademark Owner. A domain name registrant who loses a UDRP proceeding has ten business days to file a lawsuit in a court for further resolution of the domain name dispute. If the losing domain name registrant does not file a lawsuit, the registrar will implement the remedy ordered by the UDRP panel. The remedy is either cancelation of the domain name or transfer of the domain name to the trademark owner.

Likewise, a losing trademark owner may still file a lawsuit in court. Courts are not bound by the outcome of a UDRP proceeding. Losing the UDRP proceeding does not mean you will lose a court action involving the domain name under the ACPA or more traditional trademark litigation.

6.4.3. Views of the UDRP

The UDRP has many critics. They allege that the policy favors trademark owners over domain name owners. Only trademark owners can initiate the proceeding and trademark owners win overwhelmingly. Critics also complain that UDRP proceedings yield conflicting opinions from panelists with no single court of final review, that there is no evidentiary review (meaning that facts and documents presented to the panel need not be authenticated), and that the lack of oversight and accountability leads to opportunities for misuse and abuse of the system.

Additional Dispute Resolution Policies. The UDRP is applicable across all generic top level domains. Additional dispute resolution policies may apply to specific circumstances in individual top level domains.

For example, the Eligibility Requirements Dispute Resolution Policy (ERDRP) applies to domain names registered under the top level domain, .name. You may register names under the .name top level domain only if the name registered is your legal name, commonly known nick-name, or the name of a fictional character in which you hold trademark rights. Challenges to a registration in .name on the grounds that the domain name registrant does not have such a legal name, nick-name, or trademark rights are filed under the ERDRP

6.5. *Anticybersquatting Consumer Protection Act (ACPA)*

The Anticybersquatting Consumer Protection Act (ACPA), adopted in November 1999 and incorporated into the federal Lanham Act, combats cybersquatting. More specifically, the ACPA prohibits registering, trafficking in, or using a domain name that is confusingly similar to a trademark if you have a bad faith intent to profit from the trademark.

Trafficking under ACPA means selling or otherwise transferring the domain name for something of value. The congressional report accompanying the ACPA defined cybersquatters as those who register well-known brand names or trademarks as internet domain names with the intention of:

- extracting payment from the trademark owners,
- warehousing those domain names with the hope of selling them to the highest bidder,
- misusing the domain name to divert customers from the trademark owner's site to the cybersquatter's own site, or

• defrauding consumers by some other means including through counterfeiting activities.

6.5.1. Winning an ACPA Lawsuit

To win an ACPA claim, a trademark owner must show the following:

Valid Trademark. The trademark owner holds rights in a trademark that is distinctive or famous. A federally registered trademark is helpful but not absolutely necessary. The exception to the valid trademark requirement is an action under the personal name provision of the ACPA which allows you to challenge the use of your name as a domain name whether or not your name functions as a trademark. I discuss personal name ACPA actions further in Section 6.9.1 below.

Similarity of Trademark and Domain Name. The disputed domain name is identical or confusingly similar to the trademark.

Bad Faith. The domain name owner registered the domain name with the bad faith intent to profit. I discuss the bad faith requirements further in Section 6.7.

ACPA Remedies. If a trademark owner wins an ACPA action, possible remedies include forfeiture or cancellation of the domain name or transfer of the domain name to the trademark owner. Monetary damages are available as long as the registration, trafficking, and infringing activity took place on or after November 29, 1999, the effective date of the ACPA.

6.6. *Traditional Trademark Lawsuits*

Filing a lawsuit with more traditional trademark claims is slower and more expensive than a UDRP proceeding and normally involves an assortment of claims based on federal and state laws. Remedies available through a traditional trademark lawsuit include monetary damages in addition to cancellation or transfer of the domain name. Monetary damages include statutory damages and can be tripled.

6.6.1. Basis for Traditional Trademark Lawsuit Claim

Most traditional trademark lawsuits include claims based on the Lanham Act, which is a federal law that protects both registered and common law trademarks. The Lanham Act prohibits you—without the consent of the trademark owner—from using in commerce any registered trademark in a manner likely to confuse consumers. The Lanham Act also prohibits using either federally registered or common law trademarks in a false advertising context or as a false designation of origin.

The Lanham Act includes anti-dilution laws which prevent a trademark's distinctiveness from being weakened as a result of being used to identify the source of another's good or service. Anti-dilution laws also prevent the trademark's reputation from being tarnished through an association with an undesirable good or service. Dilution claims are generally available only for trademarks considered to be famous.

Most states have laws that parallel the federal Lanham Act and the federal anti-dilution laws. Many trademark lawsuits include a combination of claims based on federal law and state law. A lawsuit based on these more traditional trademark claims may also include an ACPA claim.

6.6.2. Winning a Traditional Trademark Lawsuit

To be successful in a traditional lawsuit action against a domain name owner under the Lanham Act, the trademark owner must show the following:

Valid Trademark. The trademark owner has rights in a trademark that pre-exists use of the domain name. These can be common law trademark rights so federal registration is not required.

Use of Domain Name In Commerce. The domain name registrant is using the domain name in commerce. I discuss the in commerce standard in Section 6.8.1.

Likelihood of Confusion. There is a likelihood of confusion between the trademark and the domain name. As explained further in Section 5.5.3, a likelihood of confusion exists when a consumer might confuse a proposed trademark with an existing trademark already being used to identify the source of a similar good or service. The exception is for anti-dilution claims for which the trademark owner need not show any likelihood of confusion over source of goods and services.

Bad Faith Not Necessary. In contrast to a UDRP or ACPA action, a traditional trademark infringement lawsuit carries no requirement that the domain name registrant acted in bad faith. Nevertheless, under the likelihood of confusion analysis in a traditional trademark lawsuit, one of the factors considered by a court is the intent of the registrant in choosing the potentially infringing domain name.

6.7. Bad Faith under the UDRP and ACPA

To be a successful trademark owner in either a UDRP or ACPA legal proceeding, you must show that the domain name registrant acted in bad faith. As the domain name registrant in either procedure, you want to show that your actions were not in bad faith. This requirement is markedly different from a traditional trademark lawsuit which has no bad faith requirement.

Both the UDRP Policy and the ACPA statute provide guidelines for determining whether the domain name registrant acted in bad faith. The guidelines are not exclusive. Decision makers review the totality of circumstances and may look at other indicia when evaluating the existence of bad faith.

Factors Suggesting No Bad Faith. The ACPA and UDRP guidelines suggest that the domain name registrant is not acting in bad faith if any of the following conditions exist:

> *Legal or Common Name.* The disputed domain name consists of the domain name registrant's legal name or other name by which the domain name registrant is commonly known. It is not crucial that the domain name registrant actually have trademark rights in the name.

> *Use with Goods or Services.* The domain name registrant has previously used the name to offer goods or services.

> *Non-commercial Site.* The domain name registrant uses the domain name with a non-commercial website or in a manner that qualifies as fair use. Non-commercial websites include websites offering parody, criticism, or commentary.

> *Generic Words.* The disputed domain name consists of generic or descriptive words.

Factors Suggesting Bad Faith. The UDRP and ACPA guidelines suggest that the domain name registrant is acting in bad faith if any of the following conditions exist:

> *Classic Cybersquatting.* The domain name owner registers the domain name in a strategic effort to prevent the trademark owner from being able to register a domain name with its trademark. This is classic cybersquatting and frequently involves a domain name registrant who has registered several variations of the domain name and then tries to sell them to the trademark owner.

> *Diversion of Traffic.* The domain name registrant uses the domain name in a manner that confuses consumers and diverts traffic away

from the website of the trademark owner or otherwise uses the domain name to disrupt the trademark owner's business.

Attempts to Sell. The domain name registrant attempts to sell the domain name for a cost that far exceeds the domain name registrant's initial cost of obtaining the domain name. The sale need not always be to the trademark owner. For example, it may be bad faith to offer a domain name for sale on an online auction website.

False Contact Information. The domain name registrant provides false contact information when registering the domain.

Repeated Cybersquatting. The domain name registrant has a pattern of acquiring domain names which mimic the trademarks of others.

Warehousing. If I register numerous domain names and do not construct active websites for those domain names or otherwise use the domain names, I am warehousing the domain names. Passively holding the domain name does not automatically excuse the domain name registrant from a finding of bad faith.

Real-Life Examples of Bad Faith

Just Don't Do That. Circle Group, a provider of business services to emerging technical companies, acted in bad faith when it registered and used the domain name justdoit.net for employee email addresses and as a means to redirect users to its company websites. It did not matter that Circle Group did not use the Just Do It trademark on its websites or in connection with any Circle Group products or services. (*Nike, Inc. v. Circle Group Internet, Inc.*, 318 F. Supp. 2d 688 (N.D. Ill. 2004)).

Tit-for-Tat. Flow Control, a chemical injection valve manufacturer, learned that its competitor was using its name in online advertisements. In retaliation, Flow Control registered a variation of the competitor's trademark as a domain name hoping to use the domain name as leverage to make the competitor modify the offensive advertisements. Flow Control acted in bad faith when it registered and used confusing domain names to improve its bargaining position in a commercial dispute. (*Flow Control Industries v. AMHI*, 278 F. Supp. 2d 1193 (W.D. Wash. 2003)).

Failure to Conduct a Trademark Search. A website operator did not conduct a trademark search before registering domain names unrelated to its common name and using those domain names for a commercial website. A trademark search would have uncovered a pre-existing similar trademark. The court found failure to conduct a trademark search to be bad faith. (*Eurotech v. Cosmos European Travels*, 213 F. Supp. 2d 612 (E.D. Va. 2002)).

MySpace TV. The domain name registrant of myspacetv.org acted in bad faith when he provided false contact details during registration and used the domain name as a link to his own MySpace page. (*MySpace, Inc. v. Mari Gomez*, No. D2007-1231, (WIPO UDRP Decision, Oct. 17, 2007)).

The Un-AOL. The domain name registrant of numerous domain names containing the word unaol acted in bad faith where he used the domain names to redirect internet users to his websites on which he benefited financially by collecting advertising revenue and soliciting donations. (*AOL, LLC v. Maher Osseiran d/b/a Arabian Virtual Village, LLC*, No. FA0607000758794, (NAF UDRP Decision, Sept. 11, 2006)).

Classic Cybersquatting. Registration of stanleybostitch.com, stanley-bostitch.com, and eight other variations of the Stanley Bostitch name prevented the Stanley Works company, owner of the trademarks Stanley and Bostich, from using these trademarks in its own online sites. Under those circumstances, the UDRP panel found that the domain name registrant had acted in bad faith. (*The Stanley*

Works v. Camp Creek Co., Inc., No. D2000-0113, (WIPO UDRP Decision, Apr. 14, 2000)).

Real-Life Examples of No Bad Faith

Not Every Offer to Sell Is Bad Faith. The Nissan Computer Corporation did not show bad faith by offering to sell the domain name nissan.com to the Nissan Motor Company for fifteen million dollars. Bad faith under the ACPA requires the sale offer to be made without any previous bona fide use of the domain name. In this situation, Nissan Computer Corporation had used nissan.com for its computer business for over four years prior to commencement of the domain name dispute. *(Nissan Motor Co. v. Nissan Computer Corp.*, 61 U.S.P.Q.2d 1839 (C.D. Cal. 2002)).

Auditron Electronics and Auditron Accounting. William Sloan registered Auditron as a trademark in connection with bookkeeping, accounting and tax services. Sloan later filed an ACPA lawsuit against Auditron Electronics Corporation, a manufacturer of high fidelity speakers that had registered the domain name auditron.com. The court ruled there was no bad faith by Auditron. Auditron had been using Auditron as a trademark since 1978, obtained a legal opinion prior to adopting the Auditron trademark, provided different services than Sloan, and used the domain name and website for legitimate business purposes. (*Sloan v. Auditron Elec. Corp.*, 68 Fed. Appx. 386 (4th Cir. 2003)).

Nutritional Supplements. Ultimate Living International had sold nutritional supplements under the trademark Green Miracle since 1996 and federally registered Green Miracle as a trademark in 1997. Another company, Miracle Greens Supplement, had sold nutritional supplements under the Miracle Greens trademark since 1997. When Miracle Greens began operating a website with the domain name miraclegreens.com, Ultimate Living filed a lawsuit with ACPA and traditional trademark claims. There was no bad faith by Miracle

Greens because it used the domain name to market its own product, did not deliberately divert consumers from Ultimate Living's website, never offered to sell or transfer the domain name, provided correct contact information when applying for the domain name, and did not cybersquat any other domain names. (*Ultimate Living Int'l. v. Miracle Greens Supplements*, No. 3:05-cv-1745-M (N.D. Tex., Jan. 3, 2007)).

Sierra, Sierra. Sierra Suites, a hotel lodging business, had used SIERRA SUITES as a trademark since 1995, had federally registered it, and had used the domain name sierrasuites.com since 1998. In 2008, a different company named Sierra Hospitality registered the domain names sierrahotelgroup.com and sierra-hotels.net.

Sierra Suites initiated a UDRP proceeding against Sierra Hospitality and lost. A UDRP panel held there was no bad faith by Sierra Hospitality because it was commonly known as Sierra Hospitality; was founded by Pablo Sierra in 1997; had actively conducted business as a consultant in the hotel and hospitality field for over a decade; and had used other domain names with variations of sierra, hotel, and hospitality for years prior to the filing of the UDRP complaint. Furthermore, sierra is a common word used by companies in the hotel industry. (*Lodgeworks L.P. v Sierra Hospitality*, No. FA0802001152964, (NAF UDRP Decision, Apr. 21, 2008)).

Sonograms and Images. An ultrasound clinic located in Redondo Beach, California used the federally registered trademark FIRST LOOK SONOGRAM. When a Columbia, South Carolina provider of ultrasound and sonogram services began a website with the domain name firstlookimaging.com, the California clinic initiated a UDRP proceeding. The California clinic lost. The South Carolina imager had shown no bad faith because it legitimately used the domain name in connection with the offering of a service. Furthermore, the panel did not believe First Look Imaging was confusingly similar to First Look Sonogram. (*First Look Sonogram, Inc. v. Computer Care*, No. FA0710001092259, (NAF UDRP Decision, Dec. 10, 2007)).

6.8. The Commercial Use Requirement

Commercial use versus non-commercial use of a domain name impacts whether and how a trademark owner may challenge your use of that domain name. A trademark owner can only challenge your use of a domain name under traditional trademark laws if you are using the domain name in commerce. While neither a successful UDRP nor ACPA challenge requires commercial use of the domain name, both proceedings do evaluate whether the domain name registrant is profiting as a result of the similarities of the domain name and the trademark.

6.8.1. Commercial Use As Distinct from Use in Commerce

Use in commerce is always commercial use; however, a commercial use is not always use in commerce. It is possible to use a domain name or website commercially without using the domain name in commerce as required by a traditional trademark claim. As discussed in Section 5.5.2, use in commerce is a term relevant to trademarks and means that you use the trademark in connection with selling or offering a good or service. If you offer a domain name for sale, you are using the domain name commercially. However, the activity does not require your using the domain name to identify the source of a specific good or service. Hence, you are not using the domain name in commerce according to the Lanham Act definition.

In order to win a domain name dispute through most traditional trademark litigation claims, the trademark owner must show that the domain name registrant is using the disputed domain name in commerce. If the domain name simply indicates an address on the internet or if the registrant passively holds the domain name, there is no use in commerce. If you are registering domain names and simply warehousing them without actually using them, you cannot be sued successfully in a traditional trademark lawsuit; however, you can still lose the domain name in a UDRP proceeding or ACPA lawsuit.

While the UDRP and the ACPA have no use in commerce requirement, each has a commercial inquiry component. Commercial use is not a requirement for winning the UDRP proceeding or ACPA lawsuit but commercial use is a point of inquiry. In this sense, commercial use means that the domain name registrant uses the domain name for financial benefit. One of the components of a successful ACPA inquiry includes whether the domain name registrant is attempting to profit from the trademark. Bad faith under both ACPA and UDRP may investigate whether the registrant attempts to use the domain name for profit.

Real-Life Examples of Commercial Use of Domain Name and Website

Offer to Sell. A self-proclaimed internet entrepreneur who had registered thousands of domain names used the domain name vericheck.com commercially. In addition to earning revenue by using the domain name to direct traffic to another website, the internet entrepreneur, through his representative, offered to sell the domain name for amounts exceeding $48,000. These actions also led the court to conclude that the entrepreneur acted in a bad faith attempt to profit from the domain name under the ACPA. (*Lahoti v. Vericheck*, No. C06-1132JLR (W.D. Wash. Aug. 30, 2007)).

Continental. An individual unaffiliated with Continental Airlines used the domain name continentalairlines.com commercially when he automatically redirected customers to a third party website. The third-party site charged customers a fifteen dollar purchase fee that they would not have paid if purchasing tickets from the official Continental Airlines website. (*Continental Airlines, Inc. v. continentalairlines.com*, 390 F. Supp. 2d 501 (E.D. Va. 2005)).

Ads in Washington Post. An anti-abortion website operator's offer to trade his Washington Post domain names for space on the editorial page in the *Washington Post* was an attempt to use the domain names for financial gain. (*Coca-Cola Co. v. Purdy*, 382 F.3d 774 (8th Cir. 2004)).

Real-Life Examples of Non-Commercial Use of Domain Name and Website. It is possible to use a domain name and a website in a non-commercial manner.

Criticism or Gripe Site. Your use is likely not commercial if your use is within the context of a parody, criticism, or commentary site. I discuss these forms of online works in Chapter 13.

Commercial Element Too Remote. A website was not commercial just because it had links to a discussion group which in turn contained links to a commercial website. The connection to commercial use was too remote. (*Bosley Medical Institute v. Kremer*, No. OH752WQH (S.D. Cal., April 29, 2004)).

Fan or Celebrity Website. A fan site that contains no advertising or other specifically commercial content is not commercial. I discuss fan sites further in Chapter 13. You can even use the personal name of a celebrity or other famous person as a domain name if you are using the domain name in a non-commercial manner.

6.9. Protecting Your Personal Name on the Internet

If someone is using your personal name as a domain name in an invalid manner, you can use the same domain name dispute techniques discussed in this chapter.

As explained in Section 6.3.1, success in a domain name dispute requires that you have trademark rights in the disputed name. Proving trademark rights in your personal name can sometimes be a hurdle. If your personal name is federally registered as a trademark with the Patent and Trademark Office, that is evidence that you have trademark rights in your name.

Without a federal registration, you must prove that you have common law trademark rights in your personal name. Simply having a famous or recognizable name is not sufficient to show common law trademark rights. As discussed in Section 5.5.1, trademarks primarily based on a surname fall into the distinctiveness category of merely descriptive. Merely descriptive trademarks receive little or no trademark protection unless they have acquired secondary meaning. Your personal name has secondary meaning if the public clearly associates your name with the source of a specific commercially available good or service.

Personal Names with Secondary Meaning. These are celebrities who were deemed to have developed secondary meaning in their personal names:

Pierce Brosnan is a name with secondary meaning that the public associates with Brosnan's services as an actor and producer. Brosnan is an internationally famous film and television actor who has appeared in over fifty motion pictures, television series and television programs including playing the role of James Bond. (*Pierce Brosnan v. Network Operations Center*, No. D2003-0519 (WIPO UDRP Decision, Aug. 27, 2003)).

Morgan Freeman is a personal name with secondary meaning as the source of services and goods to which his name is applied. Freeman is an actor who has appeared in more than fifty movies, numerous television shows, and plays and whose name is used in advertisements to promote these productions. (*Morgan Freeman v. Mighty LLC*, No. D2005-0263 (WIPO UDRP Decision, Apr. 28, 2005)).

Dan Marino is a personal name with secondary meaning within the American sports, entertainment and public service communities. Marino was quarterback for the Miami Dolphins professional football team and had ancillary careers as a sports commentator and major motion picture actor. (*Daniel C. Marino, Jr. v. Video Images Productions,* No. D2000-0598 (WIPO UDRP Decision, Aug. 2, 2000)).

Julia Roberts is a personal name with secondary meaning. Roberts is an Academy-award winning actress featured in numerous major motion pictures, celebrity publications, movie reviews, and entertainment publications and television shows. (*Julia Fiona Roberts v. Russell Boyd,* No. D2000-0210 (WIPO UDRP Decision, May 29, 2000)).

Personal Names with No Secondary Meaning. These are people, who even though they have widely recognizable names, were not deemed to have developed secondary meaning in their personal names:

Gene Edwards. Even though Edwards had an international Christian ministry, had appeared on television, and was an author, the UDRP panel did not find that his name was associated with goods or services. (*Gene Edwards v. David Miller,* No. D2003-0339 (WIPO UDRP Decision, July 14, 2003)).

David Pecker. Pecker was Chairman and CEO of American Media, Inc., publisher of well-known publications including the *National Enquirer, Star,* and *Sun.* However, Pecker had not used his personal name for the purpose of advertising or promoting his business or for the sale of any goods or services. (*David Pecker v. Mr. Ferris,* No. D2006-1514 (WIPO UDRP Decision, Jan. 15, 2007)).

Sting. Being well known under a particular name is not the same as having trademark rights in that name. Although singer Gordon

Sumner is world famous and known internationally under the name Sting, the UDRP panel was not convinced that he had trademark rights in the name. This result was largely due to sting being a common word in the English language, with a number of different meanings. (*Gordon Sumner, p/k/a Sting v Michael Urvan*, No. D2000-0596 (WIPO UDRP Decision, July 20, 2000)).

Ted Turner. Although a well-known personality, famous entrepreneur Ted Turner failed to convince the UDRP panel that his personal name had been used commercially as a trademark to promote goods or services. The panel did not view inclusion of the Turner name in several media companies as sufficient to make Ted Turner a common law trademark. (*R. E. 'Ted' Turner v. Mazen Fahmi*, No. D2002-0251 (WIPO UDRP Decision, July 4, 2002)).

6.9.1. Options If You Have No Trademark Rights in Your Personal Name

Most of the discussion of the ACPA in this Chapter 6 focuses on a provision of the ACPA that requires trademark rights to prevent the bad faith online use of your name as a domain name. There is another ACPA provision exclusively for the protection of personal names which lets you prevent the use of your personal name as a domain name even if you have no trademark rights in your personal name. This provision, which is titled in the federal code as Cyberpiracy protection for individuals, gives you the right to file a lawsuit against

> any person who registers a domain name that consists of the name of another living person, or a name substantially and confusingly similar thereto, without that person's consent, with the specific intent to profit from such name by selling the domain name for financial gain to that person or any third party, shall be liable in a civil action by such person.

Available remedies under the personal name ACPA provision include forfeiture or cancellation of the domain name or the transfer of the domain name. The court may also, in its discretion, award costs and attorneys' fees to the prevailing party.

The personal name ACPA provision does not require that you have trademark rights in your name. For example, in one case, a person lost under the ACPA trademark rights provision because he had no trademark rights in his name; however, he was able to win under the ACPA personal name provision. In that case, Garner Meadows registered the domain name briansalle.com as leverage in an attempt to persuade Brian Salle to pay a disputed debt. Salle sued for cybersquatting under both the trademark rights and personal name provisions of the ACPA. Salle lost the ACPA trademark rights claim because he had no trademark rights in his personal name. However, Salle won the ACPA personal name claim. The court found that cyber-extortion as a means of recovering a debt qualified as using a domain name for financial gain in violation of the ACPA personal name provision. In a later related decision, Meadows was ordered to pay Salle $24,830 in attorneys' fees and costs. (*Salle v. Meadows*, No. 6:07-cv-1089Orl-31DAB (M.D. Fla., Dec. 17, 2007)).

6.9.2. Your Personal Name on a Social Networking Site

If you find you are being impersonated on a social networking site, you may be able to remedy the situation simply by alerting the operator of the social network to the situation. Impersonating others violates the terms of use of many social networking sites and the site may de-activate the offending account in response to your alert. In extreme cases, someone's online impersonation of you may be a form of criminal cyber harassment. I discuss cyber harassment and cyber bullying in Section 9.4.

Impersonation on Social Network Sites Likely Not Actionable Under UDRP or ACPA. Impersonation or use of a name on a social networking site is likely not actionable under the Uniform Domain Name Dispute Resolution Policy or the Anticybersquatting Consumer Protection Act. On a social networking site, the name comes after the .com or other top level domain name. For example, the url for a Twitter account might be www.twitter.com/maryjanesimpson. The use of Mary Jane Simpson is not actionable under the UDRP as it is a user name issued by the individual social networking site and not part of the domain name issued by a domain name registrar.

It is also unclear whether use of the user name would be actionable under the ACPA which defines domain name as "any alphanumeric designation which is registered with or assigned by any domain name registrar, domain name registry, or other domain name registration authority as part of an electronic address on the internet". That definition may not be sufficiently broad to include user names distributed by social networking sites like MySpace, Twitter, and Facebook.

If you want to take legal action for use of a name or trademark as a user name on a social networking site, you would likely rely on the traditional trademark laws discussed in Section 6.6 with the need to prove use in commerce and likelihood of confusion. You would also need to address whether the use of your name in the post domain path of the url can constitute a trademark law violation. See Section 6.10 for a discussion of personal names and trademarks used in post domain paths and sub domains.

6.10. Use of Trademarks and Names in Post Domain and Sub Domain Paths

This chapter has focused primarily on disputes involving trademarks and names used in the second level domain name. Trademarks and names may also appear in the post domain paths and in sub domains.

The post domain path of the url is everything to the right of .com or top level domain. Very few cases have dealt with whether the use of trademarks in the post domain path constitutes trademark infringement. The few courts that have reviewed the question have concluded that the post domain path of the url does not normally signify the source, but merely indicates the manner in which information is organized. Thus, these courts concluded in those particular cases that use of a trademark in the post domain path was not a trademark law violation.

However, these cases did not deal with a third party host or social networking site giving out account user names. In the discussion in Section 6.9, I mentioned as an example the Twitter account www.twitter.com/maryjanesimpson. There are millions of Twitter accounts. Each starts with www.twitter.com. One could argue that, in this case, the portion in the post-domain path does signify source.

Likewise, the courts have not yet addressed whether trademarks appearing in a sub domain is infringement. If you have your blog as a sub domain on blog host blogsareus.com, your blog may reside on the sub domain myblog.blogsareus.com. One might successfully argue that the myblog portion of the domain does signify source.

PROTECTING YOUR TECHNOLOGY

7.1. Patent Law Basics

A patent is a property right applicable to inventions and discoveries. During the period that you have a patent on an invention, you can exclude others from making, using, offering for sale, or selling the invention in the United States or importing the invention into the United States. The Patent and Trademark Office (PTO) issues and administers patents in the United States.

Categories of Patents. United States-issued patents are divided into three categories: utility patents, design patents and plant patents.

Utility Patents. Utility patents are the most common type of patents issued. They cover inventions which function in a unique manner to produce a useful result. Utility patents include business method patents, which are the category of patents prevalent on the internet and discussed further below. The term of a utility patent is twenty years from the date on which the application for the patent was filed in the United States.

Plant Patents. Plant patents cover the discovery and asexual re-production of distinct and new varieties of plants. Plant patents last for twenty years from the date on which the application for the pat-ent was filed in the United States. The holder of a plant patent can prevent others from asexually reproducing, selling, or using the plant.

Design Patents. Design patents protect the overall appearance of an invention. While a utility patent protects the way an invention is used and works, a design patent protects the way an invention looks. Design patents include the ornamental design that appears on the side of Nike athletic footwear, the design of Samsung portable flip phones, and the design of the Nintendo control panel. Design patents last for fourteen years from the date of issuance.

7.2. Requirements for Patentability

Patent protection is available for a process, machine, manufacture or composition of matter. It is not available for laws of nature, natural phenomena, abstract ideas, or for inventions publicly disclosed or offered for sale for more than twelve months without a patent application having been filed. In addition, to qualify for patent protection, the invention or discovery must be novel, useful, and nonobvious.

7.2.1. Novelty as a Requirement for Patentability

Novel is a manner of saying new. To qualify as novel, an invention must be different from all inventions that came before it. These previous inventions are referred to as prior art. Prior art for patents includes the following:

- any published writing or patent that was made publicly available either before the date of the invention or more than one year before the patent application is filed

- any United States patent or patent application publication that has a filing date earlier than the earliest date that the invention was conceived

- any relevant method or process existing publicly before the invention or discovery was conceived

- any public or commercial use, sale, or knowledge of the invention in the United States more than one year before the patent application is filed

7.2.2. Usefulness as a Requirement for Patentability

The invention must have a purpose and be operable. Being useful means the invention must provide some benefit—even if the benefit is trivial. If the invention does not work, it is not useful and will not qualify for a patent.

Examples of Useful Invention. In a pre-mix beverage dispenser, the syrup concentrate and water are pre-mixed and the beverage is stored in a display reservoir bowl until it is ready to be dispensed. In contrast, in a post-mix beverage dispenser, the beverage syrup and water are stored in separate locations until the beverage is ready to be dispensed. The Juicy Whip beverage dispenser is a post-mix dispenser but through a patented invention, it gives the appearance that the mixture has already been made. It does this by showing a false product in a clear container above the beverage mixer. The Juicy Whip beverage dispenser displays this false product to stimulate impulse buying by providing the consumer with a visual beverage display.

Orange Bang claimed that the Juicy Whip patent was invalid for lack of usefulness as it falsely depicted the drink mixture. A federal court found the Juicy Whip invention to be useful because the post-mix dispenser imitated the visual appearance of a pre-mix dispenser. The court's rationale was consistent with previous patents found useful for making a product appear to be something it is not such as a production method for placing imitation grill marks on food without using heat and laminated flooring imitating wood. (*Juicy Whip, Inc. v. Orange Bang, Inc.*, 185 F.3d 1364 (1999)).

7.2.3. Nonobviousness as a Requirement for Patentability

The invention must be sufficiently different from what has been used or described previously that it is nonobvious to a person having ordinary skill in the area of technology related to the invention. Adapting existing electronic processes to incorporate modern internet and web browser technology is often deemed as obvious.

Example of Nonobvious Determination. Muniauction developed a system in which mass amounts of bonds can be offered to underwriters who then resell individual bonds to the public. The individual buyer bids for bonds using an electronic bid submission system offered via the internet. There was a prior art system called the Parity bid submission system with an identical function. The difference was the Parity system ran on each buyer's own computer using installed software while the Muniauction system required no separate software. According to the court, Muniauction's modification of an existing auction system to use an internet-based software application rather than software installed on a user's computer was obvious. (*Muniauction, Inc. v. Thomson Corp.*, 532 F.3d 1318 (Fed. Cir. 2008)).

7.3. Business Method Patents

Business method patents frequently combine software with business methodology for novel ways of doing business. Many of these patents involve methods of doing business online.

A Few Examples of Business Method Patents. Here are some examples of business method patents:

Priceline Online Shopping System. Priceline.com's patented system allows online shoppers to name their own price for airline tickets, hotel rooms, and other travel related services.

Search Engine Spiders. The AltaVista Company owns a patent for a method of identifying and eliminating duplicate pages in a webpage search index.

Netflix's Method of Renting Movies. Netflix, the online video rental store, offers subscribers a method for renting items on a subscription basis. The patented method ranks and delivers items available for rental according to selection criteria provided by the customer.

A Brief History of Business Method Patents. Prior to 1998, patents were not available for business methods. In that year, a federal court upheld a patent for a computer system for calculating the net asset value of mutual funds and opened the door for other business method patents (*State Street Bank v. Signature Financial Group*, 149 F.3d 1368 (Fed. Cir. 1998)). Critics claim the *State Street* decision led to the issuance of weak patents for obvious technologies, abstract ideas, and components that are not patent-worthy.

In the 2008 case, *In re Bilski*, 545 F.3d 943 (Fed. Cir. 2008), the Federal Circuit Court of Appeals re-evaluated the requirements for business method patents. While the Federal Circuit Court did not explicitly overturn the *State Street* decision, it did make it more difficult to get a business method patent by saying that portions of the *State Street* opinion could no longer be relied upon. Namely, the *Bilski* court rejected the holding that issuance of a patent is appropriate for a process that produces a useful, concrete and tangible result. Instead, the *Bilski* court said a process eligible for patent protection must either involve a physical transformation or be tied to a particular machine.

The *Bilski* court did not say that a patent must involve technology. It also rejected the argument that methods of doing business are ineligible for patent protection. Nevertheless, the *Bilski* decision could be problematic because in the ten years between *State Street* and *Bilski* nearly 15,000 business method patents have been issued in fields such as banking, finance, insurance, data processing, industrial engineering, and medicine.

As of this writing, the Supreme Court has agreed to hear an appeal of the *Bilski* decision and determine which test should be applied when determining the patentability of a process. Hence, the issue is not yet settled.

7.4. Filing a Patent Application

Obtaining a patent requires filing an application with the Patent and Trademark Office. While it is possible for an inventor to file his or her own patent application, it is advisable to use a registered patent attorney or patent agent.

Patent attorneys and agents are recognized by the PTO as having the legal, scientific and technical qualifications necessary to prepare applications for patents and represent inventors in proceedings before the PTO. Registered patent attorneys and agents have a college degree in engineering or physical science or the equivalent and have passed an examination.

At the application stage, you can file either a provisional patent application or a complete application. The government filing fees for the provisional application are significantly less and, in some cases, the provisional application may require less preparation time. The provisional application, which requires a detailed description of the invention and a simple drawing but no claims, still allows the inventor to obtain a filing date and claim patent pending status. You have one year to incorporate the provisional application into a standard patent. If you fail to do so, the provisional application expires and you lose the filing date.

7.4.1. Components of a Utility Patent Application

The complete application for a utility patent must include a transmittal form, a specification consisting of one or more claims, a drawing, and a filing fee.

Transmittal Form. The transmittal form is a letter listing the documents included in the application and providing basic information such as the name of the applicant and the title of the invention.

Specification. The most important part of the specification is the claim or claims describing how the invention functions. In addition to the claims, the specification includes the invention title, a description of the invention including how to make and use the invention, and a narrative describing the advantages of the invention and how the invention solves previously existing problems.

Claims. Claims are included with the specification and define the scope of the protection afforded by the patent. The claims are perhaps the most important part of the patent application and their wording determines whether or not the patent will be granted. Each claim is numbered. Most utility patents contain ten to twenty claims. Writing patent claims is its own art form. They are in a stylized, legalistic format. The patent claims identify the products or processes over which the patent owner will have exclusivity during the patent term. Claims can be independent or dependent. An independent claim stands on its own. A dependent claim refers back to previous claims in the application. For example, here are the first two claims of the fourteen claims in Acco Brands, Inc.'s patent for a laptop lock. The first claim is independent. The second claim is dependent.

1. A locking method for a portable electronic device, comprising the steps of: Engaging a generally rectangular security slot, having dimensions of about 3 mm x 7 mm, defined in a wall of the portable electronic device with a moveable locking member; moving said locking member to a locked position relative to said security slot to configure said locking member in a locked configuration; and maintaining said locked configuration by use of a pin proximate said locking member; wherein said pin extends into said security slot.

2. The locking method of claim 1 wherein said locking member rotates to said locked position.

Drawings. Drawings must be included in the application if they are necessary to understand the patent claim. The drawings must show every feature of the invention as specified in the claims. Typically, the drawings are in black and white

Filing Fee. The fee schedule, which changes each October, is posted on the PTO's website. The fee is non-refundable. The exact fee depends on the number of sheets of paper in the specification and drawings and the number and type of claims presented.

Fees for complete applications include search fees, examination fees, and publication fees. If the patent ultimately issues, there will be additional fees the patent owner must periodically pay throughout the duration of the patent. If the owner of the invention is an independent inventor, small business, non-profit organization, or otherwise qualifies as a small entity, many of the fees are reduced.

7.4.2. Steps for Patent Registration

The process of completing a patent application and getting it through the registration process at the PTO is referred to as patent prosecution. A detailed explanation of the patent registration process is beyond the scope of this book. Here is a simplified outline of what occurs during prosecution of a standard utility patent.

Submission of Application. You submit a completed application to the PTO. You can submit your application in hardcopy form or in electronic form. The PTO encourages electronic filings.

If the application is complete, the PTO sends you a filing date receipt. If it is not complete, the PTO notifies you of the errors or problems that must be corrected before the application is deemed complete. Issuance of the filing date receipt means that the application will be forwarded to a patent examiner for examination purposes.

Examiner's Review. The application is assigned to an examiner who determines whether it complies with the legal patentability requirements. The application process begins with a comparison of the claims listed in the patent to prior art. If no differences are found between the claimed invention and the prior art, the corresponding claims are rejected as lacking novelty. The examiner also searches through United States patents, publications of patent applications, foreign patent documents, and available literature, to determine if the claimed invention is novel, useful and nonobvious and if the application otherwise meets the requirements for patentability.

The PTO publishes the patent application eighteen months after the filing date. Prior to that publication the application is confidential. The publication of a patent application marks the date at which it is publicly available and therefore the date on which it forms prior art for other patent applications worldwide.

Office Action and Applicant's Responses. If the patent examiner finds that the claims are deficient or that the patent fails for proper patentable subject matter, obviousness, usefulness, or novelty, she sends you a letter explaining the problem. The letter is called an Office Action. Most applications receive an initial Office Action. Few patent applications are accepted as initially filed.

Typically, the applicant has three months to respond in writing to the Office Action.

Final Rejection. If the examiner and applicant do not reach agreement on the claims and patent application, rejection may become final. The applicant then has the option to appeal to the PTO's Board of Patent Appeals and Interferences. An application rejected by the Board can be appealed to the Court of Appeals for the Federal Circuit which will review the PTO record and either affirm or reverse the PTO's action. Alternatively, the applicant can file a lawsuit against the PTO Director in the United States District Court for the District of Columbia which will render a decision after the applicant has an opportunity to present testimony.

Allowance/Issuance of Patent. If the examiner is satisfied with the patentability of the application claims, the applicant receives a Notice of Allowance and Fees Due. The applicant has three months from the date of the notice to pay the fee for issuing the patent. If the applicant does not make timely payment, the application is deemed abandoned. Upon payment, the PTO issues the patent. Upon issuance, the patent file normally becomes open to the public in the event not already opened earlier by publication of the application.

Interference. When two different inventors file patent applications seeking a patent on the same invention, there is often a dispute as to who is the first inventor with the right to the patent. The dispute is resolved through an interference proceeding, an administrative proceeding conducted by a panel of administrative patent judges. The losing party of the administrative proceeding may appeal to the

Court of Appeals for the Federal Circuit or file a civil action against the winning party in the appropriate United States district court.

7.4.3. Procedures after Patent Issuance

As of the writing of this book, the opportunities for a third party to oppose a pending patent application are limited. Patent regulations allow a third party to submit documents related to a pending application; however, the third party may not include any explanations or arguments with the document. Congress has considered legislation that would create an opposition system in the United States by which third parties could oppose a patent application during its prosecution.

Third Party Objection. Any third party may request reexamination, a request that obligates the PTO to examine further an issued patent. Whoever requests reexamination must also pay the reexamination fee, which is about equal to the full cost of filing a new patent application. A benefit of reexamination is that issued patents may be either invalidated or once again deemed valid, without the considerable cost and lengthy time required for a full patent infringement lawsuit.

7.5. Protecting Technology through Trade Secrets

A trade secret is confidential information of a particular company that gives the company a competitive advantage over other businesses. The primary benefit comes from the fact that other companies do not have the same information. I discuss the elements of trade secrets further in Section 3.7.4.

The category of items qualifying for trade secret protection is broad and includes both technology-related items and non-technology-related items.

Unlike patents, trade secret claims are based primarily on state law rather than federal law. For technology, companies choose trade secrets over patent law protection when the information may not qualify for patent protection or when the company hopes to maintain exclusivity of the information for longer than patent law allows. While patents last up to twenty years, trade secret protection can potentially last forever. Also, obtaining and maintaining trade secret protection is less expensive than patent protection.

The same technology can not be protected by both patent law and trade secret law at the same time. You must choose one. However, it is possible for content to be protected by both copyright and trade secret law.

7.6. Protecting Technology through Contract

The strongest and easiest to enforce mechanism for protecting your technology may be through a contract or a licensing agreement. This is a good solution if you are uncertain whether other forms of intellectual property law protection apply to your technology. Employees, consultants, and business partners of computer-related companies often sign non-disclosure and confidentiality agreements in which they agree not to disclose or use the trade secrets of the company.

USING OTHER PEOPLE'S MATERIAL

8.1. Permissions and Rights Clearance Basics

Your online work probably includes some materials that you did not create or to which you do not own the rights. The material might be a magazine article, a line from a poem, an illustration, or a clip from a television program. You might also incorporate the names, images, and stories of real people into your online work.

Typically, there are people or organizations that possess rights in those items. Depending upon the material and how you incorporate it into your online work, the person's rights might be classified as a copyright, a trademark, a right of publicity, a right of privacy, the right not to be defamed, or other right. The proper use of such material requires obtaining proper permissions and clearances.

In this chapter, I provide a brief overview of permissions and the rights clearance process. When you clear rights, you verify that your online work contains no material that violates the rights of another person or that violates any relevant laws. For more detailed information on the permission and rights clearance process, including step-by-step instructions on determining if you need permission and obtaining permission, I recommend my book, *The Permission Seeker's Guide Through the Legal Jungle: Clearing Copyrights, Trademarks, and Other Rights for Entertainment and Media Productions.*

8.1.1. Categories of Permission Risks

There are two separate categories of rights clearance risk. There is the risk of being sued and there is the separate risk of losing a lawsuit. Many rights owners are extremely aggressive about protecting the use of their content. They may launch a lawsuit over your unauthorized use of their content even if there is a valid justification under the law for the unauthorized use. As a result, you still incur the expense and time of defending a legal action, even if you ultimately win the legal action.

When you use someone's proprietary material without permission, there is always some level of risk. While the risk may sometimes be minimal, it is never zero. To minimize this risk, producers sometimes find it worthwhile to secure a license for material even when it may arguably be legal to use the material without a license.

As a general rule, you should obtain permission before using another person's intellectual property in your online work unless you determine that an exception such as fair use or the First Amendment applies. The law sometimes allows you to use someone else's material without permission. This allowance comes with a huge caveat. Application of the law to rights clearance questions is subjective and fact specific—even fickle at times. Having the rights owner's permission is always preferable. In the next sections, I discuss circumstances under which permission may not be required.

8.2. Use Protected by the First Amendment

The First Amendment to the United States Constitution reads as follows:

> Congress shall make no law respecting an establishment of religion, or prohibiting the free exercise thereof; or abridging the freedom of speech, or of the press; or the right of the people peaceably to assemble, and to petition the government for a redress of grievances.

It is the First Amendment's protections for the freedom of speech and of the press that are most significant for the internet. You cannot use copyright, trademark, and other rights as a means to stop people from expressing themselves, from giving their opinions, and from otherwise using their First Amendment rights.

Newsworthy is a manner of saying the topic or event is a matter of public interest or that the First Amendment applies. For example, the newsworthy use of a private person's name or photograph is permissible as long as the use is reasonably related to a matter of public interest.

8.3. Copyright Fair Use

The fair use exception to copyright protection allows you to use a reasonable portion of a copyrighted work without running afoul of copyright law. There is no bright line rule in determining what qualifies as fair use. Whether or not your use qualifies as a fair use depends on the specific circumstances. Courts use a four-factor test to determine whether a specific use of a copyrighted work qualifies as a fair use. No single factor is determinative.

Factor One: Purpose and Character of the Use. The first factor is the purpose and character of the use. This factor focuses on whether the use is for a commercial purpose or for a non-profit or educational purpose and whether the use is transformative.

Favored Uses for Fair Use. The Copyright Act lists favored uses for fair use. Favored uses include criticism, commentary, news reporting, teaching, scholarship and research. While each activity on this favored list is not always a non-profit use, the list does strongly hint at copyright law's preference that fair use be for non-profit purposes. Even if your unauthorized use fits into one of the favored use categories listed in the Copyright Act, you must still weigh the remaining three factors for each individual case of fair use.

Transformative Use. Copyright law likes transformative uses. Your use of a copyrighted work is transformative if your use is creatively different from the way in which the copyright owner used it. For example, a parody of a copyrighted work typically qualifies as transformative. As a general rule, the transformed work can not serve as a substitute for the original work.

Factor Two: Nature of the Copyrighted Work. There is a hierarchy of copyright protection. Some works are closer to the core of intended copyright protection than others. The more originality and creativity embodied in a work, the more protection it enjoys. An animated cartoon and a symphony are examples of works that might fall at the top of the hierarchy and receive the most protection copyright has to offer. Fact-based works like encyclopedias and biographies are at the bottom of this hierarchy and are sometimes referred to as having thin copyrights.

Factor Three: Amount of the Work Used. There is a copyright myth that you are in a fair use safe harbor if you use fewer than eight bars of a song, fewer than 250 words of a book or fewer than five seconds of a film. This is untrue! Use of a small amount of a copyrighted work has been deemed by courts as infringement. There is no set amount of a copyrighted work that guarantees fair use. Nevertheless, it is true that the less of a copyrighted work you use, the more inclined a court will be to view your use as a fair use.

The quality of what you take is just as important as the quantity. If you use the best part, the most notable part, or the most famous part of a copyrighted work, your use may be viewed as infringement even though you may have used only a small portion of the copyrighted work. In the fair use analysis, the best part of the copyrighted work is often referred to as the heart of the work.

Factor Four: Effect on the Copyright Owner's Ability to Market the Work. If your use competes with the original copyrighted work or damages the copyright owner's ability to market the work, your use is less likely to be viewed as a fair use.

8.4. Trademark Fair Use

Trademark fair use does not use the same four-factor test used for copyright fair use. There are two types of trademark fair use: (i) traditional or classic trademark fair use and (ii) nominative trademark fair use.

Classic trademark fair use recognizes that anyone may use a trademark in its descriptive sense. For example, Apple Computer owns a registered trademark for APPLE in connection with computer goods. That does not mean the company can prevent others from using the term "apple" to describe apple sauce, an apple orchard, or apple juice.

Nominative fair use recognizes that you can use a trademark to refer to or describe the trademark owner's goods or services. Your use of a trademark qualifies as a nominative fair use if all the following conditions apply:

- You can not readily identify the good or service without using the trademark.
- You use the trademark only to the extent necessary to identify the good or service.
- Your use does not falsely suggest sponsorship or endorsement by the trademark owner.

For example, Terri Welles, Playboy's 1981 Playmate of the Year, created a website offering photos of herself for sale, membership in her photo club, and promoting her services as a spokesperson. Welles' use of the terms "Playboy", "Playmate" and "Playmate of the Year 1981," accurately described her affiliation with the magazine; were nominative; and did not infringe the Playboy trademarks. Welles could use the trademarks to describe her affiliation with the magazine. However, Welles' repeated depiction of "PMOY 81" in the wallpaper of the website was not necessary to describe Welles, and was not a nominative, fair use. (*Playboy Enterprises, Inc. v Welles*, 279 F.3d 796 (9th Cir. 2002)).

8.5. Parody

A parody is a form of commentary that borrows liberally from the original work in order to make fun of it. In order to qualify as a parody, the parody must be a commentary on the original work being quoted or copied. If you are borrowing from one work in order to comment about something else, the result is satire—not parody —and may be infringement of the work from which you borrow.

Parody of Copyrighted Works. When determining whether an unauthorized use of a copyrighted work qualifies as a parody, courts apply the same four-factor copyright fair use test discussed in Section 8.3. The nature of parody requires that the four-factor test be more flexible.

Factor One: Purpose and Character of the Use. The Copyright Act lists favored uses for fair use. The favored uses are criticism, comment, news reporting, teaching, scholarship and research. While the list does not specifically include parody, since parody is a form of commentary and criticism, courts consider parody as a favored use.

Courts applying the fair use test favor uses that are transformative and that are poor substitutes for the original work. By their very nature, parodic works are transformative. They are new works originating from pre-existing works and are typically poor substitutes for the original work they critique.

Factor Two: Nature of the Copyrighted Work. There is a hierarchy of copyright protection. Highly creative works are at the top of the hierarchy and receive the most copyright protection. Fact-based works receive less protection. Whether a work is highly creative or fact-based holds less significance in a parody case because parodies almost invariably copy popular and well-known works that are highly creative.

Factor Three: Amount of the Work Used. While the creator of a parody can be more liberal in the amount borrowed from a copyrighted work, the parody should nevertheless borrow just enough to conjure up the original in the minds of the audience. Copyright law is often more forgiving of parodies that use the heart, best part or most famous part of the copyrighted work. Copyright law recognizes that the heart is the section that most readily makes the audience think of the copyrighted work.

Factor Four: Effect of Use on the Copyright Owner's Ability to Market the Work. Typically, the parody is not a replacement for the copyrighted work. Copyright owners often claim that the parody damages the reputation of their works and thus affects their ability to market it. This argument is usually unsuccessful.

Parody of Trademarks. In cyberspace trademarks appear in parodies when people use the trademarks of the products, companies, and individuals of which they want to make fun or otherwise criticize. The trademark in question is often used in a domain name or in the text of a website.

8.6. Public Domain Materials

If a creative work is in the public domain, you may copy, distribute, perform or otherwise use the work without fear of violating any copyright laws. It is not necessary to obtain permission for the use from the work's author.

For purposes of copyright law, being in the public domain means that the copyright in the work has expired—or that no copyright ever existed in the work. Do not confuse a work in the public domain with a work that is available to the public. A book that is on sale at the bookstore is available to the public; however, its public availability does not mean necessarily that the book is in the public domain or that you may freely copy the book.

There are several routes by which creative works can meander their way into the public domain:

- The copyright expires.
- The copyright owner failed to comply with a past copyright formality.
- The work qualifies as a federal government work.

- The copyright owner deliberately places the work in the public domain.

8.6.1. Works with Expired Copyrights

Materials most commonly enter the public domain as a result of the expiration or lapse of their copyright period. Copyright protection is not indefinite. It lasts for a specified period of time. Due to changes in copyright law over the years, different creative works have different copyright terms. The copyright term depends on the creation or publication date of the specific work.

Copyright Term for Copyrighted Works Created On or After January 1, 1978. In general, a copyright in a work created on or after January 1, 1978 has a copyright duration that lasts for the lifetime of the creator plus seventy years. For example, if John Smith writes a song in 2012 and dies in 2025, the copyright in the song expires seventy years after John's death or in 2095.

If there is more than one creator, the copyright duration expires seventy years after the life of the last surviving author. For example, suppose John Smith and Susan Brown co-write a song in 2012, John dies in 2025, and Susan dies in 2029. Susan is the last surviving creator and the copyright in the song expires seventy years after Susan's death, or in 2099.

The owner of a copyright is not always a person. The copyright owner may be a company or organization that owns its employee's work as a work made for hire. I discuss the concept of work made for hire in Section 3.4. The copyright in a work made for hire lasts for ninety-five years from its first publication or for 120 years from its creation, whichever is shorter. A copyrighted work that is published anonymously or under a pseudonym has the same copyright term as a work made for hire—ninety-five years from its first publication or 120 years from its creation, whichever period is shorter.

For example, suppose John Smith writes his song in 2012. He writes the song within the scope of his employment with a video game manufacturer so the video game manufacturer owns the copyright in the song as a work made for hire. The song is included on a new videogame released by the manufacturer in 2012. Let's assume the use of the song on the videogame qualifies as publication of the song. In this case, the copyright in the song expires ninety-five years after publication. That is because 2107, the date that is 95 years after first publication, is sooner than 2132, the date that is 120 years after John's creation of the song.

Let's change the scenario. John writes the song in 2012 for his employer. However, the employer never publishes the song so there is no publication date to determine the copyright term. Hence, the copyright term runs from the creation date and expires in 2132.

Copyright Term for Works Created Prior to January 1, 1978. The above rules apply to works created on or after January 1, 1978. Different copyright terms apply to works created prior to 1978. Works published prior to 1978 have a copyright term of up to ninety-five years from the date of publication.

Pre-1978 works fall under the previous copyright law statute, the 1909 Copyright Act. The 1909 Copyright Act provided for an initial term of twenty-eight years and a renewal term. The renewal term initially provided another twenty-eight years for a total copyright term of up to fifty-six years. To keep up with changes in the current Copyright Act, the duration of this renewal term was gradually increased and is currently sixty-seven years.

If the work was published prior to 1964, the copyright owner had to file a renewal application with the Copyright Office in order to receive the additional term. If no renewal application was filed for a pre-1964 work, it fell into the public domain after expiration of the initial twenty-eight-year term. Renewal is automatic for works published between 1964 and 1977. These works receive the subsequent term even if the copyright owner failed to file a renewal application.

Summary of General Guidelines. Although there are variations, here are some general guidelines for determining whether a pre-1978 work is in the public domain. A work published prior to 1923 is now in the public domain. A work published between 1923 and 1963 has a copyright term of ninety-five years from the date of the work's publication if its copyright owner filed a timely renewal application. If the copyright owner failed to file a timely renewal application for a work published between 1923 and 1963, the copyright expired twenty-eight years after the publication date. A work published between 1964 and 1977 has a copyright duration of ninety-five years from its date of publication regardless of whether the copyright owner filed a renewal application.

The guidelines are summarized in the chart below.

Creation/Publication Date	Duration of Copyright
Created on or after Jan. 1, 1978	Life of author plus 70 years
Published between 1964–1977	95 years from date of publication
Published between 1923–1963	95 years from date of publication if renewal application filed; 28 years if not

Effect of the Sonny Bono Act On Expiring Copyright Terms. 1923 will remain the magic public domain status cut-off year for awhile. The Sonny Bono Copyright Term Extension Act amended the Copyright Act and extended copyright duration by twenty years for all works still under copyright protection as of January 1, 1999. The current general copyright duration is the life of the author plus seventy years. Prior to the Sonny Bono Act, the general copyright duration was the life of the author plus fifty years. Unless copyright law changes again, no works that were protected by copyright on January 1, 1999 will fall into the public domain as a result of an expired copyright until January 1, 2019.

8.6.2. Failure to Comply with Copyright Formalities

Currently, there are no formal actions required to obtain and maintain a copyright—but there used to be. A work could have fallen into the public domain if the copyright owner failed to take one of these required actions—such as failing to file a renewal application, an action required for works published prior to 1964, or publishing a work without a proper copyright notice, a step required for works published prior to 1989. I discuss former copyright formalities further in Section 3.5.

8.6.3. Federal Government Works

Works created by federal government employees or commissioned by the federal government as works made for hire are in the public domain. This includes the text of speeches and official papers prepared or given by federal officials *while they are in office*. State and local government works may be protected by copyright.

8.6.4. Works Placed in the Public Domain by Copyright Owners

Some copyright owners deliberately place their work into the public domain. You may use such material without the creator's permission.

There are also hybrid situations in which a copyright owner places her work somewhere in between the public domain and full copyright protection. Some organizations provide standard ways and licenses or statements for copyright owners to reserve some rights but not all. Organizations, such as The Free Software Foundation and the Open Source Initiative provide such statements for software. Creative Commons focuses on music, images, text, and video.

Creative Commons Materials. Creative Commons, a non-profit organization, offers copyright owners free documentation to assist them in placing their works in the public domain. Copyright owners that want to retain some rights can use one of a number of free Creative Commons licenses that relax the Copyright Act's exclusive rights.

For example, if a copyright owner adopts a Creative Commons Attribution License, anyone may copy, distribute, display, perform and develop derivative works from the copyright owner's work as long as the copyright owner receives attribution—or credit for the work. If a copyright owner adopts a Creative Commons Non-commercial License, anyone may use the copyright owner's work for a non-commercial purpose.

Current versions of Creative Commons Licenses do not include representations, warranties, or indemnifications. In essence, representations and warranties are guaranties by the rights owner that he is authorized to give you permission to use the material and that the material has no clearance problems. By agreeing to indemnify you, the rights owner agrees to pay or reimburse you for any monetary loss you suffer as a result of relying on a representation that ultimately turns out to be false. Without representations, warranties, and indemnification, you are taking the Creative Commons material as is and essentially using it at your own risk.

8.6.5. Other Rights Clearance Considerations When Using Public Domain Works

There may be other rights considerations required for your use of public domain material. These considerations include right of publicity, right of privacy and defamation concerns.

For example, if you find images of real people posted online under a Creative Commons License, the Creative Commons License waives only copyright restrictions. It does not waive the privacy and other personal rights of the person in the photograph. Use of a person's photograph in a commercial advertisement without obtaining the person's permission would be a privacy violation or misappropriation of the person's image.

8.7. Using Other's Copyrighted Materials

Copyright infringement occurs when someone exercises one of the copyright holder's exclusive rights without permission. For example, each of the following activities, if done without the permission of the copyright owner, is typically copyright infringement:

- posting online an entire chapter of a book
- posting online an entire newspaper or magazine article
- posting online a full, high resolution copy of an image
- posting online the full lyrics to a song

8.7.1. Using Snippets, Thumbnails, and Clips

Many online works incorporate abbreviated or miniature versions of copyrighted works. For example, many search engines include low-resolution, thumbnail-sized reproductions of visual artwork. If your use of the clip does not qualify as fair use or other exception to copyright, you need permission from the copyright owner. While the use of snippets, thumbnails and clips often qualifies as a fair use, there is no guarantee of a fair use determination. Each specific use must go through the same four-factor copyright fair use analysis discussed in Section 8.3.

Snippets of Text. A snippet or a clip is a small portion of a larger work. Snippets often refer to small portions of textual works. For example, a snippet may be thirty words from an entire book.

Although one might also use the term snippet to refer to a small portion of an audio or video work, I refer to portions of audio and audio-visual works as clips and discuss their use below.

Quoting from Other Blogs. Many bloggers borrow from other blogs. I suggest not doing a re-write or extensive paraphrasing of another blog posting even when attribution is given. It is copyright infringement. In contrast, it is likely not copyright infringement if you use quotes from a blog posting for the purpose of adding your own substantive commentary. How much you may quote depends on a fair use analysis.

Newspaper Articles. Bloggers and others frequently quote from newspaper articles in their online postings. How much may one excerpt from a news article before it goes beyond fair use? There is no magic number such as less than 200 words. Again, you want to consider the copyright fair use factors when determining how much you may excerpt.

The Associated Press has agreed that linking to and excerpting small quotes from news articles is permissible. However, the Associated Press distinguishes the activity of providing a link to an article from the activity of verbatim copying of a headline and the lead paragraph with a link to the full article. It argues that the latter practice is not fair use because the headline and lead paragraph contain a large percentage of the story's value. While the Associated Press has scuffled with some prominent blogs regarding the matter, it has not filed a lawsuit and no court has yet issued a ruling on whether it is fair use to copy the headline and lead paragraph of a news article.

Thumbnails of Images. A thumbnail is a reduced sized version of a visual work. When used on the internet, the thumbnail is frequently low resolution and accompanied by a link to the full-sized image located on another website.

Here is an example of when thumbnail use satisfied the fair use test and an example of when it did not.

Arriba's Thumbnail Use Qualifies as a Fair Use. Arriba Soft Corp. operated an internet search engine that displayed results in the form of small, low-resolution pictures. Arriba obtained its database of pictures by copying images from other web sites. A court found Arriba's use to be a transformative, fair use because Arriba's search engine improved access to images on the internet and the low-resolution thumbnail images did not serve as a substitute for the original images. (*Kelly v. Arriba Soft, Corp.* 280 F.3d 934, (9th Cir. 2002)); opinion later withdrawn for technical reasons not directly relevant to thumbnail use analysis and replaced by 336 F.3d 811 (9th Cir. 2003)).

Funeral Depot's Thumbnail Use Does Not Qualify as Fair Use. Batesville Casket manufactured caskets and sold them through a network of authorized dealers. As part of its marketing efforts, Batesville Casket created lithographs featuring images and descriptions of its caskets and allowed its authorized dealers to use the lithographs at no charge.

Funeral Depot, which sold Batesville Caskets even though it was not an authorized dealer, used several of the Batesville-created lithographs. Although Funeral Depot used low-resolution thumbnail images on its own website, those thumbnails linked to full-sized images on another website controlled by Funeral Depot. Batesville Casket sued Funeral Depot for copyright infringement.

The court ruled that Funeral Depot's use of the casket images was not a fair use. The use was not transformative or informational. Instead, Funeral Depot used high resolution versions of the images for the purpose of promoting its own sales efforts. (*Batesville Services vs. Funeral Depot*, Copyright Law Reporter P28,901 (S.D. Ind., Nov. 10, 2004)).

Audio and Audio-Visual Clips. Clips often refer to small portions of audio or video works. A clip may be a few seconds of an entire song or of a film or television program.

For films and music, your use might miss the fair use mark even if you use a very small portion of the original work. For example, Video Pipeline provided trailers for streaming on websites that sold home videos such as Yahoo!, Amazon, and Best Buy. Video Pipeline's internet clients paid a fee for the streaming service. After Disney declined to continue licensing trailers of Disney films to Video Pipeline, Video Pipeline created its own previews of Disney films by copying approximately two minutes from each of over sixty Disney movies. Finding that creation and streaming of the previews was likely not a fair use, the court enjoined Video Pipeline from making its own previews of Disney films and displaying them on the internet. (*Video Pipeline v. Buena Vista Home*, 342 F.3d 191 (3d Cir. 2003)).

8.7.2. Linking

Hypertext links are instructions that take you from one webpage to another. Visitors to your webpage do not see the instructions. They identify the link because it appears as highlighted text on your webpage. While some websites take a conservative approach and ask for permission prior to linking to another website, many other website owners link without asking permission. Linking generally does not subject you to any legal liability. The potential exceptions include deep linking, framing and linking to infringing material.

Deep Linking. When you deep link to a webpage, you skip the home page and material such as advertising the website owners want visitors to see. Deep linking may lead to consumer confusion and result in claims of copyright or trademark infringement. Some companies write into their website terms of service prohibitions against deep linking to any pages on their website. There have been lawsuits alleging copyright, trademark and related claims as a result of deep linking. Most of these lawsuits have settled prior to a trial with the defendant agreeing to stop deep linking to the other party's website. If you deep link, do not do it in a way that might mislead consumers into thinking that you are the creator of the material to which you are linking.

Framing. Framing allows visitors to your website to view content from another site without actually leaving your website. Like deep linking, framing may lead to consumer confusion and result in claims of copyright or trademark infringement.

Linking or Referring Users to Infringing Materials. Linking to a website that contains material which infringes another party's copyrights can lead to claims against you for contributory copyright infringement. You are guilty of contributory copyright infringement if you encourage or make it easier for someone else to infringe copyrighted material.

One of the provisions of the Digital Millennium Copyright Act (DMCA) provides a safe harbor immunizing you from copyright infringement for links to infringing material. I discuss the DMCA further in Sections 8.7.3 and 12.5.

8.7.3. DMCA Insulation from Copyright Infringement Claims

The Digital Millennium Copyright Act (DMCA) includes safe harbors that insulate the operators of online sites from claims of copyright infringement for material posted by their customers and online visitors as well as from claims of copyright infringement for linking to infringing material. To qualify for the safe harbor for material posted by others, you must comply with specific DMCA requirements. I discuss the DMCA further in Section 12.5.

8.8. Using Other Protected Materials

8.8.1. Trademarks

You commit trademark infringement when you create a likelihood of confusion with a pre-existing trademark. A likelihood of confusion exists when a consumer might confuse your proposed trademark with an existing trademark already being used to identify the source of a similar good or service. Section 5.5 provides an overview of trademark basics. Section 5.5.3 contains a discussion of when a particular use might create a likelihood of confusion with a trademark.

Permissible Uses of Others' Trademarks. There are several circumstances in which you can use a trademark without being liable for trademark infringement:

First Amendment Protection. Holding a trademark, copyright, or other intellectual property right is not a right to limit the manner in which people can express themselves. As a general rule, you may use trademarks in an online site that parodies, criticizes, of otherwise comments on the product, company, or people associated with those trademarks.

Trademark Fair Use. Classic trademark fair use recognizes that anyone may use a trademark in its descriptive sense. Nominative fair use recognizes that anyone may use a trademark to refer to or describe the trademark owner's goods or services. Section 8.4 contains more discussion of trademark fair use.

Reference. You may refer to a trademark in your online work as long as the reference does not falsely imply that the trademark owner is somehow sponsoring, endorsing or affiliated with you, your company, or products.

Product Appearances. Several court rulings say the unauthorized appearance of a brand-name product in your creative work such as a website is permissible as long as the appearance does not tarnish the product's reputation, draw on the goodwill associated with the product, or mislead people to believe that the product manufacturer has endorsed or sponsored you, your company, or your products.

Metatags. Metatags are index words inserted in webpages so that the page is identified when someone performs a search engine query for the word. For example, metatags for a companion webpage to *The Cyber Citizen's Guide Through the Legal Jungle* might include "internet law", "internet defamation", and "online copyright fair use". Metatags are imbedded in the code of your website and are not visible to visitors who access a site with a normal web browser.

The use of a trademark as a metatag may constitute trademark infringement if it creates a likelihood of confusion as discussed in Section 5.5.3. Most liability in this area results from a company using its competitor's trademarks as a metatag. For example, Pepsi's use of Coke as a metatag might be a problem because it would lead people searching for Coke to the site of its competitor, Pepsi.

However, using trademarks as a metatag is valid if used to describe the content and subject matter of your website. As discussed in Section 8.4, in such a case, the use of a trademark as a metatag is a fair use of the trademark.

8.8.2. Patents

A patent is a property right that applies to inventions and discoveries. Patent infringement occurs when without the patent owner's authority you make, use, offer to sell, or sell any patented invention, within the United States. It is also infringement to import into the United States any patented invention without the patent owner's authorization. I discuss patent protection further in Chapter 7.

8.8.3. Trade Secrets

A trade secret is confidential information of a particular company that gives the company a competitive advantage over other businesses. I discuss trade secrets further in Sections 3.7.4 and 7.5. Companies have filed lawsuits against operators of blogs and electronic bulletin boards complaining that the companies' trade secrets have been posted.

8.9. Mentioning Real People Online

If your online work mentions or portrays real people, you need to think about privacy rights, publicity rights, and defamation. Unlike copyright and much of trademark law, the right of privacy, the right of publicity and defamation are governed by state law. As a result, these laws vary significantly from state to state.

8.9.1. Privacy Rights

Broadly speaking, the right of privacy is a person's right to be left alone. Privacy violations often involve using hidden cameras and microphones or disclosing embarrassing private facts about a person. The more famous a person is, the less ability that person has to claim privacy rights. This is due to the First Amendment. Events and personal matters surrounding a person in public life are matters of legitimate public interest and discourse.

Deceased people have no privacy rights. However, if your online work mentions a deceased individual, you must still exercise caution so as not to violate the privacy rights of the deceased person's living relatives and associates. Also, a person's publicity rights, discussed in Section 8.9.2, may survive the person's death.

8.9.2. Publicity Rights

The right of publicity allows each individual to control and profit from the commercial value of his or her own identity. The right covers all aspects of an individual's identity including name, likeness, voice, and personally identifying characteristics.

To win a right of publicity claim, a person must demonstrate that his identity has commercial value and that you used his identity without consent for commercial purposes. If you use the person's identity in a non-commercial rather than commercial context, there is no right of publicity claim. Broadly speaking, you are using a person's identity for a commercial purpose when you use the person's identity to sell something. If you use the person's identity in connection with news, public affairs, or a political campaign with which that person is involved, you are likely using the person's identity in a non-commercial context.

While there is no right of privacy for deceased individuals, several states allow the right of publicity to extend beyond death.

8.9.3. Defamation

There is a rise in the number of defamation claims being generated by online activities. Although people may refer to internet defamation, for the most part, online defamation laws mirror offline defamation laws. The one exception is insulation provided to websites through the Communications Decency Act discussed in this section below.

What Is Defamation? You defame someone when you make a false statement about the person and the statement harms the person's reputation. While each state has its own defamation laws, certain U.S. Supreme Court rulings set specific guidelines on how states may structure their defamation laws.

Publication Required. Before you are guilty of defamation, you must communicate the false statement to someone other than the person who is the subject of the statement. For example, suppose you say or write in a private email to the board member of a non-profit organization, "You've embezzled funds from your organization." You do not share the accusation with anyone else. In that situation, there is no defamation even if the statement is false. You have shared the accusation only with the board member who is the subject of the statement. That is not a publication or a communication for purposes of defamation. Once you repeat or share your accusation with additional people, there is the possibility of a defamation action.

Negligence for Private Individuals; Actual Malice for Public Figures. To be guilty of defamation, you must have made the defamatory statement with negligence or with actual malice. Public figures and public officials must prove that you made the statement with actual malice. Actual malice is publication of a statement with knowledge that the offending statement is false or publication with reckless disregard of whether or not the statement is false.

Private figures need only show that you were negligent in making the statement. Negligence is the absence of reasonable care. You are negligent if you are slipshod and careless in putting together your statements about the person.

Who Qualifies as a Public Official or Public Figure? As a public official or public figure in a defamation lawsuit, you must prove that the other side made the damaging statement about you with malice. A private individual need only prove negligence. The distinction can make the difference between winning and losing a defamation lawsuit.

A public official is someone who holds a position of considerable importance and is responsible for governmental affairs. Most elected or appointed federal, state or territorial officials are public officials. It is often more difficult to determine whether lower-level city and state officials qualify as public officials.

You become a public figure by being famous or notorious, by attracting public attention, or by being at the center of a public issue. There are degrees of public figure status. Very famous people like Barbara Walters and Oprah Winfrey are public figures in all circumstances. On the other side of the spectrum are those who qualify as a public figure for a particular issue and remain a private individual for all other issues. These limited purpose public figures evolve either by accident or by the deliberate actions of the public figure. For example, the unlucky victim of a highly reported natural disaster might involuntarily become a public figure for a short period of time. A private individual is anyone who is not a public official or public figure.

Insulation from Online Defamation Claims through the Communications Decency Act. Operators of websites and other online works have special protection from defamation actions under the immunity created by the federal Communications Decency Act (CDA). The provision of the CDA providing insulation is often referred to as Section 230 because 230 is the code section number within the federal statute. CDA Section 230 provides that:

No provider . . . of an interactive computer service shall be treated as the publisher or speaker of any information provided by another information content provider.

In other words, if someone else posts a defamatory statement on your website, blog, community bulletin board, or online work, you are not legally responsible.

This immunity is available to all providers of interactive computer services. Courts have treated many diverse entities as "users and providers of interactive computer service" eligible for the protection offered by Section 230 of the CDA. They include operators of electronic community bulletin boards, websites, and discussion lists.

CDA Immunity Does Not Apply to Content You Provide. CDA immunity applies only if you function as an interactive computer service provider. It does not apply if you function as an information content provider. An information content provider is someone who is partially or entirely responsible for the creation of the offending content.

It is possible to function as both a service provider and a content provider. You are a service provider with respect to content that someone else creates and you passively display on your website. Such content might include comments submitted by your online visitors, entries written by guest bloggers, and information provided to you through an RSS feed.

You do not have immunity for content you create. For example, if you actively gather data from external sources and post the information on your website, you have taken an active role in creating the content and would not be insulated by the CDA if the information is defamatory.

Good Samaritan Rule Allows You to Edit User-Provided Content. You remain immune from liability even if you take an active editing role and make decisions about whether to publish, remove, or modify content. This is sometimes referred to as the Good Samaritan provision and encourages websites to self-regulate. However, if you change or edit the user provided content in a manner that changes the original meaning and results in making it defamatory, the CDA may not protect your actions.

CDA Immunity Applies Only to Content Willingly Provided for Publication. If you post content provided to you, the CDA insulates you only if the person furnishing the content intended that you publish the material online. This was not clearly the situation in a case involving potentially stolen Nazi art in the home of Ellen Batzel.

While doing some work at the North Carolina home of Ellen Batzel, handyman Robert Smith claimed to hear Batzel say that she was a descendant of a Nazi politician who was a close associate of Adolf Hitler. Smith inferred that some of the paintings in Batzel's home, which Batzel said she had inherited, were stolen Nazi art. Smith sent an email about the matter to Museum Security Network, a website and discussion forum operated by Tom Cremers and focusing on museum security and stolen art. Even though Smith was not a subscriber to the forum, Cremers published Smith's email message to the Museum Security Network, with some minor wording changes and a note that the FBI had been informed of the matter.

Batzel sued both Smith and Cremers for defamation. Smith claimed he never intended or realized that his email would be posted online. According to the court, CDA immunity applies only if the third person who created the information furnished it to the provider under circumstances in which a reasonable person would conclude that the information was provided for publication. It was unclear from the record whether Cremers' belief that Smith submitted the email for internet publication was reasonable. As a result, the court would not dismiss the case on summary judgment. (*Batzel v. Smith*, 333 F.3d 1018 (9th Cir. 2003)).

Real-Life Examples of Insulation provided by the Communications Decency Act. CDA immunity has extended beyond protection from defamation to protect online service providers from several other categories of claims:

No Liability for Sexual Assault. A fourteen year old girl lied about her age to circumvent social network site, MySpace's, protections for minors. She communicated with an older man through her online account, exchanged personal contact information with him, and was assaulted by him when the two met in person. The girl's mother sued MySpace for negligently failing to implement safety mechanisms to prevent sexual predators from using its online service. The court viewed the negligence claim as directed toward MySpace in its publishing, editorial, and screening capacities. CDA immunity applied to MySpace because MySpace had not provided the content that resulted in the assault. (*Doe v. MySpace*, 474 F. Supp. 2d 843 (W.D. Tex. 2007)).

Liability for Sale of Obscene Videotapes. When a man discussed and tried to sell obscene videotapes in one of AOL's chat rooms, AOL was not liable for the negligent distribution of obscene material. Imposing such liability on AOL would be holding AOL responsible for failing to prevent its users' from publishing allegedly illegal postings. (*Doe v. America Online*, 783 So. 2d 1010 (2001)).

No Liability for Interference with Business. OptIn claimed that Ironport's SpamCop website interfered with its business by listing OptIn as a major source of spam and, thereby, causing multiple ISPs to block its email. The CDA protected Ironport and the SpamCop list because it was content generated and derived by third parties. (*Optinrealbig.com, LLC v. Ironport Systems, Inc.*, 323 F. Supp. 2d 1037 (N.D. Cal. 2004)).

No Liability for Counterfeit Sports Memorabilia. When a seller offered falsely autographed sports memorabilia on the eBay auction site, the CDA protected eBay from a claim under California's Autographed Sports Memorabilia law. The false descriptions of the goods were supplied by a third party seller and not by eBay. (*Gentry v. eBay, Inc.*, 121 Cal. Rptr. 2d 703 (2002)).

No Liability for Negative Comments. Amazon.com was not liable for breach of contract, negligent misrepresentation, or interference with contract for failing to remove negative comments about a book. A third party, and not Amazon, had provided the negative comments. The CDA immunized Amazon even though the comments violated Amazon's terms of service and Amazon failed to act on an alleged promise to the book's author to remove the comments. (*Schneider v. Amazon.com, Inc.*, 31 P.3d 37 (2001)).

No Liability for Criminal Privacy Violation. A web host provider had no criminal liability when users of its service uploaded videotape of college athletes undressing in locker room showers and rest rooms. The web host was not the provider of the videotape content. (*John Does 1 Through 30 v. Franco Productions*, No. 99C-7885 (N.D. Ill., June 21, 2000)).

Avoiding Defamation Claims. Here are some guidelines to help you minimize the risk of your online work generating defamation claims:

Realize You Are Accountable for Your Internet Speech. Just because you say it through the internet does not mean you are not accountable for your defamatory language.

Stick to the Facts. Your risks of a defamation claim increase if you stray from verifiable facts when you discuss real people and real events.

Solicit Comments. Offer your subject an opportunity to confirm or deny any allegations. Courts view this action as a sign you are exercising journalistic objectivity. It may help to qualify you for protection of the reporter privilege and shield laws discussed in Section 11.5.1.

Write about Public Figures and Issues of Public Concern. Your risk of defamation decreases if the real people mentioned in your online work are public figures or if other people involved in events of public concern. Also, if the real people about whom you write are no longer living, note that the deceased cannot be defamed.

Do Not Think Changing Names Is Sufficient. Changing names is not always enough. Even without using real names, your readers might be able to identify the person through your mention of a nickname, geographic location, physical description, personality trait, or real-life events in which the person was involved.

Get a Release. Have the real person sign a release giving you permission to tell his story. This might be an interview release or life story rights release.

Obtain Media Liability Insurance. Media liability insurance protects you if you are accused of violating someone's rights. Coverage can vary by policy and may cover claims in addition to defamation such as copyright, trademark, and privacy violations. The insurance may also be called by a number of other names such as errors and omissions insurance, media liability insurance, media peril insurance, and producer's liability insurance. Media liability insurance does not cover you for knowingly or deliberately violating defamation, copyright, trademark, and related laws.

Use Reliable Sources. Keep notes to show that any negative impressions in your online work about a living person are truthful and that you obtained those true facts from credible sources to which you had legitimate access such as public records and newspapers.

My book, *The Permission Seeker's Guide Through the Legal Jungle*, includes a more extensive discussion on defamation including what needs to happen before you are liable for defamation, who qualifies as a public figure, and your best defenses to defamation.

8.10. Using Music on the Internet

There are some special issues that come up with respect to the use of music on the internet.

8.10.1. How Songs, Sound Recordings and Phonorecords Differ

To understand the requirements for the online use of music, it is crucial to recognize the distinction among songs, sound recordings, and phonorecords.

Song. A song consists of a melody and any accompanying lyrics. The Copyright Act refers to songs as musical works. Typically, the copyright in a song is owned by the songwriter or by the songwriter's music publishing company.

Sound Recording. A sound recording is the recorded rendition of a song. The copyright in a sound recording is typically owned by the record label that released the recording. Within the music industry, a sound recording is often referred to as a master.

Phonorecord. A phonorecord is any material object onto which sound can be recorded such as an audiocassette, a compact disc or a vinyl record. When you obtain a digital version of a phonorecord via the internet, the Copyright Act refers to the output as a digital phonorecord delivery or DPD.

A single song may have several different sound recordings. For example, a number of artists have recorded the song *Amazing Grace*. They include Aretha Franklin, Elvis Presley, and Leontyne Price. The familiar melody and lyrics make up the song. Aretha Franklin's recorded performance of *Amazing Grace* is one sound recording; Elvis Presley's recorded performance of the song is a separate sound recording; and Leontyne Price's recorded rendition of *Amazing Grace* is still a third sound recording. That is three separate sound recordings for the same song.

You can think of the phonorecord as the metaphorical carrying case for the sound recording. Owning the phonorecord does not give you any ownership interest in the sound recording or song. For example, if I walk into a store and purchase a CD with Frank Sinatra singing *That's Life*, I am now the owner of the CD. The CD in my hand as I walk out of the record store is the phonorecord. Had I purchased *That's Life* as a digital download, that is also a phonorecord in the eyes of the Copyright Act. The phonorecord is the physical object or digital file which contains the sound recording of Frank Sinatra singing the song entitled *That's Life*.

The license required to use music on the internet depends on whether you use the song, the sound recording or both and how you use them. It is not possible to use a sound recording without also using the underlying song. As a result, if you use a sound recording and the underlying song is copyright protected, you need a license from both the copyright owner of the sound recording and the copyright owner of the song.

8.10.2. Licenses for Songs

Public Performance License. A public performance license provides permission to perform a song in public. Public venues requiring public performance licenses include the internet as well as the radio, television, restaurants, and concert halls. The public venue playing the music is normally responsible for obtaining and paying for the public performance license. The performing rights organizations for songs—ASCAP, BMI, and SESAC—issue most public performance licenses.

Mechanical License. A mechanical license provides permission to reproduce and distribute a song onto phonorecords. To make and distribute a recording of an existing song, you need a mechanical license from the copyright owner of the song. You need a mechanical license whether you are making and distributing physical copies (*e.g.*, CDs, tapes) of the song or digital downloads of the song.

If the song has already been commercially released, you can obtain a compulsory mechanical license. License fees and other terms of a compulsory license are established by law. Therefore, there is no need to obtain direct permission from or negotiate license terms with the copyright owner if a compulsory license is available.

The Harry Fox Agency issues mechanical licenses on behalf of more than 22,000 music publishers. Other than relaxing certain notice and accounting requirements, the mechanical license issued by the Harry Fox Agency substantially mirrors the compulsory mechanical license.

Synchronization License. A synchronization license or synch license provides permission to reproduce or record a song onto the soundtrack of an audio-visual production such as a film or television program or multimedia production. Synchronization refers to the fact that the song is synchronized with the visual images of the audio-visual production.

Display of Song Lyrics. Song lyrics are protected by copyright law whether they are used with or without an accompanying melody. Websites offering song lyrics without permission are violating copyright laws and exposing themselves to claims of copyright infringement. Of course, if you are displaying the lyrics in a manner consistent with fair use, you are not violating any copyright laws. But, like most fair use questions, determining whether a particular use qualifies as a fair use is often subjective.

8.10.3. Licenses for Sound Recordings

Master Use License. When you obtain a master use license, you have permission to use a sound recording in an audio-visual production. The master use license is completely distinct from the synchronization license which authorizes you to use a song in an audio-visual production. You cannot use a sound recording without also using the underlying song. When you obtain a master use license in a sound recording, if the underlying song is copyright-protected, you must also obtain a synchronization license in the song.

License to Perform a Sound Recording via Digital Audio Transmission. As discussed in Section 3.2, the exclusive right of public performance by means of digital audio transmission is applicable only to sound recordings. Websites that want to stream sound recordings need a license to perform the sound recording via digital audio transmission. I discuss licenses for streaming music in Section 8.10.5.

8.10.4. Licenses Required for Downloading Music

With downloaded or compressed music, a copy of the music is placed on your computer hard drive.

Downloading the Song. Offering a song for downloading on the internet requires a mechanical license. If the song has already been commercially released, you can obtain a compulsory mechanical license. For example, an independent band that records an existing song and wants to offer those recordings as downloads needs a mechanical license in the song. A federal court has ruled that downloading a song does not qualify as a public performance of the song and, therefore, no public performance license is required. As of the writing of this book, performing rights organizations are appealing that decision and lobbying for legislation to overturn it.

Downloading the Sound Recording. Offering a recording on the internet for downloading requires a license to reproduce and distribute the recording. This is the license that Apple has with the recording labels in order to offer downloads through the itunes service. There is no central administrator that issues these licenses and compulsory licenses are available only in limited circumstances. As a result, you must negotiate these licenses directly with the copyright owner of the recording.

8.10.5. Licenses Required for Streaming Music

Streamed music, also referred to as internet radio or webcasting, does not require placement of a permanent copy of the music on your computer.

Streaming the Song. Streaming a song on the internet requires a public performance license. You can obtain the public performance license directly from the songwriter. If you stream many songs, you may need a blanket license from ASCAP, BMI and SESAC, which are the performing rights organizations (PROs) for songs in the United States. The PROs usually issue blanket licenses that allow the internet site to perform any song in the catalog of the PRO issuing the blanket license.

Streaming the Sound Recording. Streaming a recording on the internet requires a license for public performance by digital audio transmission. There is a compulsory license available for websites that offer music through non-interactive programs. In essence, non-interactive status requires that listeners are not able to choose the sound recordings they hear. There is a laundry list of requirements for the non-interactive test including a limit on the number of songs played by the same artist or from the same album within any three-hour period and a prohibition on prior announcements of songs.

SoundExchange, a performing rights organization for sound recordings, administers compulsory licenses that are available for the non-interactive streaming of sound recordings on the internet, collects the corresponding fees, and distributes those fees to artists and record labels. In addition to the compulsory license, there are several negotiated licenses that SoundExchange has negotiatiated and that set different terms from the compulsory license according to the class, size and revenue of the webcaster. To offer a sound recording as a download or as a stream in which the listener is able to choose the music played, you must obtain a license directly from the owner of the sound recording.

The following chart summarizes license requirements for a website to offer streams and downloads of music:

Activity	License Required	Available From	License Fee
Stream Song	Performance	Songwriter, Music Publisher, ASCAP, BMI, or SESAC	Typically, percentage of website revenue
Download Song	Mechanical	Songwriter, Music Publisher or Harry Fox	Compulsory license available. Current statutory rate is 9.1¢ per copy.
Stream Recording	Performance by means of Digital Audio Transmission	SoundExchange for noninter-active use; Record Company for interactive uses	Compulsory license available for nonin-teractive use. Compulsory license sets the minimum 2010 license fee at $500 per channel.
Download Recording	Reproduction and Distribution	Record Company	Negotiable. Varies greatly.

8.11. Obtaining Permission

I break obtaining permission and rights clearance into at least three steps:

- determine if you need permission;
- identify who can grant permission; and
- ask for permission.

8.11.1. Determine if You Need Permission

As discussed in Sections 8.2 through 8.6, there may be situations in which the law does not require you to get permission to use someone else's proprietary material. Application of those laws involves the analysis of facts specific to the relevant situation. If you use someone's protected material without permission, there is always some level of risk—even if it is a minimal one.

Evaluating Risk. While the risk associated with using protected material without permission may be minimal, it is never zero. Your claim that your use is protected by copyright fair use or by the First Amendment is not a guarantee that your unauthorized use will not trigger legal action from the rights owner. That is why the decision of whether to use a particular protected work without permission often revolves around a risk assessment. You must decide whether or not you can and want to accept the risk. Here are some of the questions you should ask when conducting such a risk assessment:

Would your use upset the typical rights owner? This is a reality check. Put yourself into the shoes of the rights owner. Would you be angry and want to take legal action if someone used your material without your permission in the way you want to use the rights owner's material?

Has the rights owner previously objected to similar uses of material? It is a good bet that rights owners who have been aggressive in protecting their rights in the past will continue to be aggressive in protecting their rights in the future.

Does the rights owner have the resources and knowledge to pursue an action against you—even if the action would be without merit? A well-established company with an in-house legal department can more easily make a fuss about your use than can an individual with more limited resources. Nevertheless, do not completely dismiss the cash-strapped smaller rights owner. If his claim is legitimate and offers the possibility of having the losing side pay attorneys' fees, he can probably find an attorney to assist him on a contingency basis.

How much exposure will your online work receive? The more exposure your work receives, the more likely it is that your unauthorized use will come to the attention of and spark an objection from the rights owner.

Will your unauthorized use expose other people to risk? Rights owners filing lawsuits typically sue everyone in the distribution and creation chain. Dragging your partners and customers into a lawsuit is not good for business.

Is there anyone involved in your online presence who has ample resources? People or organizations who have—or who are perceived to have—significant amounts of money make attractive targets for lawsuits.

Will you ever need anything from this rights owner? Will you need to return to the same rights owner to request rights at a later time? If yes, using the rights owner's work without authorization—even if he takes no formal action against you—can sour your future negotiations for rights you may need from that owner at a later date.

8.11.2. Identify Who Can Grant Permission

Finding the appropriate person to ask for permission is often the most difficult part of getting permission. Sometimes, you do get lucky and finding the proper rights owner simply requires reading the CD cover, the book title page, or the film credits. At other times, the search for the rights owner leads you smack into a brick wall.

Making the process more difficult is the fact that use of some material may require permission from multiple parties. I refer to those materials as materials with stacked rights.

For example, a picture of a sculpture may require permission from both the photographer and the sculptor. Music often has multiple owners. Professional film and television clips are the most difficult to clear because of clearance required from entertainment guilds that protect actors, directors, and writers. Also, this step is sometimes a challenge because ownership may have changed hands. Finding the person who can grant you permission is often a scavenger hunt. For seeking permissions related to books, try the websites of the publishers and authors. For seeking permission related to periodicals, try the publication's website or the publication itself. You can find the music publishers connected to many popular songs by searching the online song databases of music organizations such as ascap (www.ascap.com), bmi (www.bmi.com), harry fox (www.harryfox.com), and sesac (www.sesac.org).

I discuss clearing rights in greater detail in my book, *The Permission Seeker's Guide Through the Legal Jungle: Clearing Copyrights, Trademarks, and Other Rights for Entertainment and Media Productions.*

8.11.3. Ask for Permission

There is no magic method of requesting permission. Some large institutional copyright owners may offer an online permission request form. If you must draft your own request, give complete information about the material you want to use and how you want to use it.

Your permission request should include a description of your work, identification of the material you want to use, and the scope of rights you need. *The Permission Seeker's Guide Through the Legal Jungle* contains several samples of letters requesting permission as well as sample licensing fees.

Setting the License Fee. Licensing fees vary tremendously and depend on a number of factors including the scope of your use and the popularity of the material to be licensed. There is no uniform way of negotiating the license fee. There are various strategies you might use in your permission request letter:

- Do not mention a specific amount for a license fee and let the rights owner indicate the amount it wants.

- Make an offer and see if the rights owner either accepts your offer or makes a counter offer.

What Can You Do if the Rights Owner Says No? Hopefully, the rights owner will grant your permission request. However, the rights owner might say no, demand a license fee that is too high, or just not respond at all. If that happens, you can try to tailor your use so that it qualifies as a fair use. However, as noted, fair use is subjective so this approach carries some risk. Sometimes the best approach is to find alternative material or to find a creative way to complete your online work without directly using the material.

Document the Grant of Permission. The permission agreement does not need to be complicated. It is the internet age and many permission seekers wonder if it is okay to get permission via an email exchange rather than via a more formal document. All contracts do not have to be in writing. Many oral agreements can be binding. In cases where an oral agreement would suffice, I would be comfortable relying on a grant of permission via email.

The grant of a non-exclusive license does not need to be in writing—although there may be circumstances in which you still want the non-exclusive license in writing. When you seek permission to incorporate third party music, text, artwork or other material into your online work, you are usually—but not always—seeking a non-exclusive license. Non-exclusive means that the rights owner may grant the same rights to anyone else.

There are other contracts that by law must be in writing in order to be effective. They include the grant of an exclusive license in a copyright, the transfer of a copyright, and the creation of a freelance work as a work made for hire. For contracts that must be in writing, I advocate an agreement that is more formal than an exchange of emails. There is at least one court that has ruled that an exchange of emails does not satisfy the requirement that the transfer of a copyright must be in writing. As we become more reliant on digital communications, that court attitude may change—but I would not want to be the test case.

MONITORING YOUR RELATIONSHIPS WITH AND OBLIGATIONS TO ONLINE VISITORS

Privacy on the internet is largely self-regulated. Federal law generally does not require you to take any affirmative steps to protect the privacy of your online visitors. The exception is sites that take personal information from children under thirteen which requires compliance with the Children's Online Privacy Protection Act. There may also be exceptions under state law requirements.

9.1. *Online Privacy Policy*

In a privacy policy, a website or online service explains to its visitors what information it collects from them, how it will use and secure that information, and whether it will share that information with any third parties. In most cases, websites are not required to post a privacy policy.

However, if you do post a privacy policy, you are legally required to honor the promises you make. The Federal Trade Commission (FTC) uses its authority to prohibit unfair or deceptive practices to enforce promises made in privacy policies. The FTC is especially sensitive to major modifications in privacy policies without adequate notice to or consent from your online visitors.

For example, suppose you collect personal information from online visitors such as email addresses and physical mailing addresses and your privacy policy states you will not share the information with any third party. Later you change your posted privacy policy to allow sharing such information in limited circumstances. You can not share the information of consumers whose information you collected while the previous policy was posted unless you get that consumer's affirmative consent.

Exceptions to Self-Regulation. There are two notable exceptions to the standard of self-regulation of internet privacy:

Children under Thirteen. Websites that collect personal information from children under the age of thirteen must comply with the Children's Online Privacy Protection Act (COPPA). The Federal Trade Commission takes COPPA very seriously and has levied fines of up to $1,000,000 on websites that were not COPPA compliant.

State Law. Some states are becoming more aggressive in demanding privacy policies and procedures of websites. For example, the California Online Privacy Protection Act of 2003 requires posting of a privacy policy by any commercial website that collects personally identifiable information from consumers residing in California. For that reason, it may be a good idea to post a privacy policy if your online site collects, uses, or sells personal information about its visitors.

9.2. Children's Online Privacy Protection Act (COPPA)

The protection of children is an area in which the law imposes specific regulations rather than leaving sites to self-regulate. The Children's Online Privacy Protection Act (COPPA) is a federal law that went into effect on April 21, 2000 and regulates websites that collect personal information from children under thirteen years of age.

Under COPPA, personal information includes information that would make it possible for someone to identify or contact the child. That includes address information and email address as well as information collected through online tracking systems if tied to individually identifying information.

9.2.1. Which Websites Must Comply with COPPA

You must comply with COPPA if you operate a commercial website targeted to children under thirteen and you collect, use, or disclose personal information from children. You must also comply with COPPA if you have actual knowledge that your website is collecting, using, or disclosing personal information from children under thirteen. The Federal Trade Commission, the government agency that takes the lead in COPPA enforcement, considers a number of factors when determining whether a website targets children:

- Does the website's subject matter appeal to children?
- Are children depicted on the website?
- Does the website include advertisements directed to children?
- What is the age of the actual or intended audience?
- Does the website use animated characters or other child-oriented features?

9.2.2. What COPPA Compliance Requires

If COPPA applies to your website, you must do the following:

- post a privacy policy,
- provide parental notice and get parental consent before collecting personal information from children,
- allow a parent to review the information collected about the child, and
- delete the child's information upon the parent's request.

Posted Privacy Policy. If you fall under COPPA, your website must include a written privacy policy. You must post a link to the policy on the home page of the website *and* at each area where you collect personal information from children. The policy must include the following information:

- name and contact information of the person or company operating the website

- type of information collected from children
- explanation of how the information is used
- statement of whether or not you share the information with anyone else
- a statement that the parent has the option to agree to the collection and use of the child's information without consenting to the disclosure of the information to third parties
- a statement that you may not require a child to disclose more information than is reasonably necessary to participate in an activity
- a statement that the parent can review the child's personal information, ask to have it deleted and refuse to allow any further collection or use of the child's information
- instructions for how the parent can access the child's personal information

Parental Notice and Consent. A website must provide parental notice and obtain verifiable consent before collecting personal information from children. The notice must contain the same information included in the privacy policy posted on the website. You can satisfy much of the parental notice requirement by providing a link to your privacy notice. However, the notice must state that you wish to collect personal information from the child and what types of information you wish to collect. If you are seeking parental consent, the notice must state that the parent's consent is required and explain how the parent may provide consent.

Disclosure. At a parent's request, you must disclose the kinds of personal information you collect online from children. You must use reasonable procedures to ensure you are dealing with the child's parent before providing access to the child's specific information.

Deletion Upon Request. A parent may revoke consent, refuse to allow an operator to further use the child's personal information, and direct the operator to delete the information. In turn, you may terminate any service provided to the child, but only if the information at issue is reasonably necessary for the child's participation in that service.

9.2.3. COPPA Safe Harbors

In several COPPA enforcement actions, the FTC found COPPA-compliance deficiencies in websites that believed themselves to be in compliance. The FTC is often vague in its explanations of how the websites fail to comply. To minimize the risk of an unintentional COPPA violation, websites can affiliate with one of the safe harbor programs.

Safe harbor programs are industry self-regulatory guidelines that, if adhered to, are deemed to comply with COPPA. Organizations may submit guidelines that the FTC may consider authorizing as safe harbors. The FTC has approved the safe harbor applications of the Children's Advertising Review Unit (CARU) of the Council of Better Business Bureaus, Inc.; ESRB Privacy Online, a Division of the Entertainment Software Rating Board; TRUSTe; and Privo, Inc.

The safe harbor requirements substantially mirror the federal rules. The organizers of the safe harbor programs review and monitor those websites whose operators want the protection of their safe harbor.

9.3. Spam and Unsolicited Commercial Email

Electronic mail or email has become an extremely important and popular means of communication, relied on by millions of Americans on a daily basis for personal and commercial purposes. Spam is unsolicited commercial email. Too much spam threatens the usefulness of commercial email because it becomes difficult to sort out legitimate email, means consumers might miss legitimate email among the spam, and forces both consumers and internet access services to devote time and resources to dealing with spam.

9.3.1. Federal CAN-SPAM Act

The federal law designed to combat spam is called the Controlling the Assault of Non-Solicited Pornography and Marketing Act of 2003. It is often referred to as the CAN-SPAM Act and it became effective on January 1, 2004. The CAN-SPAM Act targets commercial electronic mail messages defined as email whose primary purpose is advertising or promoting a commercial product or service.

What the CAN-SPAM Act Requires. The CAN-SPAM Act does not prevent you from sending an initial email. Instead, it requires you to use honest business practices and to offer an opt-out mechanism to those who want no further email communications from you.

To comply with the CAN-SPAM Act, you must do the following:

Accurate Header Information. You cannot use false or misleading header information. The domain name, email address, and any other information in the from and to sections of your email message must be accurate and correctly identify the person sending the email.

Accurate Subject Line. You cannot use a deceptive subject line in your email message. The subject line cannot mislead the recipient about the contents or subject matter of the message. The FTC has categorized as deceptive the following types of subject lines:

- Subject lines that falsely promise free merchandise such as "Congratulations. You've won an iPod Video 4 Player" and "Confirmation required for your 6 $500 Visa Gift Card"
- Subject lines that falsely suggest that the recipient has submitted an application or opened an account such as "About Your Mortgage application" or "Your Account info"
- Subject lines with a personal greeting that suggests a pre-existing relationship such as "Movie time. Let's go." or "Response to Your Question"

- Subject lines that are vague or misleading to the underlying contents of the message such as "I found your address", "FWD: Your Software", or "Did you hear the news?"

Opt-Out Method. Your message must contain a clear and conspicuous notice that the message is an advertisement or solicitation and that the recipient can opt out of receiving more commercial email from you. You must give recipients of your email a reliable method of requesting that you cease sending them email communications. If a recipient opts out, you have ten business days to stop sending email to the requestor's email address. The opt-out mechanism must be functional and able to process opt-out requests for at least thirty days after you send your commercial email.

Postal Address. Your message must also include a valid physical postal address. There is nothing in the CAN-SPAM act that prohibits the use of a post office box to fulfill the postal address requirement.

Sexually-Explicit Content. The CAN-SPAM Act includes specific rules for sexually explicit content. If your email includes sexually-explicit content, you must eliminate sexually oriented materials from the subject line of the message and include in the subject heading the phrase "SEXUALLY-EXPLICIT" in capital letters as the first characters of the subject line.

Enforcement. The Federal Trade Commission (FTC) takes the lead in CAN-SPAM enforcement. As of this writing, the largest settlement in a case based on CAN-SPAM non-compliance was a $2.9 million civil penalty assessed to online advertiser ValueClick.

Other agencies enforce CAN-SPAM in specific industries and situations. For example, the Securities and Exchange Commission enforces CAN-SPAM with respect to securities brokers and dealers. The Federal Deposit Insurance Act enforces CAN-SPAM compliance in the banking industry. The Department of Justice enforces criminal sanctions that come into play when you spam in volume.

Additional Restrictions on Unsolicited Commercial Email. While CAN-SPAM pre-empts state law, states can pass laws that increase restrictions. Note that your website host provider may place further restrictions on sending unsolicited commercial email.

9.4. Cyber Stalking and Cyber Bullying

Sometimes the internet is used for stalking and bullying conduct. Cyber stalking and cyber bullying might include sending unsolicited email, sending threatening emails, posting false information about the person, or creating a fake internet presence in the name of the victim.

Federal and state governments are taking steps to pass legislation that directly targets cyberbullying. In the interim, state governments often take a more creative approach to punishing cyber bullies.

The Case of Megan Meier and Lori Drew. Lori Drew set up a fake MySpace account under the identity of a non-existent teen-age boy. She used the account to befriend Megan Meier, a thirteen-year old girl who was estranged friends with Drew's teenage daughter. Drew began sending cruel messages to Meier who had a history of clinical depression. Meier hanged herself in her bedroom after receiving one such message.

When state authorities initially could not find a law under which to charge Drew, federal authorities constructed a criminal case using the anti-hacking Computer Fraud and Abuse Act (CFAA). The CFAA makes it illegal to access a protected computer without permission or in a way that exceeds authorization. Federal authorities charged Drew with violating the terms of service of MySpace as a means of inflicting emotional distress.

A jury convicted Drew of three misdemeanor CFAA violations but rejected the CFAA felony charges. The court subsequently overruled the jury verdict and acquitted Drew of all charges. The court rationalized that a conscious breach of a website's terms of service by itself should not be criminalized because making such activities criminal gave too much discretion to the police and too little notice to citizens using the internet. (*U.S. v. Drew*, No. 08-0582-GW (C.D. Cal., Decision on Drew's Motion for Acquittal, August 28, 2009)).

Developing Cyber Bullying Legislation. States have begun to implement laws to combat cyber stalking and cyber bullying. They are enacting new laws and expanding existing laws to incorporate prohibitions against cyber bullying and cyber stalking by means of the internet.

For example, in response to the Meagan Meier case, Missouri passed the Internet Harassment Law, effective August 28, 2008. The law updated state laws against harassment by removing the requirement that the communication be written or over the telephone and extending it to harassment from computers, text messages and other electronic devices. Meanwhile, Congress has considered legislation that would impose federal penalties for cyber bullying.

Impersonating Someone Online. Another form of cyber harassment is impersonating someone online. This activity can result in criminal charges. A Colorado student impersonated his teacher, Billy Johnson, by creating a fake MySpace page. The student imported pictures from Johnson's own MySpace page and used inappropriate captions on those photos. The student allegedly then sent sexually suggestive and threatening email messages to other students from the fake MySpace page. Johnson was suspended from his job and was investigated by law enforcement. Eventually, the messages were tracked to a seventeen-year-old minor who was arrested for felony criminal libel, felony criminal impersonation, and misdemeanor computer crime.

PART THREE
Engaging in Specific Online Activities

Part Three offers a discussion of legal issues related to specific online activities such as fan sites, blogs, podcasts and social networking sites; explains some of the special considerations for these activities; and provides examples of how the concepts explained in Part Two apply to specific types of internet activities.

Many of the concepts discussed are applicable to more than one type of internet activity. Hence, placement of certain topics in particular chapters is sometimes arbitrary.

Chapters in Part Three:

SERVICES USED BY CYBER CITIZENS

10.1. Web Hosts and Other Service Providers

There are many providers that offer software and infrastructures for you to set-up websites, blogs, podcasts, instant messaging, discussion forums, and internet bulletin boards. Some are free; some charge a fee. If you are particularly concerned about how the hosting service will use your posted information, it is worthwhile to read the provider's terms of service and privacy policy. The companies that cater specifically to a particular type of online activity such as podcasting or blogging will have unique terms catering to that particular service.

As a very general rule, providers of free services take more liberties with the use of information than providers of paid services. Here are common provisions you often find in the terms of hosting and service provider companies:

- Your content may be made browsable in search engines or on the web.

- Provider takes a license to use your content in the promotion or marketing of the provider's service.

- Providers often reserve the right to delete your content under certain circumstances.

- Providers often reserve the right, but not the obligation, to monitor content in multiple-group communications in order to determine that communications are not pornographic, harassing or otherwise inappropriate.

- Many service providers adhere to the Digital Millennium Copyright Act safe harbors and will remove your content if they receive a takedown notice from a copyright owner indicating your posted material is infringing.

10.2. Sample Terms Used by Service Providers

Hosting companies periodically change their terms. What follows is a description of terms in effect as of the writing of this book for some well-known hosts:

Google Discussion Groups. Google claims no ownership or control over any of your content. Google does take a worldwide, non-exclusive, royalty-free license to reproduce, adapt and publish your content on the service for the purpose of displaying, distributing and promoting any of its services. The license terminates when you delete the content. Google also reserves the right to post any of your content through its other services.

Typepad Blogging. Six Apart offers Typepad, an infrastructure for blogging. Six Apart does not claim ownership of any of your blog content. Six Apart does take a world-wide, royalty-free, and non-exclusive license to reproduce, modify, adapt and publish your blog content. However, Six Apart may take these actions solely for the purpose of displaying, distributing and promoting your blog on Six Apart's websites. This license exists only for as long as you are a Six Apart customer and terminates when you stop maintaining a blog on Typepad.

Vertical Response. Vertical Response is a service for sending email newsletters. While Vertical Response has no obligation to monitor the content sent through its service, it reserves the right to monitor and remove any content that violates the Vertical Response User Agreement.

AOL Instant Messenger Software. AOL Instant Messenger (AIM) is an instant messaging software that allows users to communicate in real time. AOL does not read private online communications transmitted using AOL communication tools such as AOL instant messenger software. You retain ownership of all right, title and interest in content you post to any public areas of AOL. However, by submitting or posting content to public areas such as a message board, you grant AOL the irrevocable, perpetual, worldwide right to reproduce, display, perform, distribute, adapt and promote the content in any medium. Once you submit or post content to any public area, AOL does not need to give you any further right to inspect or approve uses of such content or to compensate you for any such uses.

In this case, AOL takes all ownership in any compilation, collective work or other derivative work created by AOL using or incorporating content posted to public areas.

Podcasting Services. One popular free podcasting hosting service recognizes that you maintain the intellectual property ownership of all material placed on its site but grants itself a very generous license in the use of your material:

> When you give us content, you grant us a non-exclusive, worldwide, perpetual, irrevocable, royalty-free, sublicensable (through multiple tiers) right to exercise the copyright, publicity, and database rights (but no other rights) you have in the content, in any media known now or in the future. (We need these rights to host and display your content.)

Here is the license a paid podcasting hosting service takes in your content:

> You hereby grant to podcast host a non-exclusive, royalty-free, worldwide right and license for so long as you use the service to do the following to the extent necessary in the performance of services under this Agreement: digitize, convert, install, upload, select, order, arrange, compile, combine, synchronize, use, reproduce, store, process, retrieve, transmit, distribute, publish, publicly display, publicly perform and hyperlink your content; and make archival or back-up copies of your content. Except for the rights expressly granted above, podcast host is not acquiring any right, title or interest in or to your content, all of which shall remain solely with you.

Facebook. You own all content you post on Facebook and you control how it is shared through your privacy preferences. Subject to your privacy preferences, Facebook takes a non-exclusive, transferable, sub-licensable, royalty-free, worldwide license to use your posted content. The license ends when you delete the content or terminate your account unless your content has already been shared with others, and they have not deleted it. Facebook can remove any content that it believes violates its terms.

BLOGS AND PODCASTS

For convenience, I have somewhat arbitrarily decided to discuss several issues in this chapter designated for blogs and podcasts even though these issues are applicable to a broader array of online works.

11.1. What Is a Blog?

A blog is a web-based publication authored by an individual or group of individuals that functions as an online journal. People who write blogs are called bloggers. The blog's postings are typically arranged in reverse chronological order. While blogs are frequently text based, they can also focus on artwork, video or other media. There are blogs on every topic imaginable.

The word "blog" is a blend of the words web and log. A blog maintained by a lawyer on a legal topic is sometimes called a blawg. A blog that features video is sometimes called a vlog.

11.2. Who Owns the Blog Content?

Ownership of blog content follows the rules of copyright ownership discussed in Section 3.4. That means if you are the sole writer of the blog postings, you are the sole copyright owner of those blog postings. If you blog as a function of your employment, your blog postings are owned by your employer as a work made for hire. If the blog is ghost written or created by a freelancer, the freelancer is the copyright owner of the blog postings unless there is a written agreement signed by the freelancer indicating otherwise.

Ownership questions can become complicated if a company becomes involved in publication of an already existing blog. For example, suppose Jack begins the Great Skiing Blog that profiles ski resorts and provides other information of interest to avid skiers. The Great Skiing Blog develops a loyal audience and attracts the attention of Whirlwind Enterprises, a manufacturer and distributor of skiing equipment and other outdoor gear. Whirlwind believes Jack's Great Skiing Blog would be a good marketing vehicle for the company.

Whirlwind approaches Jack and the parties decide that Whirlwind will adopt the Great Skiing Blog into its marketing campaign and will retain Jack to continue writing the blog on behalf of the company. Whirlwind and Jack should clearly indicate—preferably in writing—whether Jack is an employee of the company or a freelancer and what is the ownership disposition of the Great Skiing Blog postings written prior to Whirlwind's involvement and the blog postings written after Whirlwind's involvement. Otherwise disputes can arise. Without a written agreement, there are good arguments that Jack owns the postings written prior to his relationship with Whirlwind. With respect to blog postings written after Whirlwind's involvement, if there is no written agreement, there are good arguments that Jack owns the postings if he works as a freelancer and Whirlwind owns the postings if Jack works as an employee.

Comments. Most blogs have an interactive element and invite readers to submit comments to each of the postings. Copyright ownership extends to the person creating the comments. That means the commenter owns any copyright in his comments. Most agree that the blogger has an implied license to post reader comments even if the blogger has no written terms of service giving him an express license to post the comments. Sometimes, the blogger will want to do more with the comments than simply post them in the blog comment section. For example, a blogger might want to use some comments in marketing materials for the blog or in a subsequent book based on the blog. To take such actions, the blogger should have provisions included in the blog's terms of service authorizing such use of the comments by the blogger.

Scraping Blog Content. Some bloggers are in the habit of taking entire articles and postings from other blogs and posting them. This act of taking content from a blog is sometimes referred to as scraping. This is copyright infringement unless you have the permission of the article's copyright owner. If you are a victim of scraping and your content has been posted without your permission onto a blog, try some of the resolutions suggested in Section 3.8.

11.3. Blogging Anonymously

Under the First Amendment, you have the right to speak anonymously. This includes the right to blog anonymously. However, not all categories of speech are entitled to First Amendment protection. Unprotected speech includes speech that violates another person's rights. Anonymous internet statements can trigger lawsuits filed by individuals or companies for a range of claims including defamation, breach of employment or confidentiality agreements, misappropriation of trade secrets, and interference with a prospective business advantage. If you engage in unprotected online speech anonymously, a person harmed by your speech may be able to uncover your identity by serving a subpoena upon any service provider you use for blogging and internet activity.

Standards for Subpoenas. The person who seeks the identity of an anonymous online poster through a subpoena must prove that he has a valid claim against the anonymous poster. The standard to receive a subpoena for identification of an anonymous poster varies from state to state. Here are three of the standards applied, listed from easiest to most difficult to prove from the perspective of the party seeking the information under a subpoena:

Good Faith. Under the good faith standard, you must show a legitimate, good faith basis to believe that you are the victim of actionable conduct and that you need the identity of the anonymous poster in order to pursue your claim.

Motion to Dismiss. Under the motion to dismiss standard, you must provide facts that would be sufficient for your lawsuit to survive a motion to dismiss. A court generally dismisses a lawsuit only if it is reasonably certain that you could not prove any set of facts that would entitle you to win the lawsuit. Nevertheless, allegations that are vague or lack detail may still satisfy the motion to dismiss test.

Summary Judgment. Under the summary judgment standard, you must support your claim with facts that would be sufficient for your lawsuit to survive a summary judgment motion. This means you must produce *prima facie* evidence supporting each element of your claim. *Prima facie* evidence is evidence which if unexplained or uncontradicted is sufficient for you to win a lawsuit. Most states confronting a subpoena request for an anonymous internet poster's identity have applied the summary judgment standard.

The anonymous poster must have an opportunity to oppose or quash the subpoena. This means someone must attempt to notify the anonymous poster that he is the subject of a subpoena request. Some states require the person seeking the subpoena to notify the anonymous poster. Such notification attempts typically include posting a notice on the blog, message board, or other internet location where the anonymous poster initially posted his objectionable statements. Sometimes the recipient of the subpoena request—which is typically an ISP or the operator of the forum on which the anonymous poster posted such as Yahoo or AOL—provides the notice.

11.4. Can You Be Fired for Blogging?

The short answer is yes, you can be fired for blogging. The legality of firing you for blogging and other online activity depends in part on whether you are a private or government employee and on the subject matter of your blog.

Private Employees. If you are employed by a private company that is not unionized, you are likely an at-will employee. As an at-will employee, you can be fired at any time for any reason and even for no reason. The exception is your employer may not fire you for a reason that violates federal or state laws. For example, your employer may not fire you based on your race or gender since such a firing decision violates federal and state employment discrimination laws.

Your employer may fire you for your blogging and internet activity as long as the blogging-related firing is not a pretext covering an illegal reason for the firing. An employer might fire an employee whose blog or internet activities include disclosing the employer's confidential information, making defamatory comments about the employer, threatening people in the work place, or materially violating any social networking or other employment policies maintained by the company. Those are all legal reasons to fire an employee for blogging. In contrast, an employer cannot fire an employee who blogs to advocate better working conditions for himself and co-workers as that action would likely violate federal laws prohibiting the firing of employees for activities designed to produce better work conditions.

Government Employees. Restrictions imposed by government employers may constitute government censorship and thus trigger constitutional scrutiny to make sure the restrictions do not violate the First Amendment. Hence, a government employer must consider the First Amendment and your right to free speech in termination decisions.

Nevertheless, your free speech rights as a public employee are weaker than your free speech rights as an ordinary citizen. Courts have held that government employers may impose certain restraints on the speech of its employees, even if those restraints would be unconstitutional if applied to the general public. You can be terminated for blogging or other online speech if the subject matter of your speech interferes with your government employer's ability to provide services. The following real-life cases illustrate the application of this principle.

Dible Versus City of Chandler. Ronald Dible, a police officer with the Chandler, Arizona City Police Department, maintained and participated in a sexually explicit website with his wife. Even though Dible took steps to hide his association with the website, members of the public learned of his participation. The police department fired him because his participation with the website violated the department's regulation prohibiting officers from bringing discredit to the city service. In rejecting Dible's First Amendment arguments, the court determined that Dible was not protected by the First Amendment because he did not contribute speech on a matter of public concern; his activities were simply vulgar and indecent. (*Dible v. City of Chandler*, 515 F.3d 918 (9th Cir. 2007)).

Blogging about Clients. Kristine Ann Peshek, an assistant public defender in Winnebago County, Illinois, disclosed confidential information about her clients. While she did not provide the full names of clients, her use of first names, variations of first names and jail identification numbers made her clients potentially identifiable to anyone who wanted to review public records. Here is an excerpt of one of Peshek's blog postings about a college student prosecuted for drug possession:

> #1111111 (the client's jail identification number) This stupid kid is taking the rap for his drug-dealing dirtbag of an older brother because "he's no snitch." I managed to talk the prosecutor into treatment and deferred prosecution, since we both know the older brother from prior dealings involving drugs and guns.

The public defender's office fired Peshek after a supervisor discovered the blog. Peshek also faced disciplinary action by the Illinois Bar for violating attorney ethical rules through her blog. (*In the Matter of Kristine Ann Peshek*, No. 09CH89 (Hearing Board of the Ill. Att'y Reg. and Disc. Comm'n, Complaint filed on August 25, 2009)).

11.4.1. Employee Blogging and Social Networking Policies

It has become increasingly common for companies to have policies concerning employee blogging and other online activities. A blogging policy cannot prevent employees from exercising the right to talk about improving work conditions, or organizing a union as such restrictions would violate federal laws. Most company blogging policies cover the following principles:

- The employee's postings must not disclose any of the employer's confidential or proprietary information.

- If the employee comments on an aspect of the employer's business in which the employee has responsibility, the employee must identify himself as an employee of the company and make it clear that he is speaking on behalf of himself and not the company.

- If the employee identifies himself as an employee of the company, refers to the company's work or provides a link to the company, the employee must include a disclaimer such as the following: "the views expressed on this post are mine and do not necessarily reflect the views of the ABC Company."

- The employee should not include the employer's logos or trademarks.

11.5. Bloggers as Journalists

Laws applicable to journalists include reporter's shield laws, fee waivers for Freedom of Information Act requests, and campaign finance laws. The overarching question is whether these laws apply to bloggers and others who provide newsgathering services via the internet.

11.5.1. Laws That Apply to Journalists

Reporter Privilege and Shield Laws. Reporter privilege and shield laws protect reporters from having to divulge their sources and from claims such as defamation.

First Amendment Reporter Privilege. The reporter's privilege under the First Amendment excuses news gatherers from disclosing the source of any information procured in connection with their journalistic endeavors. Courts have applied the First Amendment privilege to bloggers.

State Shield Laws and Constitutions. The basis of reporter's privileges may be the state constitution or a state statute. While many states' shield laws and their courts' application of state constitutional provisions have not addressed whether the protections offered apply to non-traditional news gatherers, some state laws and constitutions are sufficiently broad to allow for inclusion of bloggers. For example, the District of Columbia's shield law applies to non-traditional news gatherers. Its definition of news media, includes any printed, photographic, mechanical, or electronic means of disseminating news and information to the public.

Freedom of Information Act. The Freedom of Information Act (FOIA) requires federal agencies to disclose records upon written request. Although FOIA is not applicable to state agencies, every state has an open records law similar to FOIA. Under FOIA, representatives of the news media pay reduced duplication fees and do not have to pay search fees for the agency to locate requested documents.

Bloggers can be included as media under FOIA. FOIA defines representative of the news media to include "any person or entity that gathers information of potential interest to a segment of the public, uses its editorial skills to turn the raw materials into a distinct work, and distributes that work to an audience." The definition also explicitly says it is designed to include methods of news delivery and alternative media as they evolve.

Campaign Finance Laws. The Federal Election Campaign Act (FECA) regulates the money spent on federal elections so that wealthy individuals and special interest groups cannot wield disproportionate influence on the outcome of federal elections. Specifically, FECA limits contributions to federal elections and requires certain individuals and groups to file periodic reports disclosing the money they raise and spend for federal elections. FECA targets a limited group actively involved in federal elections such as candidates for federal office, candidate committees, party committees, and political action committees.

Some FECA laws and regulations impact internet activity. However, FECA is not designed to interfere with the everyday online or offline activity of individuals, even when the activities of those individuals are political in nature. While the vast majority of internet activities are free from campaign finance law, some internet activities may be viewed as political contributions or expenditures and trigger FECA compliance. Under FECA, a contribution or expenditure includes not just money but anything of value given with the purpose of influencing any election for federal office. Hence, internet activities such as the following might be viewed as a contribution or expenditure and be subject to FECA:

- Providing a service to a candidate free of charge or at a charge that is less than the usual charge. For example, if you normally sell advertising space on your site and you give free advertising space to a candidate, that action may be viewed as a contribution.

- Giving an asset with value to a political party. For example, if you give an email mailing list to a political party, that transfer may be viewed as a contribution.

- Paying to republish a candidate's campaign materials on another person's site. However, republishing a candidate's campaign materials on your own site would not trigger FECA compliance requirements.

FECA is not designed to prevent the ordinary citizen from engaging in political dialogue. Most internet activity that is designed to reflect your political views and to influence federal elections falls outside of FECA through one of the following exemptions:

Uncompensated Internet Activities Exemption. Your internet activities designed to influence a federal election are not regulated by FECA if you are not compensated to perform those internet activities. Internet activities is defined fairly broadly and includes sending email, providing links, blogging, and creating a website. The exemption covers the value of the time devoted to the internet activities as well as your use of equipment or services for the activities such as a domain name and ISP services. This exemption applies regardless of whether you are engaging in these internet activities with the knowledge and approval of a campaign or a political party committee.

Press or Media Exemption. FECA does not regulate the cost of covering or carrying a news story, commentary, or editorial by a broadcast station, website, newspaper, magazine, or other periodical publication, including any internet or electronic publication unless the facility is owned or controlled by a political party, political committee, or candidate. An entity that would otherwise qualify for the media exemption does not lose its eligibility because it features news and commentary lacking objectivity or expressly advocates in its editorials the election or defeat of a candidate.

Volunteer Exception. The value of your volunteer activities on behalf of a candidate or political party is not a contribution. This exemption is similar in application to the uncompensated internet activities exemption.

11.5.2. When Is a Blogger a Journalist?

Whether bloggers qualify as journalists is a developing question. The trend is that disseminating news through a blog or other new media forum does not disqualify you from treatment as a journalist. If you act like a journalist, the courts are more inclined to treat you like a journalist.

By the same reasoning if you do not conduct yourself as a legitimate journalist would, the courts will be disinclined to treat you as one. The person seeking reporter privileges must be engaged in the activity of gathering and reporting news. Depositing information or making a comment as a casual visitor to an open forum such as a newsgroup, chat room, bulletin board system, or discussion group may not qualify as the publication of news.

For example, Shellee Hale was accused of defamation for her postings on an internet message board accusing a company and its officers of criminal behavior. The court rejected Hale's argument that the postings were part of her newsgathering mission to report information about criminal activity in the adult entertainment industry. According to the court, Hale did not follow standard journalistic practices such as allowing the company to tell its side of the story. The court also found that Hale had no journalism degree, was never employed by a news agency, and had never been paid for the information she placed on her blogs and websites. Hence, she was not a journalist protected under the New Jersey Shield Law and could not refuse to disclose the sources for her postings. (*Too Much Media v. Hale*, No. MON-L-2736-08, (N.J. Super. Ct., June 30, 2009)).

11.5.3. Blogger Endorsements and Testimonials

One of the Federal Trade Commission's (FTC) roles is to take action against deceptive and misleading advertising. In late 2009, the FTC revised its Guides Concerning the Use of Endorsements and Testimonials in Advertising to include guidelines specifically targeted to blogging and new media.

The FTC guidelines are interpretations of the law intended to help advertisers comply with the Federal Trade Commission Act. The guidelines are not themselves binding law. Nevertheless, failure to adhere to the guidelines can prompt the FTC to review your online activity and initiate an action against you if it determines your failure to follow the guidelines has resulted in a business practice that deceives or misleads consumers.

Disclosure of Compensation Required. Bloggers who receive compensation for endorsing or recommending products and services are to disclose such compensation. You are endorsing a product if consumers believe your communications about the product or service reflect your personal views and experiences. If you are paid for such endorsement, the FTC expects you to disclose the fact you have received such compensation. This includes compensation in the form of free products. If companies send you free copies of their products to sample with the request that you write online reviews of those products, you should disclose that you received the item for free. The disclosure can be as simple as "ABC Company gave me this product to try."

Examples Provided by the FTC. Here are examples provided by the FTC in its guidelines. A college student with a popular blog about video games is given a newly released video game system by the manufacturer who asks the student to blog about the video game. The student tests the new gaming system and writes a favorable review. The FTC reasons that the typical consumer might not realize the student received the product free of charge in exchange for the review so the student should disclose such relationship—especially given the value of the system.

In the FTC example, the blogger received an expensive product. The example made me question whether a blogger must make such disclosures for a more modestly priced product such as a book, a cd, a tube of shampoo, or a lipstick. The FTC has not yet clearly stated that receipt of such modest products should **not** be disclosed. Hence, the conservative approach is to disclose if you receive a steady stream of such products from one or more companies and review those products online.

In another FTC-provided example, a well-known professional tennis player has a contractual relationship with a clinic that performs laser vision correction surgery under which she is paid to speak publicly about her surgery at the clinic. The tennis player discusses the clinic on a blog or social networking site that allows her fans to follow what is happening in her life. According to the FTC guidelines, she should disclose her relationship with the clinic. The FTC reasons that consumers might not realize that a celebrity discussing a medical procedure on a social network has been paid for doing so, and knowledge of such payments would likely affect the weight or credibility consumers give to the celebrity's endorsement.

Blogger Must Provide Truthful and Substantiated Descriptions.
As a blogger endorsing products, you are also expected to give
truthful and substantiated descriptions of the products. Suppose a
manufacturer sends you its new lotion to review. The advertiser does
not make any specific claims about the lotion's ability to cure skin
conditions and you do not ask about any specific claims. Nevertheless, you write that the lotion cures eczema and recommend that
your readers suffering from the condition try the product. Both you
and the lotion manufacturer are potentially liable for misleading or
unsubstantiated advertising.

11.6. What Is a Podcast?

Podcasts are short radio shows, audio blogs, or audio-visual pre-
sentations offered through websites. They can be downloaded and
played back on a computer or a portable music player like Apple's
ipod. There are as many variations in podcast programming as there
are in radio and television programming. Some podcasts are all music. Other podcasts have formats similar to talk radio.

Offering a podcast differs from simply offering a downloadable file. Podcasts are subscription-based. Technically, podcasts are
downloaded—not streamed—and then listened to or viewed by the
subscriber on the subscriber's computer or portable music player.

A technology referred to as RSS, really simple syndication, makes
the subscription feature of podcasts possible. The podcaster creates
an RSS feed for the program. The RSS automatically alerts users' systems that a new program is available and makes downloads available.

11.6.1. Using Music in a Podcast

Podcasts that include music raise the music licensing issues which I
discuss in Section 8.10. If you use music that is protected by copyright, you need a license in order to incorporate the music into your
podcast. The license needs to describe how you will distribute the
podcast. If you combine video or images with music, you need a

synchronization license and a master use license. To reduce the music licensing administrative work, consider using material under a Creative Commons License as discussed in Section 8.6.4. For a broader discussion of obtaining music including originally commissioned music or music from a production library, I recommend my book, *The Permission Seeker's Guide Through the Legal Jungle: Clearing Copyrights, Trademarks and Other Rights for Entertainment and Media Productions.*

11.7. Interview Releases

Some blogs and podcasts involve interviews of guests. You should get an interview consent from your interviewee. A release is part of the rights clearance process discussed in Chapter 8. The purpose of the release is to protect you from claims that you defamed an interviewee or violated his privacy, publicity, or other rights by including him in your blog or podcast.

Consent can be explicit or implied, written or verbal. Although verbal consents can be valid, I personally prefer that all consents be in writing. If you later need to prove that consent was given, it is easier to do so if you can produce a signed release.

Express Consent. Express consent is better than implied consent. In this sense, express means clear, direct, explicit, and unambiguous. Express consent can be verbal or written.

Implied Consent. A person can give implied consent through his conduct. For example, if the person realizes he is being recorded for broadcast on your podcast and makes no objection, he has arguably provided implied consent. If a person grants an interview with an accurate understanding of how the interview is to be used, you likely have implied consent to use the interview.

My book, *The Permission Seeker's Guide Through the Legal Jungle*, discusses interview and personal releases in greater detail.

SOCIAL NETWORKING SITES AND USER GENERATED CONTENT

12.1. What Is a Social Networking Site?

A social networking site is an online community of people who share common interests and activities. Most social networking sites are web-based and allow users to interact through email, instant messaging, and online forums.

People use social networking to expand their business associations and personal networks. There are hundreds of social networking sites. Facebook, MySpace, Twitter, and YouTube are among the most popular.

Your participation in a social networking site typically begins by your becoming a member and creating an online profile. Your online profile can contain such items as a personal statement, photographs, videos, and other personal information you choose to share. After creating a profile, you can invite other people on the social networking site to connect with you. This connection is called by different names on different social networks including friend, fan, and network connection.

12.2. What Is User Generated Content?

Broadly, user generated content is online content that is produced by everyday people as opposed to content provided by the mainstream, traditional media. User generated content, abbreviated as UGC, is sometimes referred to as consumer generated media, user created content, user provided content, or web 2.0. Although UGC is provided by everyday people, UGC often incorporates content from traditional, mainstream media. While social networking sites are commonly associated with user generated content, UGC pops up in many other online locations including standard websites, blogs, and podcasts.

While you retain ownership to any UGC you produce and post, the terms of use of most social networking sites provide that you grant the site a license to use, reproduce, distribute, prepare derivative works of, display, and perform the UGC. See discussion and samples of hosting terms of use provisions in Section 10.2.

12.3. Best Practices for Creators of User Generated Content

If you are a creator of user generated content and your UGC incorporates others' proprietary material or mentions real people, you are vulnerable to potential copyright, trademark, privacy, publicity, defamation, and other rights violations. To minimize your exposure, you should follow the suggestions offered for builders of fan sites in Section 13.2.

Posting on a social networking site does not absolve you of potential liability. Normally, in the social networking site's terms of use, you warrant that you have the appropriate rights in all content you post to the site.

12.4. Best Practices for Sites That Allow Online Visitors to Post User Generated Content

Posting user generated content on a social networking site does not absolve the poster of potential liability. However, from a practical perspective, rights owners may choose to pursue the social networking site rather than individual users for copyright infringement and similar infractions. Here are some best practices for sites that allow their online visitors to post UGC:

Know the Risks. Publication of user generated content can implicate copyright and trademark rights. When the UGC incorporates or mentions real people, it can implicate defamation, privacy, and publicity rights. See Chapter 8 for further discussion on these issues.

Incorporate Filter and Other Technologies. Social networking sites are developing and implementing tools which allow them to identify, locate, and remove infringing content. One technique scans a digital, audio, or video file and compares the electronic fingerprints to databases of copyrighted material.

License Content from Rights Owners. If the social networking site owner is able to license content from rights owners, then users can post copyrighted material under the terms of that license. For example, some social networking sites have entered into revenue sharing agreements with major content owners such as the NBA, Vivendi Universal Music Group, and CBS to address the posting of copyrighted materials. Some rights owners like CBS and LucasFilms provide materials for user generated content and create partnerships with companies that are based on user generated content.

Benefit from the Digital Millennium Copyright Act Safe Harbors. Take advantage of the safe harbor provisions offered by the Digital Millennium Copyright Act (DMCA) as discussed in Section 12.5.

Require Users to Enter Click-Wrap Agreements. Click-wrap agreements include representations that content is appropriate for the website, explains what type of content is inappropriate, and grants the social networking website a license in the material being posted. See Section 3.7.1 for a discussion of how to verify that your click-wrap agreement is enforceable.

Provide a Disclaimer. Your disclaimer would state that you are not responsible for the intellectual property status of the content provided by third parties.

12.5. *Digital Millennium Copyright Act Protection*

The Digital Millennium Copyright Act (DMCA) includes safe harbor provisions that insulate websites from claims of copyright infringement for material posted by their customers and online visitors. These posting safe harbor provisions are available for interactive service providers. The term "interactive service provider" covers companies such as AOL and Comcast that offer connections to the internet. The term is defined broadly enough that it includes operators of websites, electronic bulletin boards, blogs, social networking websites, and news groups.

The DMCA protects you only from claims of copyright infringement for material posted by other people. The DMCA does not protect you from claims of copyright infringement for material you place online yourself. The DMCA's safe harbors apply only to copyright. It does not protect you from claims of defamation, trademark, privacy, trade secret or other intellectual property claims.

Qualifying for the Safe Harbor. To qualify for the DMCA safe harbor for material posted by others, your website must comply with specific DMCA requirements which include the following:

- Remove infringing material upon the request of the copyright owner. The request, referred to by the DMCA as a takedown notice, must provide specific information including a description of the copyrighted work and the online location of the infringing material. The Appendix includes an example of a takedown notice.

- Remove or block access to any posted material that you discover infringes someone's copyright—even if you do not receive a takedown notice from the copyright owner.

- Designate an agent to handle claims of copyright infringement, register the name of the agent with the Copyright Office, and post the agent's contact information on your website.

• Have no knowledge that infringing material is on your website and gain no financial benefit from the infringing material.

• Adopt a policy of removing or terminating the accounts of individuals who repeatedly infringe copyrighted material and make your customers and visitors aware of that policy.

The DMCA also offers remedies for the improper removal of material. A customer may submit a counter notice requesting that improperly removed material be reposted. Also, there is liability for anyone who submits a fraudulent takedown notice claiming that non-infringing material is infringing.

Pending lawsuits are putting the DMCA safe harbors to the test. Content owners claim that many websites generate significant traffic and revenues through infringing content which they take few actions to prevent. While the websites adhere to the DMCA takedown provisions, many content owners complain the process shifts the entire burden and high cost of monitoring copyright infringement to the content owners.

Linking or Referring Users to Infringing Materials. One of the provisions of the Digital Millennium Copyright Act (DMCA) provides a safe harbor immunizing you from copyright infringement for links to infringing material. The requirements for this linking safe harbor are very similar to the requirements for the safe harbor provision for storing information provided by a user discussed immediately above. You must remove or disable the link to infringing material upon receiving a request from the copyright owner. One distinction between this linking safe harbor and the posting safe harbor is that you do not need to designate an agent to rely on the linking safe harbor.

12.6. *Impersonation and Use of Celebrity Names on Social Networking Sites*

Celebrities who have been impersonated on social networking sites include Kanye West, Levar Burton, and Tony La Russa, manager of the St. Louis Cardinals. In response, some social networking sites have instituted policies limiting the ability to use someone else's name or trademark and validation procedures for those who claim to be celebrities.

The policies of each social networking site differ. For example, on one popular social networking site, you must use your real name to establish an account. While unofficial fan pages violate the service's terms of use, the service does allow you to create an interest group for fans of the subject or person. Hence, you could still have a presence on the social networking site to share your thoughts and impressions about the person or product. It would just be very clear that you were an unaffiliated fan and not the actual person or his designated representative.

Impersonation on Social Network Likely Not Actionable Under UDRP or ACPA. As discussed in Section 6.9.2, such impersonation or use of celebrity names on a social networking site is likely not actionable under the Uniform Domain Name Dispute Resolution Policy or the Anticybersquatting Consumer Protection Act. Instead, any legal action would rely on traditional trademark laws.

User and Not Site Liable for Celebrity Impersonation. The social networking site or online service itself is frequently insulated from liability for third party impersonations under Section 230 of the Communications Decency Act. Instead, a successful action would need to be made against the person actually doing the impersonation. I discuss Section 230 of the Communications Decency Act in detail in Section 8.9.3.

An example is the case of actress, Christianne Carafano. After an unknown prankster impersonated Carafano on an online dating site, provided her home address, and suggested that she was looking for an unconventional liaison, Carafano sued the dating site for publishing the unauthorized profile. The site asserted and received immunity under Section 230 of the Communications Decency Act. (*Carafano* v. *Metrosplash.com, Inc.*, 339 F.3d 1119 (9th Cir. 2003)).

12.7. Wikis

A wiki, pronounced wick-ee, is a collaborative website that normally serves as an informational resource. Many people contribute content to it. Traditionally, anyone is allowed to add content or edit existing content on a wiki. Wikis store the history of each page so recovery is simple in the event of editing errors or vandalism.

Who Owns Wiki Content? You own your contribution. However, since wikis are collaborative efforts, they can become joint works. Copyright joint works are discussed in Section 3.4. The provider of the wiki infrastructure may specify ownership in its terms of service.

How May You Use Wiki Content? This depends on the terms of the specific wiki. Some wikis only grant you personal use of the material. For example, wikiAnswers.com, a community written Q&A forum structured as a wiki, grants you a personal, non-exclusive, non-transferable, revocable license to use the services. You may not modify, publish, transmit, participate in the transfer or sale, create derivative works, or in any way exploit any of the content.

Wikipedia. Wikipedia, the online free encyclopedia, is one of the most popular wikis. All Wikipedia contributors must grant broad rights for the commercial or non-commercial use of their content. In general, anyone may use your Wikipedia content as long as they give you attribution. The specific licenses used for text by Wikipedia at the time of this writing were the Creative Commons Attribution/Share-Alike License and the GNU Free Documentation License.

The Wikimedia Foundation does not claim copyright ownership of Wikipedia content. You may copy, modify, and redistribute Wikipedia content as long as the new content you create grants the same freedoms to others and acknowledges the authors of the Wikipedia article used. If using Wikipedia content in another online forum, you can provide this acknowledgement through a direct link to the Wikipedia article used as a source.

FAN SITES, GRIPE SITES, AND PARODY SITES

13.1. Commentary Sites

Since the advent of the internet there have been websites run by both fans and critics of various groups, individuals, and works. Such commentary sites may be offered as standard websites or through blogs, social networking sites, and other forums.

13.1.1. Types of Commentary Sites

Fan sites, gripe sites, and parody sites are all commentary sites meaning that they express a point of view about a person, product, company, movement, or other cultural phenomenon.

Fan Site. A fan site is a website or other online work that focuses on a celebrity, book, musical group, television program, movie, game, or other cultural phenomenon. Fan sites range from simple pages listing the dates of your favorite recording artists' upcoming concerts to massive networks such as the Harry Potter site, Mugglenet, which attracts millions of visitors every month and contains exhaustive information covering every aspect of Harry Potter's universe.

Gripe Site. Gripe or criticism sites express a negative viewpoint about products, services, organizations, companies, or individuals. Criticizing a person, product or service through a website is often referred to as cybergriping.

Parody Site. A parody site makes fun of a person, organization, company, or product. The parody site may be a spin on the gripe site offering a negative viewpoint of its object in a humorous way. I discuss the concept of parody further in Section 8.5.

13.1.2. First Amendment Protection for Commentary Websites

Commentary sites receive strong protection from the First Amendment. Holding a trademark, copyright, or other intellectual property right is not a right to limit the manner in which people express themselves. People may still parody, criticize, and comment on products, companies, organizations and other individuals. A legitimate commentary site may even use celebrity names and trademarks as its domain name and elsewhere on the website.

Commentary sites can go beyond what is permissible under the First Amendment and other laws and, in those cases, rights owners may take action against them. Commentary sites can lose their First Amendment protection if they become commercial; if they become defamatory; or if they confuse people into believing the site is sponsored by or affiliated with the celebrities, companies, or products on which they focus.

A key characteristic of a legitimate commentary site is being noncommercial. It is not a legitimate commentary site worthy of First Amendment protection if the site generates a financial benefit for the operator. The operator may derive the financial benefit by selling products on the site, displaying advertisements, or selling a domain name containing a celebrity name or trademark for a profit.

13.2. Safe and Risky Content for an Unofficial Fan Site

There are millions of fan sites. While some fan sites are official and created by those who hold rights in the phenomenon, most fan sites are unofficial and have no input or approval from the people or companies who hold rights in the subject matter of the fan site. As a result, many of the images, artwork, and other media contained on fan sites are used without permission from the rights owners and may be infringing uses.

Much of the following discussion concerning safe and risky content for a fan site is equally applicable to safe and risky content for your postings on a social networking site. I discuss social networking sites and user generated content in Chapter 12.

13.2.1. Safe Fan Site Content

The following elements should be safe to place on your unofficial fan site. Note that all of the writing should be the original creation of the fan site operator or, if not, used with permission of the writer. It should not be written material copied without permission from another source.

Schedule of Upcoming Events and Description of Recent Events. You may share information about upcoming and recent related events.

Celebrity's Biography. As discussed in Section 8.9.1, the more famous a person is, the fewer privacy rights he has. A person in the public eye or involved in public events does not have exclusive rights to his biography. Anyone may write information concerning events and people who are in the public eye—even if the individuals involved object to the publication of such information.

Nevertheless, you must be careful not to defame or disclose private facts in your discussion of such events. See Section 8.9 for a discussion of defamation and privacy rights. If the information you post is from a public record or is otherwise generally known to the public, it is not private.

Trivia Facts and Questions. You may provide information and pose questions about the celebrity's background. Your trivia can be humorous. Again, you do want to be careful with respect to defamation and the disclosure of private facts if the subject of your fan site is a person.

Reviews and Commentary of the Celebrity's Work. If you are providing reviews and commentary, you have justification for using small portions of the subject's copyrighted material under the fair use exception. Commentary is one of the favored uses of the four-factor copyright fair use test discussed in Section 8.3.

Material Provided by the Rights Owner. Some rights owners offer images, icons and other items that you may incorporate into your website. You may use such content without requesting permission. However, you should read the license terms to determine if there are any restrictions on the use. For example, some rights owners may allow use of the content only for non-commercial uses.

For example, the official *Star Wars* site made available a data bank of official video clips and sounds from the films that it encourages fans to "mash up" with their own videos to create new Star Wars-related films. Social networking and video sites like YouTube and Hulu offer tools that allow you to share clips on websites and blogs. They often allow you to embed the video into your own website.

Links to Other Websites. While some websites take a conservative approach and ask for permission prior to linking to another website, many other website owners link without asking permission. Linking generally does not subject you to any legal liability. The possible exceptions are deep linking, framing, and linking to infringing material which I discuss in Section 8.7.2.

13.2.2. Risky Fan Site Content

Commercial Advertising. While many rights owners turn a blind eye to non-commercial fan sites, making your fan site commercial is a good way to attract the negative attention of the rights owners. For example, Mugglenet, a fan site devoted to Harry Potter books and movies, was forced to cease marketing its own products featuring Warner's registered trademarks related to Harry Potter.

Official Site Designation. Do not refer to your unofficial fan site as an official site. This could confuse consumers and may be viewed as a trademark violation or unfair advertising and business practice.

Confusing Domain Names. If your fan site is a legitimate non-commercial fan site, you have a fair use argument justifying your use of the trademark or celebrity name as part of your domain name or within the site. If your fan site is not a legitimate, non-commercial fan site, a celebrity name can be a protectable trademark and the celebrity may be able to stop use of the domain name through a Uniform Domain Name Dispute Resolution Policy Proceeding or through a trademark infringement lawsuit. I discuss such actions in Section 6.9.

Detailed Plot Summaries Without Original Commentary. If you review or provide commentary on a creative work such as a movie or book, it is legitimate to include some dialogue and discussion of the plot in your review. You are using the excerpts in a transformative manner that would likely qualify as a fair use. On the other hand, if you simply aggregate significant amounts of fictional moments and dialogue from a particular work, you would likely be called an in-fringer. See Sections 8.3 and 8.7.1 for further discussion of fair use.

Links to Infringing Material. Linking to a website that contains material which infringes another party's copyrights can lead to claims against you for copyright infringement.

Song Lyrics. Song lyrics are protected by copyright law regardless of whether they are used with an accompanying melody. Website operators offering song lyrics without permission are violating copy-right laws and exposing themselves to claims of copyright infringe-ment. Of course, if you are displaying the lyrics in a manner that qualifies as fair use, you are not violating any copyright laws. Like all fair use questions, you must consider the copyright fair-use factors discussed in Section 8.3 to evaluate whether your use of the lyrics is a fair use.

13.2.3. Images of Cover Art and Celebrities

Your right to use cover art and celebrity images on your commentary site is often unclear. Using low resolution, thumbnail images of cover art as part of a review or commentary may be permissible. See the discussion of thumbnails in Section 8.7.1.

Using images of celebrities raises privacy, publicity, and copyright concerns. No celebrity images should be used without permission in the context of advertising. As a general rule, you can use a person's image without violating privacy or publicity rights where the use is part of news reporting.

For example, a blogger attended a farmer's market sponsored by First Lady Michelle Obama. The blogger took photos of the First Lady, the Washington, DC mayor, and other high-profile individuals in attendance. Later, she wondered if she could post the photos as part of her blog report of the event without violating anyone's publicity or privacy rights. These were photos that the blogger took of public figures attending a public and newsworthy event. Under those circumstances, the blogger could use the photos to accompany her report on the event. On the other hand, if the blogger wanted to use the photos in an advertising context—that would require a different analysis.

Also, in this example, the blogger took the photographs herself so she was the copyright owner of the photographs. In contrast, if you use images of celebrities that you find elsewhere—even if they are images of news worthy and public events, you do need to be concerned about the copyright claims of the photographer. You should try to use images of celebrities distributed by the celebrity for promotional use.

13.3. Criticism, Gripe and Parody Sites

Criticizing a person, product or company through a website is often referred to as cybergriping. Safe content for your criticism site includes complaints based on factual and truthful accounts of experiences with the person, product, or company. You may even use a negative domain name as long as it is not a domain name that confuses people.

Content to avoid on your criticism site includes any material that would confuse the consumer into believing that the targeted person or company is the sponsor of your website. You should also avoid any activity that attempts to divert online visitors away from the targeted person or company's official website.

13.3.1. Defamation and Commercial Disparagement

Even if the use of the domain name generates no trademark infringement problems, you can be liable for other actions if your cybergriping site goes too far. If your cybergriping site targets a person, you can be liable for defamation if your commentary strays too far from factual accounts. I discuss defamation and how to avoid defaming someone in Section 8.9.3.

If your comments about a company or its products stray too far from fact, you can be liable for commercial disparagement or a similar claim such as trade libel, product disparagement, slander of goods, unfair competition or interference with prospective business advantage. Commercial disparagement claims are generally state law claims so their elements vary from state to state.

Commercial disparagement has many similarities with defamation discussed in Section 8.9.3. You are guilty of commercial disparagement if you publish an untrue, derogatory statement of fact about a company or its products and the statement directly results in the company's financial loss. The financial loss typically relates to influencing people not to conduct business with the company or purchase its products. Some state laws require that the statement be made with malice.

13.4. Use of Trademarks and Celebrity Names in Commentary Sites

As a general rule, you may use trademarks in a commentary site provided that the use does not confuse consumers into incorrectly thinking the trademark owner sponsors or is affiliated with your site.

Celebrity Name as Domain Name. Some celebrities may have trademark rights in their name. Nevertheless, you should be able to use a celebrity name for a legitimate commentary site. See Section 6.9 for more discussion on domain name disputes involving celebrity names and personal names. See Section 12.6 for a related discussion of impersonating and using celebrity names on social networking sites.

Use of Trademarks as Domain Names for Criticism, Gripe and Parody Sites. Using a trademark as a domain name on a non-commercial website is generally acceptable and protected by the First Amendment as long as the use of the domain name signals that the site is a commentary or gripe site and does not confuse consumers into thinking that the trademark owner operates or endorses the website. I discuss domain names and domain name disputes in depth in Chapter 5 and Chapter 6.

Domain names for cybergriping sites often consist of the trademark and a negative dictionary word. Sucks is a popular negative word used in gripe site domain names. The domain name for a gripe site abut the XYZ Company might be www.XYZCompanysucks. com. Most courts would not view the domain name, www.XYZ-Companysucks.com, as infringing the trademark XYZ Company. That is because the domain name does not create a likelihood of confusion with the trademark company name as required for domain name dispute actions. No one is likely to believe that the XYZ

Company is the sponsor or operator of a site that criticizes the company and carries a domain name like XYZCompanysucks.

It can depend on the negative term as to whether or not the domain name is deemed to be confusingly similar with the trademark. Domain names with the words "truthabout" or "stop" before the trademark and "fraud" or "theft" after the trademark have been viewed as not confusing. Dictionary terms that are not clearly negative may be viewed as confusing. For example, the domain name XYZCompanyExposed.com is not clearly a source of criticism about the XYZ Company.

13.5. Disclaimers for Commentary Sites

Disclaimers are a way of showing your good faith effort to not violate anyone else's rights and not mislead or confuse consumers. A proper disclaimer may shield you from claims and persuade a court to conclude that your commentary site is legal.

However, if you do everything wrong, a disclaimer is not going to save you. You can invalidate your disclaimer by your conduct. For example, if your disclaimer indicates that your fan site is unofficial and not endorsed by the rights owners, yet, your website pages and advertisements state or imply your site is an official fan site, no court is going to give your disclaimer serious consideration.

To be effective, your disclaimer must be noticeable, clearly stated, and command the average viewer's attention. Your disclaimer should indicate that the website is not affiliated with the product, company or person on which it comments. You can also provide a link to the official website of the product, company, or person.

Here is a potential disclaimer one might use for a fan site:

This website is an unofficial fan site made by a fan of Heroes for the enjoyment of other Heroes fans. This site is NOT authorized by or affiliated with NBC, Universal Media Studios, Tailwind Productions or any entity or person involved with the Heroes television program. Heroes, its characters, and all related images and content are the proprietary material of NBC and its affiliated entities.

Here is a potential disclaimer one might use for a gripe site:

This site offers a critique of the services provided by the XYZ Company and is not affiliated with or sponsored by the XYZ Company. You can visit the website of the XYZ Company at the following link: www.XYZCompany.com

13.6. Real-Life Examples of Acceptable and Unacceptable Commentary Sites

Real-Life Examples of Acceptable Commentary Sites

Anna Nicole Smith Fan Site. Anna Nicole Smith lost a Uniform Domain Name Dispute Resolution Policy (UDRP) proceeding regarding the domain name annanicolesmith.com. The domain name owner had registered the domain name for the express purpose of establishing a fan club site for Smith and operated a fan site for at least two years prior to Smith launching the UDRP proceeding. The domain name owner did not derive any commercial benefit from the site and the site contained a clear disclaimer indicating that it was not an official Anna Nicole Smith site. (*Anna Nicole Smith v. DNS Research, Inc.*, No. FA0312000220007 (NAF UDRP Decision, Feb. 21, 2004)).

Bally's. The owner of a criticism website about Bally's health club business was not liable for trademark infringement. The url included the phrase "Bally Sucks". The opening page presented Bally's trademark with the word "sucks" printed across it, stated the website was unauthorized, and included the statement "Bally Total Fitness Complaints! Un-Authorized." According to the court, no reasonable consumer could assume Bally's was the source of the website or was in anyway associated with it. (*Bally Total Fitness Holding Corp. v. Faber*, 29 F. Supp. 2d 1161 (C.D. Cal. 1998)).

Reverend Falwell. A gripe website critical of Reverend Jerry Falwell was located at the url, www.fallwell.com. Although the interior pages of the gripe site contained no disclaimer, the homepage prominently stated, "This website is NOT affiliated with Jerry Falwell or his ministry"; advised "If you would like to visit Rev. Falwell's website, you may click here"; and provided a hyperlink to Reverend Falwell's official website. According to the court, there was no likelihood of confusion for a trademark infringement claim. No reasonable online visitor would believe that Reverend Falwell was affiliated with or sponsored a site that criticized him, his positions, and his interpretations of the Bible. (*Lamparello v. Falwell*, 420 F.3d 309 (4th Cir. 2005)).

Griping about Contractors. Joseph Maxwell created the website trendmakerhome.com, on which he complained about his consumer experiences with TMI, Inc., a construction company which had a website at trendmakershome.com. The site also included a page on which readers could share and obtain information about contractors and tradespeople. Maxwell's website was not commercial and did not violate federal or state anti-dilution laws or the Anticybersquatting Consumer Protection Act. The court based its decision that the site was not infringing on several factors. Specifically, Maxwell's website included a disclaimer at the top of the homepage indicating that it was not TMI's site, charged no fees related to the contractor recommendations, and accepted no paid advertisements. (*TMI v. Maxwell*, 368 F.3d 433 (5th Cir. 2004)).

Real-Life Examples of Unacceptable Commentary Sites

Real Estate Competitors. Her, Inc. and Re/Max, both residential real estate companies operating in Ohio, were direct competitors. Re/Max registered and used domain names incorporating the slogans of Her, Inc. and the personal names of its principals. Although the websites contained critical content about Her, Inc., the websites were commercially misleading. The criticism websites gave no indication that they were not associated with Her, Inc. and did not identify themselves as criticism sites. (*Her, Inc. v. Re/Max First Choice, LLC* , 468 F. Supp. 2d 964 (S.D. Ohio 2007)).

Tanning Exposed. Sunlight Saunas was a retailer of personal saunas. One of its competitors constructed a website critical of Sunlight Sauna under the domain name sunlightsaunas-exposed.com. The competitor also sent emails to consumers encouraging consumers to visit the sunlightsaunasexposed.com site. The competitor's website did not qualify as a protected criticism website. Sunlightsaunasexposed did not signal to consumers that it was a criticism site as a website with a name such as sunlightsaunassucks would have. According to the court, the term "exposed" does not send the same unequivocal negative message as "sucks" and may not immediately alert an internet user that he or she is at a gripe site. The court also found that the competitor intended to divert traffic from Sunlight Sauna's website. (*Sunlight Saunas v. Sundance Sauna*, 427 F. Supp. 2d 1032 (D. Kan. 2006)).

PEER-TO-PEER FILE SHARING

14.1. What Is Peer-to-Peer File Sharing?

Peer-to-peer (P2P) file sharing is a method of sharing computer files by making them available for other users to access and download onto their own computers. You store the files on your own computer. Other people can then access those files and make copies of them.

The peer-to-peer infrastructure provides a network so that you can see which files are available for download on other computers in the network. Companies that have provided file sharing networks, software, and applications include Napster, Grokster, and BitTorrent.

14.1.1. Is Peer-to-Peer File Sharing Legal?

There are uses of P2P systems that are accepted as legal. For example, people in an academic setting or colleagues within a work place may use P2P systems to facilitate exchanging drafts of documents on which they are collectively working.

Despite the available legal P2P applications, many people use P2P systems to exchange copyright protected works such as music, films, television programs, and books. The Motion Picture Association of America (MPAA) and the Recording Industry Association of America (RIAA) have filed lawsuits against companies and individual sharers of unauthorized files.

While many copyright experts support liberalizing the law and frown on content companies suing individual consumers, most agree that P2P file sharing of copyrighted works is infringement—even if you are downloading the work for your personal, non-commercial use.

14.2. Media Industry Actions against Individual File Sharers

Beginning in 2003, the RIAA sued or threatened to sue over 35,000 individuals who participated in P2P file sharing. Most of these lawsuits never went to trial and resulted in settlements in which the accused file sharer paid a settlement fee of several thousand dollars. Due in part to complaints against RIAA's methods and the failure of the lawsuits to deter piracy significantly, the RIAA is phasing out its strategy of suing individual file sharers.

14.2.1. The Making Available Issue

There are questions as to whether the single act of uploading a file to a P2P network constitutes copyright infringement.

As discussed in Section 3.2, there are six exclusive rights held by a copyright owner. Copyright infringement requires that you exercise one of these exclusive rights without the copyright owner's permission. While distribution is listed as one of the six exclusive rights, making available and publication are not. Traditionally, publishing a work or making a work available for distribution have been viewed as being synonymous with distribution. Battles over P2P file sharing have called into question whether it is accurate to view making a work available as synonymous with distributing the work. Here is a story about Jack and Jill that illustrates why.

Jack, a P2P file sharer, uses a decentralized system to place a file in a folder located on Jack's computer. The file might contain a copyrighted recording, or a television program. By doing this, Jack makes the file available for another P2P file sharer to acquire. Jill is another P2P file sharer who uses the same P2P infrastructure that Jack uses. If and when Jill comes along and takes a copy of the file made available by Jack, there has been a distribution of the file. However, there is no guarantee that Jill or any another P2P file sharer will take a copy of the file that Jack has made available. The file could simply sit undisturbed on Jack's computer. Hence, if no one takes a copy of the file that Jack has made available, has the file been distributed?

This question has become very important to music and content industries attempting to combat the unauthorized sharing of their content through P2P file sharing systems. Content owners argue that making the file available is equivalent to distributing the file and if distribution is unauthorized, the distribution constitutes copyright infringement. Others argue placing content in a peer-to-peer file is not equivalent to distribution if no one actually takes a copy of the file.

Real-Life Cases Deciding the Making Available Issue

Peer-to-Peer File Sharing. Even if Jeffrey Howell placed copyrighted recordings in a Kazaa shared folder on his computer, the record labels could not prove that any other P2P user had accessed Howell's shared folder and copied the recordings. As a result, there was no proof that Howell had distributed the recordings. (*Atlantic Recording Corp. v. Howell*, 554 F. Supp. 2d 976 (D. Ariz. 2008)).

Jammie Thomas and Jury Instruction No. 15. Jammie Thomas lost a copyright infringement lawsuit to the tune of $222,000 for recordings she allegedly placed on Kazaa, a peer-to-peer file sharing network. The Minnesota District Court granted a new trial due to an error in one of the jury instructions. Jury Instruction No. 15 instructed the jury that Thomas was guilty of infringement if she made copyrighted recordings available for electronic distribution without permission on a peer-to-peer network—regardless of whether there had been actual distribution of those recordings. (*Capitol Records v. Thomas*, 579 F. Supp. 2d 1210 (D. Minn. 2008)).

In the second trial, jury instructions indicated that Thomas was guilty of copyright infringement if Thomas infringed the reproduction or distribution rights in the recordings. The jury in the second trial also found Thomas liable for infringement and awarded 1.92 Million Dollars in monetary damages to the record labels. In the second trial, the jury did not specify whether Thomas infringed the distribution right or the reproduction right and the jury instructions did not define distribution.

14.3. Media Industry Actions against Internet Companies

Content owners have been successful in shutting down several companies that facilitate peer-to-peer file sharing by filing lawsuits against them. Closures occur sometimes as a result of judicial order and sometimes through the fledgling P2P company succumbing to the demands of expensive litigation.

Examples of specific infractions by P2P companies resulting in claims by copyright owners include the following:

- providing software or operating an internet-based service that allows users to share videos and other files
- providing a search feature and recommendation engine and linking to files elsewhere on the internet
- providing a virtual locker where users can sync their own music collections to access at any location or device on which they have an internet connection

The internet company typically asserts a defense in reliance on the Digital Millennium Copyright Act's (DMCA) safe harbor provisions. I discuss DMCA safe harbor provisions further in Section 12.5. Even though the DMCA faces ongoing criticism, it has been effective in insulating many companies from liability resulting from the copyright infringement activities of their online visitors.

14.4. Other Media Industry Responses to Peer-to-Peer File Sharing

Content owners have pursued other mechanisms to combat piracy through P2P file sharing. They include legislative action and efforts to work with websites.

Legislation. Content owners have pursued stricter legislation which contain protection provisions for a broad number of assets and industries. For example, legislation has included proposals to increase civil penalties for infringement, appoint an anti-piracy czar, and increase enforcement by the U.S. Department of Justice.

While the United States has not seriously considered three-strikes legislation, some European and Asian countries have passed or are considering three-strike legislation. Here is how three-strike legislation works: In response to complaints from copyright holders, a government agency would track down the internet addresses of infringing individuals and send warning emails and registered letters to first-time and second-time infringers. In the most aggressive proposals, upon the third violation, the infringer's internet connection would be cut off for a period of time.

Legalize P2P File-Swapping. Legalizing file-swapping is an often-discussed concept. While this has not been seriously considered as an option within the United States, the Songwriters Association of Canada (SAC) has made such a proposal. The SAC proposal defines file sharing as sharing music without financial gain. In return for legalizing the sharing of their music, music owners would receive a monthly fee from internet service providers in Canada. While music owners could opt out of the system, if they participated and accepted license fees, they would waive the right to sue Canadians who share music. Individual broadband internet and wireless subscribers could opt out of the license fee if they do not share music files and if they agree to pay a predetermined amount of damages if they are caught file sharing. If implemented the amount of the license fee would be set by a regulatory or judicial process. Previous versions of the proposal set the monthly license fee at five dollars.

Filtering Technology. Some internet companies are trying to work with content companies and are developing filtering systems that detect and decrease unauthorized sharing of copyrighted works.

Email was perhaps the first breakthrough application that brought millions of people to cyberspace. Email is short for electronic mail, the exchange of messages on the internet. Email is often text-based meaning it contains text only. Email can also be provided in hypertext markup language, or html for short, which allows one to include images and more sophisticated formatting in the emails.

Cyberspace offers a motley assortment of ways for us to communicate with each other beyond standard email. Online communication methods include discussion forums, instant messaging, bulletin boards, and chat rooms. Some of these communication methods have developed their own jargon. For example, LOL stands for Laugh Out Loud and HRU stands How Are You.

Email communication does not occur in real time. In other words, with email communication, the communication takes place at disparate times. You send a message and the recipient receives it the next time he logs onto the internet and checks his email. Other online communications take place in real time. This communication may be one-way or two-way, involving two individuals or multiple users.

15.1. Online Communication Methods

Chats. Chat is a technology that allows real-time, text-based communication between two or more participants via the internet or via an intranet. A chat occurs in real time in a virtual room typically among many users who do not necessarily know one another. All participants in the chat must be online at the same time; however, transcripts from chats are often archived and made available for review after the live chat. Since chat occurs in real time, it is much more like having a conversation with someone than email which requires waiting for a response. Within seconds of your writing a comment online, everyone else logged into the chat system can view and immediately respond to your remarks.

Chat rooms are used for online learning and for business world applications as well as for personal use. For example, newspapers host chats on various topics in which their subscribers can participate. Internet service providers offer chat rooms on specific topics.

Sometimes the chat room is moderated. Sometimes, it is not. A chat room can be a noisy place. Many people may be talking at the same time.

Instant Messaging. Instant messaging or IM is communication between two individuals. While the terms instant messaging and chatting are sometimes used interchangeably, there are distinctions between the two methods. Like chats, individuals using IM communicate in real time. The people instant messaging type messages to each other online and can receive an immediate response.

A traditional chat requires a virtual chat room which is a website or online area onto which you log on for the online chat. Instant Messaging relies on an online software application. For example, AOL Instant Messenger (AIM) is a popular IM software application. Once you download the software and create a handle or name, you can instant message with anyone else on the AOL Instant Messenger network whose IM account name you have. You can also send IM messages to your friends' mobile phones and personal digital assistants.

Discussion Forums. While a live online chat might last a few hours, a discussion forum is an ongoing online conversation. Discussion forums typically focus on a particular topic such as publishing, marketing, starting a business, sewing, or being a good pet owner.

In a discussion forum, you send a message to the group and people respond to you. The discussion does not occur in real time which means all members of the discussion forum do not have to be online at the same time. A discussion forum consists of threads and posts. Each question or reply is referred to as a post. Each new topic of conversation is a thread. A thread can consist of many posts by multiple participants.

Sometimes the discussion forum is a website or internet bulletin board. Sometimes, the discussion takes place via email in which case it may be referred to as a discussion group. Discussion groups often give you the option of choosing how to participate. You can read and post messages online. Alternatively, you can use your email account to read and respond to messages. Discussion boards are usually read through a web browser. Newsgroups are similar to discussion forums but take place on usenet and require a special program for access called a newsgroup reader.

Sometimes you must register or become a member in order to participate in the discussion forum. Many discussion forums have their own rules and do not allow spam, overt advertising nor attachments.

Every Discussion Forum Is Not a Listserv. Some people refer to discussion forums as a Listserv. However, every discussion forum is not a listserv. LISTSERV is a registered trademark owned by Eric Thomas, the founder and CEO of L-Soft. L-Soft develops and sells LISTSERV email list management software. To prevent the trademark from going generic and losing the ability to be protected as a trademark, L-Soft encourages people not to refer to discussion forums as a Listserv.

Mailing Lists or Email Newsletter. Mailing lists are generally a message sent by one person or organization to many people. It might be a store announcement, a newsletter, or a news alert. The communications generally go one-way. The group does not send messages back to the person or organization originating the mailing list or newsletter.

You might think of these communications as subscribing to a magazine or newsletter. Instead of being delivered to your postal mailbox, the announcement is delivered to your email inbox.

15.2. Legal Issues Common to Online Communication Methods

Copyright Issues. The same copyright issues as discussed in Section 8.7 apply to online communication methods. For example, instead of posting an entire article, it is better cyber etiquette to post links to articles that you want to share with others.

If you are the administrator or host of a group communications method, you can insulate yourself from liability caused by the copyright infringement of others by complying with the Digital Millennium Copyright Act discussed in Section 12.5. Also, consider whether any of the best practices for website operators who allow user generated content, discussed in Section 12.4, would benefit you.

Defamation. You are responsible for any defamatory statements that you make. If you are the provider or administrator of a forum for group communications, you likely qualify as an interactive service provider. That means you qualify for the Communications Decency Act which insulates you from liability for defamatory comments made by others. I discuss defamation and the Communications Decency Act in Section 8.9.3.

Ownership of Comments. The person who creates the comment is the copyright owner of the comment or posting. Under current copyright law, the creator has a valid copyright as soon as the work is fixed in a tangible medium of expression. As soon as the person writes the message, the person has a copyright to the extent the material is eligible for copyright protection. Some comments may be ineligible for copyright protection if they are too short or simply a recitation of facts—such as a list of ten pizza restaurants in town.

Some uses of others' comments and postings are likely good candidates for the fair use exception to copyright protection. For example, it is common to include an excerpt of the original message when responding so that other readers know the context of the conversation or thread. Forwarding someone else's comment, posting someone's comment elsewhere, or distributing multiple copies of it is copyright infringement.

Forum Administrator's Use of Comments. If you want to use the comments for other purposes, you can obtain such rights by placing the right to re-use the comments in your terms of service for participation in the forum.

CAN-SPAM. If you use the communications method for advertising purposes such as a company email marketing newsletter—you should comply with the CAN-SPAM Act provisions discussed in Section 9.3.

APPENDICES
Resources, Forms and Glossary

The appendices include resources, forms, and a glossary of terms used in this book.

Appendices:

RESOURCES AND FORMS

A.1. General Resources for the Cyber Citizen

A.1.1. General

United States Copyright Office, 101 Independence Avenue, SE, Washington, DC 20559, (202) 707-3000 (information specialists available on weekdays from 8:30 a.m. to 5:00 p.m., EST; recorded information available 24 hours per day), (202) 707-9100 (forms and publication hotline). Forms and publications are also available online at www.copyright.gov. To find current processing time for copyright registration applications, visit the electronic copyright office section of www.copyright.gov.

United States Patent and Trademark Office (PTO), 2900 Crystal Drive, Arlington, VA 22202, general information: (703) 308-HELP, www.uspto.gov. You can search trademarks that are federally registered and pending for federal registration on the PTO's free online database, Trademark Electronic Search System (TESS), available on the PTO's website. The PTO Website also offers the Patent Full-Text and Imaging Database (PatFT), a searchable database of issued patents. The Google search engine offers an alternative database of issued patents at www.google.com/patents which some may find more user-friendly and easier to navigate than PatFT.

The Federal Trade Commission (FTC), 600 Pennsylvania Avenue, NW, Washington, DC 20580, (202) 326-2222, www.ftc.gov. The FTC issues regulations for and enforces the Children's Online Privacy Protection Act, the CAN-SPAM Act, and numerous other consumer protection laws. The FTC also issues guidelines concerning the use of endorsements and testimonials in advertising. You can find informational publications, documents from enforcement actions, and related reports and congressional testimony at the FTC's website.

Internet Corporation for Assigned Names and Numbers (ICANN), www.icann.org. ICANN has United States offices in Marina del Rey, California and Washington, DC. The ICANN website offers a list of ICANN-accredited registrars.

A.1.2. Domain Names Resources

Registrars and TLDs. You can find a listing of ICANN-accredited registrars and generic top level domains (gTLDs) at ICANN's website at www.icann.org. You can find a listing of country code top level domains (ccTLDs) at www.iana.org/domains/root/db/.

UDRP Policy and Rules. You can find links to the full text and the accompanying rules for the Uniform Domain Name Dispute Resolution Policy (UDRP) as well as information about the other dispute resolution policies administered by ICANN online at www.icann.org/en/udrp/.

UDRP Dispute Resolution Service Providers. There are currently four providers who administer UDRP Proceedings. They are referred to as Dispute Resolution Service Providers:

- the Asian Domain Name Dispute Resolution Centre (www.adndrc.org)
- the Czech Arbitration Court (www.adr.eu)
- the National Arbitration Forum (domains.adrforum.com/)
- the World Intellectual Property Organization (www.wipo.int/amc/en/domains)

The National Arbitration Forum (NAF) and the World Intellectual Property Organization (WIPO) administer most UDRP proceedings among United States trademark owners and domain name registrants. In the policies section of its domain name disputes website, NAF offers model forms for initiation of UDRP proceedings.

UDRP Decisions. The full text of all UDRP decisions is available online. Here are some internet search tools to aid you in finding decisions of interest to you:

- www.adr-decisions.eu for Czech Arbitration Court decisions
- Domain Fight (www.domainfight.net) for both NAF and WIPO decisions
- Domains ADR Forum (domains.adrforum.com/decision.aspx) for NAF decisions
- www.wipo.int/amc/en/domains/index.html for WIPO decisions

A.1.3. Resources for Compliance with the Children's Online Privacy Protection Act (COPPA)

The Federal Trade Commission (FTC), the government agency that administers and enforces COPPA, strives to educate the public on COPPA compliance. One FTC publication offered at www.ftc.gov useful to website operators drafting privacy policies is *You, Your Privacy Policy and COPPA*. To ask the FTC additional questions about COPPA, you can call the FTC toll free at (877) FTC-HELP or (877) 382-4357, or write Consumer Response Center, Federal Trade Commission, 600 Pennsylvania Avenue, NW, Washington, DC 20580.

The Direct Marketing Association offers an online tool that leads website operators through a series of questions to generate a draft of a COPPA-compliant privacy policy. The online tool is available at www.the-dma.org.

A.1.4. Resources for Freedom of Information Act (FOIA) Requests

The Reporters Committee for Freedom of the Press, 1101 Wilson Boulevard, Suite 1100, Arlington, VA 22209, www.rcfp.org, is a nonprofit organization dedicated to providing free legal help to reporters and news organizations. It offers *The Federal Open Government Guide*, a booklet available online and in print describing how to use FOIA and other federal open access laws.

All fifty states and Washington, DC have enacted open records laws similar to the Freedom of Information Act. The Reporters Committee for Freedom of the Press offers the *Open Government Guide*, a comprehensive state-by-state guide to open records and meetings laws.

The National Security Archive, Suite 701, Gelman Library, the George Washington University, 2130 H Street, NW, Washington, DC 20037, (202) 994-7000, is an independent non-governmental research institute and library located at the George Washington University. The Archive collects and publishes declassified documents obtained through FOIA. The Archive devotes an entire section of its website to the subject of FOIA, including the publication *Effective FOIA Requesting for Everyone*.

A.2. Tips and Sample Forms for Registering the Copyright in Your Online Work

A.2.1. Copyright Registration Tips

You should read these copyright registration tips in conjunction with the discussion of copyright registration in Chapter 4.

Copyright Office Registration Resources. The Copyright Office provides instructions for completing each part of the application.

When filing online, read the instructions on the screen and in the help text. The Copyright Office offers several publications that explain copyright registration. The publications most helpful to the cyber citizen include Circular 62a, *Group Registration of Newspapers and Newsletters*; Circular 62b, *Copyright Registration of a Group of Serial Issues*; Circular 65, *Copyright Registration for Automated Databases*; and Circular 66, *Copyright Registration for Online Works*.

Nature of Authorship. As part of the application, you must describe the elements of the work you created and in which you claim copyright. List elements that are eligible for copyright protection. Appropriate descriptions include *text, artwork, photograph, music, lyrics, sound recording*, and *motion picture*. Do not list elements that are not eligible for copyright or that are ambiguous such as *idea, concept, look and feel, interface, layout, plot, structure, style*, and *technique*.

Publication Date. Do not list a publication date if you are registering the copyright in an unpublished work. If you are registering the copyright in a published work, the publication date you indicate on your application must be prior to the date of your application. The Copyright Office will not accept an application for a published work before the publication actually takes place.

Limitation of Copyright Claim. Complete the *Limitation of Copyright Claim* portion of the application only if your work contains preexisting material in which you do not claim copyright ownership. For example, if your website features an arrangement of both public domain photographs and your original photographs, you can not claim copyright ownership in the public domain photographs. Do not complete the *Limitation of Copyright Claim* section if the work you are registering is completely new, even if the work is a compilation of new works.

Submitting the Correct Deposit. For online works, make sure the deposit has a date that is consistent with the date you provide on the application. The date of publication specified on your application and the date indicated on the deposit should be consistent.

Author Information. The *Author Information* portion of the application asks for the author's birth date. Providing a birth date is optional. The Copyright Office likes to have birth date information to use as a form of identification. If given, this information will appear in the public record. If the author is deceased, the year of death must be included on the application.

Filing Fees. Registration fees change periodically. Check the Copyright Office's website to verify you have the most current fee information. Fees also vary depending on method of registration and the number of claims being filed.

Free Form Responses. When using online registration or Form CO, you respond to most questions by selecting a response from a limited number of options. If you use paper application forms or provide free-form responses during online registration, be brief and clear.

A.2.2. Registration of Your Online Work as a Basic Claim, Sample One, Appropriate for Blogs and Websites

This sample copyright registration is provided on the Copyright Office's Fill-In Form CO. If you use the Copyright Office's online registration system, you will provide substantially the same information on the multiple screens presented to you during the online registration process.

In this example, Virtual Flights, LLC, registers the copyright in its company website, www.virtualflights.com. In the Chapter 4 discussion of copyright registration, I mention that websites with frequently changing content can sometimes be registered using the group registration method for automated databases. In this example, Virtual Flights does not select that option and instead registers its website as a basic claim. This registration example is also appropriate for a blog registered as a basic claim.

For the response to 1a, *Type of work being registered*, you should select the type of work that best describes the material you are registering. In this example, Virtual Flights' website is mostly text so the company selects *Literary work* to describe the work being registered. As an alternative example, if your website were an online portfolio of your artwork and was primarily photographs, the better response to 1a would be *Visual arts work*. The Copyright Office uses your description primarily for its internal classification purposes so there is no wrong answer to this question. The exception is that any applicant claiming ownership in a sound recording should select *Sound recording* to describe the work being registered.

For this sample registration, Virtual Flights employees created the html (computer programming behind the website) and the text for the website. As a result, the website html and text qualify as works made for hire owned by Virtual Flights and Virtual Flights lists itself as the author in part 2b and selects made for hire in part 2g of the first entry for *Author Information*. The first entry for *Author Information* covers authorship of the html and text.

Virtual Flights' website also incorporates photographs. Although Virtual Flights is the copyright claimant of the photographs on its website, the company is not the work made for hire author of those photographs. The author of the photographs is a freelance photographer, Heather Reynolds, who sold (or assigned) the copyright in the photographs to Virtual Flights. This information is reflected in the second entry for *Author Information* that provides authorship information for the photographs. In response to 3.e of *Copyright Claimant Information*, Virtual Flights checks *Written agreement* to indicate the company is not the author of the website photography and acquired the copyright in those photographs through a written agreement with Heather Reynolds.

Since all the material on the www.virtualflights.com website is new, original material, Virtual Flights leaves part 4 of the application, *Limitation of Copyright Claim*, blank. Jeremy Wright, a Virtual Flights employee authorized to act on behalf of the company, signs the application in part 8, *Certification*.

UNITED STATES COPYRIGHT OFFICE
Form CO · Application for Copyright Registration

APPLICATION FOR COPYRIGHT REGISTRATION   TX

* Designates Required Fields

1 WORK BEING REGISTERED

1a. * Type of work being registered (*Fill in one only*)

☒ Literary work   ☐ Performing arts work

☐ Visual arts work   ☐ Motion picture/audiovisual work

☐ Sound recording   ☐ Single serial issue

ApplicationForCopyrightRegistration

1b. * Title of this work (*one title per space*)

THE VIRTUALFLIGHTS.COM WEBSITE

WorkTitles

1c. For a serial issue: Volume [   ] Number [   ] Issue [   ] ISSN [   ]

Frequency of publication: [   ]

1d. Previous or alternative title

[   ]

1e. * Year of completion [2][0][1][0]

Publication (*If this work has not been published, skip to section 2*)

1f. Date of publication [01/25/2010] (*mm/dd/yyyy*)   **1g.** ISBN [   ]

1h. Nation of publication   ☒ United States ☐ Other

1i. Published as a contribution in a larger work entitled

[   ]

1j. If line 1i above names a serial issue   Volume [   ] Number [   ] Issue [   ]

On pages [   ]

1k. If work was preregistered   Number PRE-[ ][ ][ ][ ][ ][ ][ ][ ]

C UNITED STATES COPYRIGHT OFFICE
Form CO · Application for Copyright Registration

For Office Use Only

WorkBeingRegistered

2 AUTHOR INFORMATION

2a. Personal name   *complete either 2a or 2b*

First Name | Middle | Last

2b. Organization name   VIRTUAL FLIGHTS, LLC

2c. Doing business as

2d. Year of birth   **2e.** Year of death

2f. *   ☒ Citizenship   ☒ United States   ☐ Other
☐ Domicile

2g. Author's contribution: ☒ Made for hire   ☐ Anonymous
☐ Pseudonymous

Continuation of Author Information

2h. * This author created (*Fill in only the authorship that applies to this author*)

☒ Text/poetry   ☐ Compilation   ☐ Map/technical drawing   ☐ Music
☐ Editing   ☐ Sculpture   ☐ Architectural work   ☐ Lyrics
☒ Computer program   ☐ Jewelry design   ☐ Photography   ☐ Motion picture/audiovisual
☐ Collective work   ☐ 2-dimensional artwork ☐ Script/play/screenplay ☐ Sound recording/performance

Other:

For Office Use Only

AuthorInformation

Privacy Act Notice
Sections 408-410 of title 17 of the *United States Code* authorize the Copyright Office to collect the personally identifying information requested on this form in order to process the application for copyright registration. By providing this information you are agreeing to routine uses of the information that include publication to give legal notice of your copyright claim as required by 17 U.S.C. § 705. It will appear in the Office's online catalog. If you do not provide the information requested, registration may be refused or delayed, and you may not be entitled to certain relief, remedies, and benefits under the copyright law.

Page 2 of 7

Sample Copyright Registration of Your Website as a Basic Claim (continued)

UNITED STATES COPYRIGHT OFFICE
Form CO · Application for Copyright Registration

2 AUTHOR INFORMATION - Entry Number 2

2a. Personal name   `* complete either 2a or 2b`

First Name	Middle	Last
HEATHER		REYNOLDS

2b. Organization name

2c. Doing business as

2d. Year of birth   **2e.** Year of death

2f. * ☒ Citizenship   ☒ United States   ☐ Other
       ☐ Domicile

2g. Author's contribution: ☐ Made for hire   ☐ Anonymous
                ☐ Pseudonymous

Continuation of Author Information

2h. * This author created (*Fill in only the authorship that applies to this author*)

☐ Text/poetry   ☐ Compilation   ☐ Map/technical drawing   ☐ Music
☐ Editing   ☐ Sculpture   ☐ Architectural work   ☐ Lyrics
☐ Computer program   ☐ Jewelry design   ☒ Photography   ☐ Motion picture/audiovisual
☐ Collective work   ☐ 2-dimensional artwork ☐ Script/play/screenplay   ☐ Sound recording/performance

Other:

For Office Use Only

AuthorInformation

3 COPYRIGHT CLAIMANT INFORMATION

Claimant   `* complete either 3a or 3b` - If you do not know the address for a claimant, enter "not known" in the Street address and City fields.

3a. Personal name

Sample Copyright Registration of Your Website as a Basic Claim (continued)

UNITED STATES COPYRIGHT OFFICE
Form CO · Application for Copyright Registration

First Name	Middle	Last

3b. Organization name
VIRTUAL FLIGHTS, LLC

3c. Doing business as

3d. Street address *
100 MAIN STREET

Street address (line 2)

City *	State	ZIP / Postal code	Country
ANYPLACE	ANYSTATE	00000	United States

Email	Phone number	
LEGAL@VIRTUALFLIGHTS.COM	(999) 555-1212	(Add "+" and country code for foreign numbers)

3e. If claimant is **not** an author, copyright ownership acquired by: ☒ Written agreement ☐ Will or inheritance ☐ Other

For Office Use Only

CopyrightClaimantInformation

4 LIMITATION OF COPYRIGHT CLAIM

Skip section 4 if this work is all new.

4a. Material excluded from this claim (Material previously registered, previously published, or not owned by this claimant)

☐ Text ☐ Artwork ☐ Music ☐ Sound recording/performance ☐ Motion picture/audiovisual

Other:

4b. Previous registration(s)   Number   Year

Number   Year

4c. New material included in this claim (This work contains new, additional, or revised material)

☐ Text   ☐ Compilation   ☐ Map/technical drawing   ☐ Music

☐ Poetry   ☐ Sculpture   ☐ Architectural work   ☐ Lyrics

☐ Computer program   ☐ Jewelry design   ☐ Photography   ☐ Motion picture/audiovisual

☐ Editing   ☐ 2-dimensional artwork   ☐ Script/play/screenplay   ☐ Sound recording/performance

Sample Copyright Registration of Your Website as a Basic Claim (continued)

UNITED STATES COPYRIGHT OFFICE
Form CO · Application for Copyright Registration

Other: [   ]

For Office Use Only

LimitationOfCopyrightClaim

5 RIGHTS AND PERMISSIONS CONTACT

☐ Check if information below should be copied from the **first** copyright claimant

First Name	Middle	Last
JEREMY		WRIGHT

Name of organization
VIRTUAL FLIGHTS, LLC

Street address
100 MAIN STREET

Street address (line 2)

City	State	ZIP / Postal code	Country
ANYPLACE	ANYSTATE	00000	United States

Email	Phone number	
LEGAL@VIRTUALFLIGHTS.COM	(999) 555-1212	(*Add "+" and country code for foreign numbers*)

For Office Use Only

RightsAndPermissionsContact

Privacy Act Notice
Sections 408-410 of title 17 of the *United States Code* authorize the Copyright Office to collect the personally identifying information requested on this form in order to process the application for copyright registration. By providing this information you are agreeing to routine uses of the information that include publication to give legal notice of your copyright claim as required by 17 U.S.C. § 705. It will appear in the Office's online catalog. If you do not provide the information requested, registration may be refused or delayed, and you may not be entitled to certain relief, remedies, and benefits under the copyright law.

Sample Copyright Registration of Your Website as a Basic Claim (continued)

UNITED STATES COPYRIGHT OFFICE
Form CO · Application for Copyright Registration

6 CORRESPONDENCE CONTACT

☐ Copy from **first** copyright claimant ☒ Copy from rights and permissions contact

First name *	Middle	Last *
JEREMY		WRIGHT

Name of organization
VIRTUAL FLIGHTS, LLC

Street address *
100 MAIN STREET

Street address (line 2)

City *	State	ZIP / Postal code	Country
ANYPLACE	ANYSTATE	00000	United States

Email *	Daytime phone number	
LEGAL@VIRTUALFLIGHTS.COM	(999) 555-1212	*(Add "+" and country code for foreign numbers)*

For Office Use Only

CorrespondenceContact

7 MAIL CERTIFICATE TO:

* Complete either 7a, 7b, or both

☐ Copy from **first** copyright claimant ☒ Copy from rights and permissions contact ☐ Copy from correspondence contact

7a. First Name	Middle	Last
JEREMY		WRIGHT

7b. Name of organization
VIRTUAL FLIGHTS, LLC

7c. Street address *
100 MAIN STREET

Street address (line 2)

City *	State	ZIP / Postal code	Country
ANYPLACE	ANYSTATE	00000	United States

Sample Copyright Registration of Your Website as a Basic Claim (continued)

UNITED STATES COPYRIGHT OFFICE
Form CO · Application for Copyright Registration

For Office Use Only

MailCertificateTo

8 CERTIFICATION

17 U.S.C. § 506(e): Any person who knowingly makes a false representation of a material fact in the application for copyright registration provided for by section 409, or in any written statement filed in connection with the application, shall be fined not more than $2,500.

I certify that I am the author, copyright claimant, or owner of exclusive rights, or the authorized agent of the author, copyright claimant, or owner of exclusive rights, of this work, and that the information given in this application is correct to the best of my knowledge.

Jeremy Wright

8a. Handwritten signature

JEREMY WRIGHT   2/21/2010

8b. Printed name   **8c.** Date signed

8d. Deposit account number   Account holder

8e. Applicant's internal tracking number (optional)

For Office Use Only

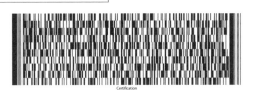

Certification

Sample Copyright Registration of Your Website as a Basic Claim (continued)

A.2.3. Registration of Your Online Work as a Basic Claim, Sample Two, Appropriate for Podcasts and Audio Programs

This sample copyright registration is provided on the Copyright Office's Fill-In Form CO. If you use the Copyright Office's online registration system, you will provide the same information on the multiple screens presented to you during the online registration process.

In this example, Francine McDonald registers the copyright in her podcast recording of a seminar entitled *Marketing Goals for the New Century*. Francine is the author and copyright claimant of the seminar content as well as the recording itself. This example is also appropriate for seminars, lectures, or other audio programs you distribute online as podcasts, streams, mp3 files, or other formats.

Francine chooses *Sound recording* in part 1a, *Type of work being registered*. *Sound recording* is the option you should choose whenever you claim copyright in a recording even if your copyright claim in the application includes other types of works.

If you are the producer of the podcast but not the author of the underlying content, claim ownership only in the sound recording. If you are also the author of the underlying material, you can claim ownership in both the sound recording and the underlying material. To indicate a claim in both the sound recording and the underlying content:

- You select sound recording in part 1a as the *Type of work being registered*.
- In the 2h description of your author contribution, you select *Sound recording* as well as the description that accurately reflects the underlying content such as *Text/poetry*, *Script/play/screenplay*, *Music*, or *Lyrics*.

In this example, Francine describes her authorship in part 2h as *Sound recording/performance* and *Text*.

By registering the underlying content and sound recording together, you pay one filing fee instead of two. If you are claiming only the underlying material and not the sound recording, do not choose *Sound recording* in part 1a as the *Type of work being registered*. Choose the category that best reflects the underlying work.

UNITED STATES COPYRIGHT OFFICE
Form CO · Application for Copyright Registration

APPLICATION FOR COPYRIGHT REGISTRATION   SR

* Designates Required Fields

1 WORK BEING REGISTERED

1a. * Type of work being registered (*Fill in one only*)

☐ Literary work   ☐ Performing arts work

☐ Visual arts work   ☐ Motion picture/audiovisual work

☒ Sound recording   ☐ Single serial issue

1b. * Title of this work (*one title per space*)

MARKETING GOALS FOR THE NEW CENTURY

1c. For a serial issue: Volume [   ] Number [   ] Issue [   ] ISSN [   ]

Frequency of publication: [   ]

1d. Previous or alternative title

1e. * Year of completion [2] [0] [1] [0]

Publication (*If this work has not been published, skip to section 2*)

1f. Date of publication 02/03/2010   (*mm/dd/yyyy*)   **1g.** ISBN [   ]

1h. Nation of publication ☒ United States ☐ Other

1i. Published as a contribution in a larger work entitled

1j. If line 1i above names a serial issue   Volume [   ] Number [   ] Issue [   ]

On pages [   ]

1k. If work was preregistered   Number PRE- [ ][ ][ ][ ][ ][ ][ ][ ]

UNITED STATES COPYRIGHT OFFICE
Form CO · Application for Copyright Registration

For Office Use Only	
	WorkBeingRegistered

2 AUTHOR INFORMATION

2a. Personal name   *complete either 2a or 2b*

First Name	Middle	Last
FRANCINE		MCDONALD

2b. Organization name

2c. Doing business as

2d. Year of birth 1 9 8 2   **2e.** Year of death

2f. ☒ Citizenship   ☒ United States ☐ Other
☐ Domicile

2g. Author's contribution: ☐ Made for hire   ☐ Anonymous
☐ Pseudonymous

Continuation of Author Information

2h. * This author created (*Fill in only the authorship that applies to this author*)

☒ Text/poetry	☐ Compilation	☐ Map/technical drawing	☐ Music
☐ Editing	☐ Sculpture	☐ Architectural work	☐ Lyrics
☐ Computer program	☐ Jewelry design	☐ Photography	☐ Motion picture/audiovisual
☐ Collective work	☐ 2-dimensional artwork	☐ Script/play/screenplay	☒ Sound recording/performance

Other:

For Office Use Only	
	AuthorInformation

Privacy Act Notice
Sections 408-410 of title 17 of the *United States Code* authorize the Copyright Office to collect the personally identifying information requested on this form in order to process the application for copyright registration. By providing this information you are agreeing to routine uses of the information that include publication to give legal notice of your copyright claim as required by 17 U.S.C. § 705. It will appear in the Office's online catalog. If you do not provide the information requested, registration may be refused or delayed, and you may not be entitled to certain relief, remedies, and benefits under the copyright law.

Sample Copyright Registration of Your Podcast as a Basic Claim (continued)

UNITED STATES COPYRIGHT OFFICE
Form CO · Application for Copyright Registration

3 COPYRIGHT CLAIMANT INFORMATION

Claimant   *complete either 3a or 3b* - If you do not know the address for a claimant, enter "not known" in the Street address and City fields.

3a. Personal name

First Name	Middle	Last
FRANCINE		MCDONALD

3b. Organization name

3c. Doing business as

3d. Street address *
99 CENTER DRIVE

Street address (line 2)

City *	State	ZIP / Postal code	Country
ANYPLACE	ANYSTATE	00000	United States

Email	Phone number	
FRANCINEM@QUIKMAIL.COM	(999) 555-1212	(Add "+" and country code for foreign numbers)

3e. If claimant is **not** an author, copyright ownership acquired by: ☐ Written agreement ☐ Will or inheritance ☐ Other

---

For Office Use Only

CopyrightClaimantInformation

---

4 LIMITATION OF COPYRIGHT CLAIM

Skip section 4 if this work is all new.

4a. Material excluded from this claim (*Material previously registered, previously published, or not owned by this claimant*)

☐ Text   ☐ Artwork   ☐ Music   ☐ Sound recording/performance   ☐ Motion picture/audiovisual

Other:

Sample Copyright Registration of Your Podcast as a Basic Claim (continued)

UNITED STATES COPYRIGHT OFFICE
Form CO · Application for Copyright Registration

4b. Previous registration(s)   Number [ ]   Year [ ][ ][ ][ ]

Number [ ]   Year [ ][ ][ ][ ]

4c. New material included in this claim (*This work contains new, additional, or revised material*)

- ☐ Text
- ☐ Poetry
- ☐ Computer program
- ☐ Editing

- ☐ Compilation
- ☐ Sculpture
- ☐ Jewelry design
- ☐ 2-dimensional artwork

- ☐ Map/technical drawing
- ☐ Architectural work
- ☐ Photography
- ☐ Script/play/screenplay

- ☐ Music
- ☐ Lyrics
- ☐ Motion picture/audiovisual
- ☐ Sound recording/performance

Other: [ ]

For Office Use Only

LimitationOfCopyrightClaim

5 RIGHTS AND PERMISSIONS CONTACT

☒ Check if information below should be copied from the **first** copyright claimant

First Name	Middle	Last
FRANCINE		MCDONALD

Name of organization
[ ]

Street address
99 CENTER DRIVE

Street address (line 2)
[ ]

City	State	ZIP / Postal code	Country
ANYPLACE	ANYSTATE	00000	United States

Email	Phone number	
FRANCINEM@QUIKMAIL.COM	(999) 555-1212	(*Add "+" and country code for foreign numbers*)

Privacy Act Notice
Sections 408-410 of title 17 of the *United States Code* authorize the Copyright Office to collect the personally identifying information requested on this form in order to process the application for copyright registration. By providing this information you are agreeing to routine uses of the information that include publication to give legal notice of your copyright claim as required by 17 U.S.C. § 705. It will appear in the Office's online catalog. If you do not provide the information requested, registration may be refused or delayed, and you may not be entitled to certain relief, remedies, and benefits under the copyright law.

Sample Copyright Registration of Your Podcast as a Basic Claim (continued)

UNITED STATES COPYRIGHT OFFICE
Form CO · Application for Copyright Registration

For Office Use Only

RightsAndPermissionsContact

6 CORRESPONDENCE CONTACT

☒ Copy from **first** copyright claimant ☐ Copy from rights and permissions contact

First name *   Middle   Last *
FRANCINE   MCDONALD

Name of organization

Street address *
99 CENTER DRIVE

Street address (line 2)

City *   State   ZIP / Postal code   Country
ANYPLACE   ANYSTATE   00000   United States

Email *   Daytime phone number
FRANCINEM@QUIKMAIL.COM   (999) 555-1212   (Add "+" and country code for foreign numbers)

For Office Use Only

CorrespondenceContact

7 MAIL CERTIFICATE TO:

* Complete either 7a, 7b, or both

☒ Copy from **first** copyright claimant ☐ Copy from rights and permissions contact ☐ Copy from correspondence contact

7a. First Name   Middle   Last
FRANCINE   MCDONALD

Sample Copyright Registration of Your Podcast as a Basic Claim (continued)

UNITED STATES COPYRIGHT OFFICE
Form CO · Application for Copyright Registration

7b. Name of organization

7c. Street address *

99 CENTER DRIVE

Street address (line 2)

City *	State	ZIP / Postal code	Country
ANYPLACE	ANYSTATE	00000	United States

For Office Use Only

MailCertificateTo

8 CERTIFICATION

17 U.S.C. § 506(e): Any person who knowingly makes a false representation of a material fact in the application for copyright registration provided for by section 409, or in any written statement filed in connection with the application, shall be fined not more than $2,500.

I certify that I am the author, copyright claimant, or owner of exclusive rights, or the authorized agent of the author, copyright claimant, or owner of exclusive rights, of this work, and that the information given in this application is correct to the best of my knowledge.

Francine McDonald

Sign Here

8a. Handwritten signature

FRANCINE MCDONALD   2/21/2010

8b. Printed name   **8c.** Date signed

8d. Deposit account number   Account holder

8e. Applicant's internal tracking number (optional)

Privacy Act Notice
Sections 408-410 of title 17 of the *United States Code* authorize the Copyright Office to collect the personally identifying information requested on this form in order to process the application for copyright registration. By providing this information you are agreeing to routine uses of the information that include publication to give legal notice of your copyright claim as required by 17 U.S.C. § 705. It will appear in the Office's online catalog. If you do not provide the information requested, registration may be refused or delayed, and you may not be entitled to certain relief, remedies, and benefits under the copyright law.

Sample Copyright Registration of Your Podcast as a Basic Claim (continued)

UNITED STATES COPYRIGHT OFFICE
Form CO · Application for Copyright Registration

For Office Use Only

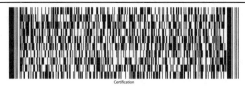

Certification

Sample Copyright Registration of Your Podcast as a Basic Claim (continued)

A.2.4. Registration of Your Online Work as an Automated Database

This example is on Form TX. As I mention in Chapter 4, as of this writing, online registration is not yet available for group registration. This situation may change very soon. The Copyright Office is considering proposed rules that would make online registration mandatory for group registration. The proposed rules also anticipate that the information required for online registration would be substantially the same as the information currently required on paper applications for group registrations.

In this sample copyright application, Virtual Flights, LLC registers the copyright in its company blog as an automated database. The company registers updates made to the blog between September 15 and December 7. Virtual Flights employees write the text of the blog within the scope of their employment. Hence, the text is a work made for hire and Virtual Flights lists itself as both author and claimant of the entire text. The blog includes previously published and public domain photographs and footage as indicated in part 6, *Derivative Work or Compilation.*

Jeremy Wright signs the application as the authorized agent of Virtual Flights, LLC.

Form TX
For a Nondramatic Literary Work
UNITED STATES COPYRIGHT OFFICE

REGISTRATION NUMBER

_____

TX	TXU

EFFECTIVE DATE OF REGISTRATION

_____

Month	Day	Year

DO NOT WRITE ABOVE THIS LINE. IF YOU NEED MORE SPACE, USE A SEPARATE CONTINUATION SHEET.

1

TITLE OF THIS WORK ▼
GROUP REGISTRATION FOR AUTOMATED DATABASE TITLED THE VIRTUAL FLIGHTS BLOG, PUBLISHED UPDATES FROM SEPTEMBER 15, 2009 TO DECEMBER 7, 2009

PREVIOUS OR ALTERNATIVE TITLES ▼
DECEMBER 7, 2009, MATERIAL UPDATED DAILY

PUBLICATION AS A CONTRIBUTION If this work was published as a contribution to a periodical, serial, or collection, give information about the collective work in which the contribution appeared.   **Title of Collective Work ▼**

If published in a periodical or serial give: **Volume ▼**   **Number ▼**   **Issue Date ▼**   **On Pages ▼**

2
a NAME OF AUTHOR ▼
VIRTUAL FLIGHTS, LLC

DATES OF BIRTH AND DEATH
Year Born ▼   Year Died ▼

Was this contribution to the work a "work made for hire"?
☑ Yes
☐ No

AUTHOR'S NATIONALITY OR DOMICILE
Name of Country
OR { Citizen of ▶ UNITED STATES
{ Domiciled in ▶

WAS THIS AUTHOR'S CONTRIBUTION TO THE WORK
Anonymous? ☐ Yes ☑ No
Pseudonymous? ☐ Yes ☑ No
If the answer to either of these questions is "Yes," see detailed instructions.

NOTE

Under the law, the "author" of a "work made for hire" is generally the employer, not the employee (see instructions). For any part of this work that was "made for hire" check "Yes" in the space provided, give the employer (or other person for whom the work was prepared) as "Author" of that part, and leave the space for dates of birth and death blank.

NATURE OF AUTHORSHIP Briefly describe nature of material created by this author in which copyright is claimed. ▼
TEXT; COMPILATION OF PHOTOGRAPHS AND FOOTAGE

b NAME OF AUTHOR ▼

DATES OF BIRTH AND DEATH
Year Born ▼   Year Died ▼

Was this contribution to the work a "work made for hire"?
☐ Yes
☐ No

AUTHOR'S NATIONALITY OR DOMICILE
Name of Country
OR { Citizen of ▶
{ Domiciled in ▶

WAS THIS AUTHOR'S CONTRIBUTION TO THE WORK
Anonymous? ☐ Yes ☐ No
Pseudonymous? ☐ Yes ☐ No
If the answer to either of these questions is "Yes," see detailed instructions.

NATURE OF AUTHORSHIP Briefly describe nature of material created by this author in which copyright is claimed. ▼

c NAME OF AUTHOR ▼

DATES OF BIRTH AND DEATH
Year Born ▼   Year Died ▼

Was this contribution to the work a "work made for hire"?
☐ Yes
☐ No

AUTHOR'S NATIONALITY OR DOMICILE
Name of Country
OR { Citizen of ▶
{ Domiciled in ▶

WAS THIS AUTHOR'S CONTRIBUTION TO THE WORK
Anonymous? ☐ Yes ☐ No
Pseudonymous? ☐ Yes ☐ No
If the answer to either of these questions is "Yes," see detailed instructions.

NATURE OF AUTHORSHIP Briefly describe nature of material created by this author in which copyright is claimed. ▼

3
a YEAR IN WHICH CREATION OF THIS WORK WAS COMPLETED This information must be given in all cases.
2009   ◀ Year

b DATE AND NATION OF FIRST PUBLICATION OF THIS PARTICULAR WORK
Complete this information ONLY if this work has been published.
Month ▶ DECEMBER   Day ▶ 7   Year ▶ 2009   ◀ Nation

4

See instructions before completing this space.

COPYRIGHT CLAIMANT(S) Name and address must be given even if the claimant is the same as the author given in space 2. ▼
VIRTUAL FLIGHTS, LLC
100 MAIN STREET, ANYPLACE, ANYSTATE USA 00000

TRANSFER If the claimant(s) named here in space 4 is (are) different from the author(s) named in space 2, give a brief statement of how the claimant(s) obtained ownership of the copyright. ▼

DO NOT WRITE HERE OFFICE USE ONLY

APPLICATION RECEIVED

ONE DEPOSIT RECEIVED

TWO DEPOSITS RECEIVED

FUNDS RECEIVED

MORE ON BACK ▶ · Complete all applicable spaces (numbers 5-9) on the reverse side of this page.
· See detailed instructions.   · Sign the form at line 8.

DO NOT WRITE HERE
Page 1 of _____ pages

EXAMINED BY

CHECKED BY

CORRESPONDENCE
Yes

FORM TX

FOR
COPYRIGHT
OFFICE
USE
ONLY

DO NOT WRITE ABOVE THIS LINE. IF YOU NEED MORE SPACE, USE A SEPARATE CONTINUATION SHEET.

PREVIOUS REGISTRATION Has registration for this work, or for an earlier version of this work, already been made in the Copyright Office?
☐ Yes ☑ No If your answer is "Yes," why is another registration being sought? (Check appropriate box.) ▼

a. ☐ This is the first published edition of a work previously registered in unpublished form.

b. ☐ This is the first application submitted by this author as copyright claimant.

c. ☐ This is a changed version of the work, as shown by space 6 on this application.

If your answer is "Yes," give: **Previous Registration Number** ▶   **Year of Registration** ▶

5

DERIVATIVE WORK OR COMPILATION
Preexisting Material Identify any preexisting work or works that this work is based on or incorporates. ▼

PREVIOUSLY PUBLISHED AND/OR PUBLIC DOMAIN PHOTOGRAPHS AND FOOTAGE

Material Added to This Work Give a brief, general statement of the material that has been added to this work and in which copyright is claimed. ▼

TEXT; COMPILATION OF PHOTOGRAPHS AND FOOTAGE

a

b

6

See instructions
before completing
this space.

DEPOSIT ACCOUNT If the registration fee is to be charged to a Deposit Account established in the Copyright Office, give name and number of Account.
Name ▼   Account Number ▼

CORRESPONDENCE Give name and address to which correspondence about this application should be sent.   Name/Address/Apt/City/State/Zip ▼
JEREMY WRIGHT
VIRTUAL FLIGHTS, LLC
100 MAIN STREET, ANYPLACE, ANYSTATE 00000

Area code and daytime telephone number ▶ (999) 555-1212   Fax number ▶ (999) 555-1234

Email ▶ LEGAL@VIRTUALFLIGHTS.COM

a

b

7

CERTIFICATION* I, the undersigned, hereby certify that I am the

Check only one ▶

☐ author
☐ other copyright claimant
☐ owner of exclusive right(s)
☑ authorized agent of VIRTUAL FLIGHTS, LLC

of the work identified in this application and that the statements made
by me in this application are correct to the best of my knowledge.

Name of author or other copyright claimant, or owner of exclusive right(s) ▲

Typed or printed name and date ▼ If this application gives a date of publication in space 3, do not sign and submit it before that date.

JEREMY WRIGHT   Date ▶ DECEMBER 10, 2009

Handwritten signature ▼

Jeremy Wright

8

Certificate
will be
mailed in
window
envelope
to this
address:

Name ▼
JEREMY WRIGHT/VIRTUAL FLIGHTS, LLC

Number/Street/Apt ▼
100 MAIN STREET

City/State/Zip ▼
ANYPLACE, ANYSTREET 00000

YOU MUST:
· Complete all necessary spaces
· Sign your application in space 8
**SEND ALL 3 ELEMENTS
IN THE SAME PACKAGE:**
1. Application form
2. Nonrefundable filing fee in check or money
order payable to *Register of Copyrights*
3. Deposit material
MAIL TO:
Library of Congress
Copyright Office
101 Independence Avenue SE
Washington, DC 20559-6222

9

*17 USC §506(e): Any person who knowingly makes a false representation of a material fact in the application for copyright registration provided for by section 409, or in any written statement filed in connection
with the application, shall be fined not more than $2,500.

Form TX – Full   Rev: 11/2006   Print: 11/2006 — 30,000   Printed on recycled paper   U.S. Government Printing Office: 2008-xx-xxx/60,xxx

Sample Copyright Registration of Your Online Work
as an Automated Database (continued)

A.2.5. Registration of Your Online Work as a Newsletter

This example is on Form G/DN. See the discussion in Section A.2.4 regarding the Copyright Office's potential adoption of online registration only for group registrations.

In this example, Virtual Flights, LLC registers the copyright in the company's newsletter, *The Virtual Flights Newsletter*, which the company publishes Monday through Friday. Virtual Flights employees produce the newsletter within the scope of their employment. Hence, the newsletter is a work made for hire and Virtual Flights is the author and copyright claimant. This is the same form one would use for registration of one's online work as a newspaper. Jeremy Wright signs the application as the authorized agent of Virtual Flights, LLC.

Form G/DN
For Group/Daily Newspapers and Newsletters
UNITED STATES COPYRIGHT OFFICE

REGISTRATION NUMBER

EFFECTIVE DATE OF REGISTRATION
(Assigned by Copyright Office)

| Month | Day | Year |

APPLICATION RECEIVED

EXAMINED BY   ONE DEPOSIT RECEIVED

CORRESPONDENCE   FEE RECEIVED
❏

DO NOT WRITE ABOVE THIS LINE.

1

If no previous registration under identical title, check here ❏

TITLE OF THIS ❏ NEWSPAPER AS IT APPEARS ON THE COPIES ▼   City/State▼
☒ NEWSLETTER
THE VIRTUAL FLIGHTS NEWSLETTER   ANYPLACE/ANYSTATE

Month and year date on copies ▼   Number of issues in this group ▼   ISSN▼   Edition▼
JANUARY 20XX   20   9999-9999

2

NAME AND ADDRESS OF THE AUTHOR/COPYRIGHT CLAIMANT IN THESE WORKS MADE FOR HIRE
VIRTUAL FLIGHTS, LLC
100 MAIN STREET
ANYPLACE, ANYSTATE 00000

AUTHOR'S CONTRIBUTION (check all that apply)
☒ Editing   ☒ Compilation   ☒ Text   ❏ Other

3

(First)

DATE OF PUBLICATION OF THE FIRST AND LAST ISSUES IN THIS GROUP   Important: Give month, day, and year

JANUARY   1   20XX   (Last)   JANUARY   30   20XX
Month ▲   Day▲   Year▲   Month ▲   Day▲   Year▲

CERTIFICATION*: I, the undersigned, hereby certify that I am the copyright claimant or the authorized agent of the copyright claimant of the works identified in this application, that all the conditions specified in the instructions on the back of this form are met, and that the statements made by me in this application are correct to the best of my knowledge.

Handwritten
signature (X) _Jeremy Wright_   Typed or printed
                                       name of signer   JEREMY WRIGHT

PERSON TO CONTACT FOR CORRESPONDENCE ABOUT THIS CLAIM   DEPOSIT ACCOUNT
Name JEREMY WRIGHT   Account number
Daytime telephone number (999) 555-1212   Name of account
Address (if other than given below)

Fax (999) 555-1234   Email LEGAL@VIRTUALFLIGHTS.COM

Certificate
will be
mailed
in window
envelope
to this
address

Name▼
JEREMY WRIGHT/VIRTUAL FLIGHTS, LLC

Number/Street/Apt ▼
100 MAIN STREET

City/State/Zip▼
ANYPLACE, ANYSTATE 00000

YOU MUST:
• Complete all necessary spaces
• Sign your application
SEND ALL 3 ELEMENTS
IN THE SAME PACKAGE:
1. Application form
2. Nonrefundable filing fee in check or
   money order payable to Register of
   Copyrights
3. Deposit material
MAIL TO:
Library of Congress, Copyright Office-SE
101 Independence Avenue SE
Washington, DC 20559-6226

*17 USC §506(e): Any person who knowingly makes a false representation of a material fact in the application for copyright registration provided for by section 409, or in any written statement filed in connection with the application, shall be fined not more than $2,500.

Form G/DN Rev: 07/2008   Print: 07/2008—xx,000   Printed on recycled paper   U.S. Government Printing Office: 2008-xxx-xxx/xx,xxx

A.3. Tips and Sample Form for Registering Your Domain Name as a Trademark

A.3.1. Trademark Registration Tips

You should read these trademark registration tips in conjunction with the discussion of trademark registration in Section 5.5.5.

PTO Trademark Registration Resources. The United States Patent and Trademark Office (PTO) provides instructions for completing each part of the trademark registration application. When filing on-line, read the instructions on the screen and in the help text. The PTO also offers several publications that explain the registration process on its website at www.uspto.gov. Those who want very detailed information about the registration process can review the *Trademark Manual of Examining Procedure*, which outlines procedures that examiners are required or authorized to follow when reviewing trademark registration applications.

International Classes. The PTO uses the international classification of goods and services as its primary trademark classification system. For trademark registration purposes, the PTO categorizes all goods and services into one of the forty-five international classes. While any class may potentially be appropriate for your trademark, classes frequently used for trademarks associated with the internet include Class 35, advertising and business services; Class 41, education and entertainment services; Class 42, computer and scientific services; and Class 45, personal services. It is common for a trademark owner to use a single trademark with multiple classes of goods and services. You can find a listing of all the international classes on the PTO's website.

Identification of Goods and Services. One challenge in preparing a trademark registration application is the description of the goods and services. In trademark law jargon, the description of goods and services is called the identification. You want an identification for the goods and services that is both adequate for your needs and acceptable to the PTO. The examiner's objection to the identification is a common reason for the issuance of Office Actions in the trademark registration process. *The Acceptable Identification of Goods and Services Manual*, available online at the PTO's website, lists identifications for specific goods and services that the trademark examiner will accept without further inquiry as long as the specimens submitted with your application are consistent with the identification. While you are not required to do so, using language directly from the manual helps avoid objections by trademark examiners to the identification.

Submitting the Correct Specimens. A specimen is a real-world example of how you use the trademark with your goods and services. Acceptable specimens for goods show the trademark on the actual good or on the packaging for the good such as a tag, label, or container. Invoices, announcements, order forms, bills of lading, leaflets, brochures, publicity releases, letterhead and business cards generally are not acceptable specimens for goods. Acceptable specimens for services show the trademark used in the sale or advertising for the service and include items such as signs, brochures, and advertisements.

Need for a Lawyer/No Material Changes. While you can file the trademark application yourself without the assistance of a lawyer, trademark applications appear deceptively simple. There are mistakes which can only be corrected by filing a new registration application and an experienced trademark lawyer can be instrumental in helping you avoid such potentially expensive mistakes. Once you submit your trademark registration application, there are several elements that you cannot correct or change. You cannot make any material changes to the trademark you are registering. For example, if you register the trademark ROOFTOP INN, you cannot later change the trademark to RED ROOFTOP INN on your pending application. While you can narrow the description of goods and services, you cannot broaden the description. You cannot change the applicant;

however, under certain circumstances, you can transfer the application to another person or company.

Filing Fees. The filing fee for the application is based on the number of classes in the application and the version of the trademark application form you use. The PTO offers lower filing fees if you file electronically. You can find current trademark registration filing fees at the PTO's website, www.uspto.gov.

A.3.2. Trademark Registration Application for Domain Name

During the online trademark registration process, you fill in information on multiple screens. The samples included here show the format of two options offered in the online registration process for reviewing the data you have entered. The first is the input form. The second is a text file which includes the applicant's declaration in addition to data entered by the applicant.

In this example, Eco Travels, Inc., registers the trademark HERETHENTHERE.COM which is the domain name of one of the company's websites. The description of the goods and services for the trademark falls into Class 39 which is the service class for transportation and storage services including transport, packaging and storage of goods, and travel arrangements. In the *Identification* section, Eco Travels describes the service it offers as "arranging and coordinating travel arrangements for individuals and groups, namely, destination stays, honeymoons, family vacations, and destination weddings".

As I note in the tips in Section A.3.1, the goods or services you offer determine the appropriate identification. For example, if Eco Travels' services were more focused on providing information, the company might classify its services in Class 41, education and entertainment services, and describe the services in the *Identification* section as "providing a website featuring information on eco-travel".

Eco Travels has used the trademark in commerce since February 5, 2009. That means the company files an in use trademark application and selects section 1(a) as its *Filing Basis*. If Eco Travels were not yet using the trademark in commerce but had a bona fide intention to use the trademark, it would file an intent to use application and select section 1(b) as its *Filing Basis*.

In the sample application, Eco Travels files the application through its attorney, Jayne Reynolds, whose contact information appears in the *Attorney Information* and *Correspondence Information* portions of the registration form. Kenneth Donalds, the President of Eco Travels, signs the application on behalf of the company.

PTO Form 1478 (Rev 9/2006)
OMB No. 0651-0009 (Exp 12/31/2011)

Trademark/Service Mark Application, Principal Register
NOTE: Data fields with the * are mandatory. The wording "(if applicable)" appears where the field is only mandatory under the facts of the particular application.

The table below presents the data as entered.

Input Field	Entered
SERIAL NUMBER	N/A
MARK INFORMATION	
*MARK	mark.jpg
STANDARD CHARACTERS	YES
USPTO-GENERATED IMAGE	YES
LITERAL ELEMENT	HERETHENTHERE.COM
MARK STATEMENT	The mark consists of standard characters, without claim to any particular font, style, size, or color.
APPLICANT INFORMATION	
*OWNER OF MARK	Eco Travels, Inc.
*STREET	100 Main Street
*CITY	Anyplace
*STATE (Required for U.S. applicants)	Maryland
*COUNTRY	United States
*ZIP/POSTAL CODE (Required for U.S. applicants only)	00000
LEGAL ENTITY INFORMATION	
TYPE	corporation
STATE/COUNTRY OF INCORPORATION	Delaware
GOODS AND/OR SERVICES AND BASIS INFORMATION	
*INTERNATIONAL CLASS	039
*IDENTIFICATION	Arranging and coordinating travel arrangements for individuals and groups, namely, destination stays, honeymoons, family vacations, and destination weddings
FILING BASIS	SECTION 1(a)
FIRST USE ANYWHERE DATE	At least as early as 02/05/2009

FIRST USE IN COMMERCE DATE	At least as early as 02/05/2009
SPECIMEN FILE NAME(S)	spec-9762206112-161127545_._HERETHENTHERE.COM_TM_Specimen.pdf
SPECIMEN DESCRIPTION	Pages from the website advertising the travel arrangement services
ATTORNEY INFORMATION	
NAME	Jayne Reynolds
FIRM NAME	Reynolds & Forrester, PLLC
STREET	68 Commerce Drive, Suite 17A
CITY	Anyplace
STATE	Maryland
COUNTRY	United States
ZIP/POSTAL CODE	00000
PHONE	(999) 555-1212
FAX	(999) 555-1234
EMAIL ADDRESS	JReynolds@AnyplaceLaw.com
AUTHORIZED TO COMMUNICATE VIA EMAIL	Yes
CORRESPONDENCE INFORMATION	
NAME	Jayne Reynolds
FIRM NAME	Reynolds & Forrester, PLLC
STREET	68 Commerce Drive, Suite 17A
CITY	Anyplace
STATE	Maryland
COUNTRY	United States
ZIP/POSTAL CODE	00000
PHONE	(999) 555-1212
FAX	(999) 555-1234
EMAIL ADDRESS	JReynolds@AnyplaceLaw.com
AUTHORIZED TO COMMUNICATE VIA EMAIL	Yes
FEE INFORMATION	
NUMBER OF CLASSES	1
FEE PER CLASS	325

Sample Trademark Registration of Your Domain Name; Input File (continued)

*TOTAL FEE DUE	325
*TOTAL FEE PAID	325
SIGNATURE INFORMATION	
SIGNATURE	/Kenneth Donalds/
SIGNATORY'S NAME	Kenneth Donalds
SIGNATORY'S POSITION	President
DATE SIGNED	02/03/2010

Back		View/Save Data as PDF

Sample Trademark Registration of Your Domain Name; Input File (continued)

PTO Form 1478 (Rev 9/2006)
OMB No. 0651-0009 (Exp 12/31/2011)

Trademark/Service Mark Application, Principal Register
To the Commissioner for Trademarks:

MARK: HERETHENTHERE.COM (Standard Characters, see mark)
The literal element of the mark consists of HERETHENTHERE.COM.
The mark consists of standard characters, without claim to any particular font, style, size, or color.

The applicant, Eco Travels, Inc., a corporation of Delaware, having an address of
    100 Main Street
    Anyplace, Maryland 00000
    United States
requests registration of the trademark/service mark identified above in the United States Patent and Trademark Office on the Principal Register established by the Act of July 5, 1946 (15 U.S.C. Section 1051 et seq.), as amended, for the following:

International Class 039: Arranging and coordinating travel arrangements for individuals and groups, namely, destination stays, honeymoons, family vacations, and destination weddings In International Class 039, the mark was first used at least as early as 02/05/2009, and first used in commerce at least as early as 02/05/2009, and is now in use in such commerce. The applicant is submitting one specimen(s) showing the mark as used in commerce on or in connection with any item in the class of listed goods and/or services, consisting of a(n) Pages from the website advertising the travel arrangement services.
Specimen-1 [spec-9762206112-
161127545_._HERETHENTHERE.COM_TM_Specimen.pdf]

The applicant hereby appoints Jayne Reynolds of Reynolds & Forrester, PLLC
   68 Commerce Drive, Suite 17A
   Anyplace, Maryland 00000
   United States
to submit this application on behalf of the applicant.
   Correspondence Information: Jayne Reynolds
                   Reynolds & Forrester, PLLC
                   68 Commerce Drive, Suite 17A
                   Anyplace, Maryland 00000
                   (999) 555-1212(phone)
                   (999) 555-1234(fax)
                   JReynolds@AnyplaceLaw.com (authorized)

A fee payment in the amount of $325 will be submitted with the application, representing payment for 1 class(es).

Declaration

The undersigned, being hereby warned that willful false statements and the like so made are punishable by fine or imprisonment, or both, under 18 U.S.C. Section 1001, and that such willful false statements, and the like, may jeopardize the validity of the application or any resulting registration, declares that he/she is properly authorized to execute this application on behalf of the applicant; he/she believes the applicant to be the owner of the trademark/service mark sought to be registered, or, if the application is being filed under 15 U.S.C. Section 1051(b), he/she believes applicant to be entitled to use such mark in commerce; to the best of his/her knowledge and belief no other person, firm, corporation, or association has the right to use the mark in commerce, either in the identical form thereof or in such near resemblance thereto as to be likely, when used on or in connection with the goods/services of such other person, to cause confusion, or to cause mistake, or to deceive; and that all statements made of his/her own knowledge are true; and that all statements made on information and belief are believed to be true.

Signature: /Kenneth Donalds/   Date Signed: 02/03/2010
Signatory's Name: Kenneth Donalds
Signatory's Position: President

Sample Trademark Registration of Your Domain Name; Text File (continued)

A.4. Sample DMCA Takedown Notices and Counter Notices

A.4.1. Requirements for Takedown Notice and Counter Notice

As I discuss in Section 12.5, the Digital Millennium Copyright Act (DMCA) insulates interactive service providers from claims of copyright infringement for material posted by their customers and online visitors. Promptly removing infringing material upon the request of the copyright owner is a requirement to getting that insulation so interactive service providers generally respond fairly quickly to takedown notices.

However, your takedown notice **must** have the proper information or the interactive service provider can just ignore it.

Takedown Notice Requirements. Here is the information you must include in a DMCA takedown notice:

- the electronic or physical signature of the copyright owner or the person authorized to act on the owner's behalf
- identification of the copyrighted work that you claim has been infringed
- identification of the infringing material and the website location of the infringing material
- your contact information such as an address, telephone number, and email address
- a statement that you have a good faith belief that the disputed use is not authorized by the copyright owner, its agent or the law
- a statement that the information in the notice is accurate and a statement, made under penalty of perjury, that you are the copyright owner or are authorized to act on behalf of the copyright owner

Counter Notice Requirements. If content you post online is improperly removed as a result of a DMCA takedown notice, you may submit a counter notice requesting that the content be reposted. Your counter notice must include the following:

- your electronic or physical signature
- identification of the material removed and the website location at which the material appeared prior to removal
- your name, address, and telephone number
- a statement, made under penalty of perjury, that you have a good faith belief that the material was removed as a result of mistake or misidentification
- a statement that you consent to the jurisdiction of Federal District Court for the judicial district in which your address is located (or if your address is outside of the United States, consent to the jurisdiction of any judicial district in which the service provider may be found) and that you will accept service of process from the person who provided the takedown notice

A.4.2. Sample DMCA Takedown Notice One

Email to legal@virtualflights.com
Subject: Notice of Copyright Infringement

I am providing a takedown notice pursuant to the Digital Millennium Copyright Act. Please note the following:

The copyrighted work that has been infringed is my article entitled "Touring Virtually" which was originally published with my authorization in the November 20XX issue of *Outdoors Again Magazine*. The article has been posted in its entirety to one of the Virtual Flights forums at the following url:

[url at which infringing material is located]

I have a good faith belief that the posting of the "Touring Virtually" article on the Virtual Flights' website is not authorized by the copyright owner, its agent, or the law. Furthermore, I swear, under penalty of perjury, that the information in this notification is accurate and that I am the copyright owner of the article.

If you need additional information from me, you can contact me via email at Samantha@email.com, via phone at (999) 555-1122, or via regular mail at 99 Center Drive, Anyplace, Anystate. My electronic signature appears below.

Thank you,
Samantha West

A.4.3. Sample DMCA Takedown Notice Two

Email to Online Network
Subject: DMCA Takedown Notice

Dear Sir or Madam:

I am contacting you on behalf of Virtual Flights, LLC. Under penalty of perjury, I submit that I am authorized to act on behalf of Virtual Flights in matters related to copyright infringement and that the information provided in this notice is accurate.

A user on your network is offering an infringing sound recording for download at the following url location:

[url at which infringing material is located]

The sound recording entitled "Your Virtual Friend in Flight" is the property of Virtual Flights and is used in Virtual Flights' advertising campaigns.

I have a good faith belief that this activity is not authorized by Virtual Flights, its agent, or the law. Accordingly, we request the immediate removal or disabling of access to the infringing sound recording.

If you have any questions, please feel free to contact me via email at legal@VirtualFlights.com, via telephone at (999) 555-1212, or via mail at Virtual Flights, 100 Main Street, Anyplace, Anytown, 99999.

Thank you,
Jeremy Wright
On behalf of Virtual Flights, LLC

A.4.4. Sample DMCA Counter Notice

Email to copyright@myblogs.com
DMCA Counter Notice

To Whom It May Concern,

You recently provided me with a copy of Notice of Infringement from the XYZ Company requesting the takedown of a photograph appearing on my subscriber blog account. As a result of XYZ Company's takedown request, you disabled access to that photograph. This letter is my counter notice as authorized in § 512(g) of the U.S. Copyright Act.

Here is the url of the website location at which the disputed photograph previously appeared:

[url at which material was located prior to removal]

I swear, under penalty of perjury, that I have a good faith belief that the photograph was removed due to mistake or misidentification. I therefore request that the photograph be reposted. My full name, address, and phone number appear in my electronic signature block below. I consent to the jurisdiction of the Federal District Court for Anyplace, Anystate (solely for the purposes of the resolution of this dispute), and I agree to accept service of process from the XYZ Company.

Thank you,
James Cooper
54 Dekker Circle
Anyplace, Anystate
(999) 555-2121
James.C@email.com

A.5. Sample Website Development Agreement

This website development agreement is appropriate for use with a simple, fairly static website. Development for a website with e-commerce functionality, user interactivity, or database functionality would likely require a more complicated agreement. In this example, the website developer assigns all rights in the website to the company. In other contracts, the website developer may transfer narrower rights through a license arrangement.

The agreement should outline in as much detail as practical the services the developer will provide. Services to be provided will vary significantly from one website development arrangement to the next. The website owner and developer will determine the scope of services during preliminary discussions. In this example, the company and website developer have outlined the parameters of the services to be provided in a written development plan that is attached to the agreement. A sample development plan is not included as an attachment to this sample agreement.

Website Development Agreement

This Website Development Agreement ("Agreement") is by and between _____ ("Company") and _____ ("Website Developer"). Company hereby engages Website Developer as an independent contractor to develop the Company's website (the "Website") pursuant to the terms set forth in this Agreement and Website Developer accepts such engagement. Website Developer understands that Company intends the Website to be a simple, intuitive, user-friendly informational website about outdoor sports activities.

1.   Services. Website Developer shall provide the development, graphics, functionality, coding, and page layout for the Website using the specifications and guidelines agreed upon by the parties and set forth in the attached Development Plan. After delivery, Website Developer shall be available to correct at no charge (a) any failure to meet the requirements of the Development Plan and (b) any software anomalies that occur because of defects in the files comprising the Website.

2.   Content. Company shall provide all text and certain graphic content for the website (the "Client Content"). Company shall provide Website Developer with the Client Content in the form of a Word file, jpeg file, gif file, or other digital format mutually agreeable to Company and Website Developer.

3.   Technical Specifications. The Website shall operate properly with widely used web browsers, including the most recent two versions of Internet Explorer and Mozilla Firefox.

4.   Delivery Schedule. Website Developer shall make all commercially reasonable efforts to complete and deliver the Website by June 15, 20XX. Website Developer shall upload and install the Website on the server on which Company plans to host the Website. Company acknowledges its responsibility to make its own arrangements for web hosting and to provide Website Developer with the necessary access and authorization to upload the Website. Website Developer shall also deliver to Company the Website as a digital file including the html, graphics, and all other content that comprise the Website.

5.   **Approvals.** The Development Plan outlines the components of each development phase of the Website. Upon completion of the applicable development phase, Website Developer shall submit for review to Company a schematic design of the Website (the "Schematic Design") and a fully functional demonstration version of the Website (the "Demo") and obtain Company's written approval before moving to the next development phase. The Company agrees to review and act on all work submitted for approval in a timely manner and in no event more than fourteen (14) calendar days after submission. The Company understands that after approval of each phase, additional changes are contingent on further arrangements or fee charges.

6.   **Payment.** As full compensation for all services provided and rights granted hereunder, Company shall pay Website Developer the amount of _____ Dollars ($_____), according to the following payment schedule:

(a)   Twenty-five percent (25%) shall be due upon the full execution of this Agreement

(b)   Twenty-five percent (25%) shall be due upon completion and approval of the Schematic Design

(c)   Twenty-five percent (25%) shall be due upon completion and approval of the Demo

(d)   Twenty-five percent (25%) shall be due within five days of Website Developer's installation of the Website on Company's server

7.   **Ownership of Website.** Upon full payment by Company to Website Developer, all rights, title and interest in and to the Website shall be vested solely and exclusively in Company. The services provided by Website Developer hereunder shall be deemed a commissioned work, and Website Developer acknowledges and agrees that all services provided hereunder are a work made for hire, as that term is defined in the United States Copyright Act of 1976, as amended.

To the extent that Website Developer's services are not properly characterized as a work made for hire, Website Developer hereby irrevocably assigns to the Company all of Website Developer's right, title and interest in and to the Website including ownership of all copyright, trademark and other intellectual property rights therein throughout the universe in perpetuity, in all languages and media (whether now known or hereafter devised). Website Developer agrees to cooperate in the preparation of any documents necessary to demonstrate this assignment of rights.

8.   Representations. Website Developer represents and warrants that the Website shall be Website Developer's original work (except for materials used with the written permission of others or materials from the public domain), and that any content provided for the Website by Website Developer and work performed on the Website by Website Developer shall not infringe the intellectual property rights of any person. Company represents and warrants that all Client Content provided to Website Developer for inclusion in the Website shall be owned by Company (except for materials used with the written permission of others or materials from the public domain). Each party shall indemnify the other party for any loss suffered by the other party as a result of its breach of this representation.

9.   Independent Contractor. The Company retains Website Developer's services as an independent contractor. Website Developer shall be responsible for any and all applicable taxes with respect to payments made by Company to Website Developer.

10.   Governing Law. This Website Development Agreement shall be governed in accordance with the laws of the state of _____ (*insert state*), applicable to contracts made and to be performed wholly in _____ (*insert state*), without regard to principles of conflicts of laws.

IN WITNESS WHEREOF, the parties hereto have executed this Website Development Agreement.

Company

By: _____

(Signature of Authorized Representative)

_____

(Printed Name of Authorized Representative)

Title: _____

Website Developer

_____

(*Signature of Website Developer*)

A.6. Sample Terms of Service for Website

This sample Terms of Service is appropriate for a simple website. In this example, Virtual Flights provides information and a forum for visitors interested in travel. Virtual Flights allows posting of user generated content in its online forums. Virtual Flights does not sell any products or services directly through its website so there are no terms related to e-commerce.

Terms of Service

Thank you for visiting virtualflights.com (the "Website"), a website created and operated by Virtual Flights, LLC, 100 Main Street, Anyplace, Anystate 00000. Virtual Flights, LLC provides access to the Website, subject to these Terms of Service, which may be updated from time to time without advance notice.

1.   Copyrights. All content included on the Website is the property of Virtual Flights, LLC or its content suppliers, and is protected by United States and international copyright laws.

(a)   Permissible Uses of Copyrighted Material. You may download a single copy of any portion of the content for your personal, non-commercial entertainment, information or use. Members of the media may use brief quotations from the content provided that Virtual Flights and/or the respective author is credited.

(b)   Prohibited Uses of Copyrighted Material. All other uses of the content on the Website are prohibited without the written consent of Virtual Flights, LLC. Prohibited uses include, but are not limited to, the reproduction, sale, publication, distribution, modification, display, reposting or framing of any portion of the content.

2.   Trademarks. YOUR VIRTUAL FRIEND IN FLIGHT is a trademark of Virtual Flights, LLC. Our trademarks may only be used in connection with products or services that are provided by Virtual Flights, LLC.

3.   Linked Pages. You may hyperlink to the homepage or any other page of the Website; however, you may not (and may not authorize any other party) to frame the Website or link to the Website in any manner suggesting the content originates from any party other than Virtual Flights. Virtual Flights is not responsible for the content of any website that is linked to us or the content of any website to which we link, whether or not we are affiliated with the operator or owner of such website. Any links from the Website to any other sites are for your convenience only.

4.   Use of Virtual Flights Forums. Virtual Flights offers messaging services, chat services, bulletin boards, message boards, blogs, and other forum services (the "Forums") through the Website

(a)   Content You Submit. If you upload, post or submit any content to the Forums, you represent that you have all the necessary legal rights to upload, post or submit such content and that such content does not violate any law or the rights of any person. Although Virtual Flights does not claim ownership of content that its users post, by submitting content, you automatically grant, and you represent and warrant that you have the right to grant, to Virtual Flights, and anyone authorized by Virtual Flights, a royalty-free, perpetual, non-exclusive, worldwide license to copy, publish, modify, translate, transmit, exploit, distribute, publicly perform, publicly display, or otherwise use such material, in any and all media, in whole or in part, provided that such use is on or in connection with the Website.

(b)   Right to Monitor Submissions. You understand that Virtual Flights has no obligation to monitor any Forums, or other areas of the Website through which users can submit content. However, Virtual Flights reserves the right to monitor use of the Forums and the Website to determine compliance with these Terms of Service, as well as the right to remove any content for any reason. Notwithstanding these rights, you remain solely responsible for the content of your postings.

(c)   Malicious Code. Virtual Flights does not guarantee that the Website or Forums are free of any viruses, trojan horses, or malicious code that may be transmitted through user submitted content. Your use of the Website and the Forums is at your own risk.

5.   Notifying Virtual Flights of Copyright and Intellectual Property Infringement Claims. Virtual Flights respects the intellectual property rights of others, and we ask our online visitors to do the same. Virtual Flights adheres to the Digital Millennium Copyright Act. If you believe that your work has been copied in a way that constitutes copyright infringement, or your intellectual property rights have been otherwise violated by material on the Website, please provide Virtual Flights' copyright agent, with the following information:

- a description of the copyrighted work that has been infringed and a description of the infringing activity
- the exact url location of the infringing content on the Virtual Flights website
- your name, address, telephone number and email address
- a statement that you have a good faith belief that the disputed use is not authorized by the copyright owner, its agent, or the law
- a statement by you that the information provided in the notice is accurate and a statement, made under penalty of perjury, that the person submitting the notice is the copyright owner or is authorized to act on the behalf of the copyright owner
- an electronic or physical signature of the copyright owner or the person authorized to act on the copyright owner's behalf

Virtual Flights' agent for notice of claims of copyright or other intellectual property infringement can be reached as follows: Jeremy Wright, Virtual Flights, LLC, 100 Main Street, Anyplace, Anystate, 00000, legal@VirtualFlights.com, Phone: (999) 555-1212.

6.   Disclaimer. Virtual Flights provides the information on the Website in good faith as a service to the travelling and tourist community. While Virtual Flights uses reasonable care to provide accurate and up to date information, Virtual Flights makes no guarantee of the accuracy of the information provided on the Website. Virtual Flights and the authors and organizations contributing to the Website disclaim all liability of any kind arising directly or indirectly from any use of the information conveyed on the Website or any loss or damage incurred from such use.

For Additional Information. You can find additional information about Virtual Flights, LLC, by visiting our Frequently Asked Questions Page. If you have additional questions about the Website or Virtual Flights, LLC, please contact us at info@VirtualFlights.com.

GLOSSARY OF TERMS

Anticybersquating Consumer Protection Act. A federal law enacted in 1999 that gives trademark owners a method to dispute domain names that are confusingly similar to their trademarks.

basic claim (copyright) application. As used by the Copyright Office, a reference to a copyright registration application for a single work such as a single song, single book, or single website; for multiple unpublished works by the same person; or for multiple published works published at the same time and owned by the same person. Basic copyright claim applications do not include group registrations such as a registration for a group of newsletters or group of automated database updates.

bots. *See* **spider**.

claimant. In the context of copyright law, the person who owns the copyright. The claimant may or may not be the author who created the copyrighted work.

collective work. In the context of copyright law, a work that includes a number of independent contributions. Many newspapers, magazines, and periodicals qualify as collective works because they contain numerous articles and materials from multiple authors.

compulsory license. A license that is established by law and that sets the fees and other terms for use of particular material. When a compulsory license is available, there is no need to acquire direct permission from or negotiate license terms with the owner of the material. Compulsory licenses offered through the Copyright Act include mechanical licenses for songs and licenses to perform a sound recording publicly via digital audio transmission. Also called *statutory license*.

crawlers. *See* **spider**.

criticism site. *See* **gripe site**.

cybersquatting. The registration of a domain name identical to or very similar to a well-known trademark with the intention of selling the domain name to the trademark owner or to someone else at a significant profit. One who engages in cybersquatting is a cybersquatter. Cybersquatting is a violation of trademark law. *Contrast* **domaining.**

deposit. For copyright registration purposes, a copy of the work in which you claim copyright. You submit a deposit with your copyright registration application.

derivative work. A new work based on or derived from another pre-existing work.

Digital Millennium Copyright Act. A federal law that amended the Copyright Act for the purposes of conforming United States law to various treaty obligations and addressing issues raised by emerging digital technologies.

domaining. The registration of a domain name with the intention of re-selling it for a profit. One who engages in domaining is often called a domainer. While both domainers and cybersquatters deal in domain names for profits, domaining can be legal if the domainer deals in generic words like fastcar.net and tool.com that do not mimic or infringe upon well-known brand names and trademarks. *Contrast* **cybersquatting.**

domain name system. A system administered by **ICANN** in which mnemonics are used for website addresses to eliminate the need to remember the string of numbers that comprise the **internet protocol address** for each website you want to visit.

download. Transferring a file from another computer to your computer. For the cyber citizen, to download usually means to transfer a file from the internet to the computer of the cyber citizen. Downloading does not actually *transfer* the same file. Instead, the download process produces a copy of the file and that copy is placed on the computer of the person requesting the download. *Contrast* **upload.**

ftp. For *file transfer protocol*. A method of exchanging files among computers. Commonly used by website operators to upload the pages of their website to the **web server**. While one method of using ftp includes entering commands on your computer, many cyber citizens use one of many commercial ftp programs that offer a more user-friendly graphical interface.

gripe site. A category of commentary website that offers negative opinions about a product, service, person, or organization. Also called *criticism site.*

homepage. The opening page or beginning page of a website that appears when you select the home button on a website. It is normally not necessary to enter a website from the homepage.

html. For *hypertext markup language.* One of the computer programs used to create webpages and websites.

hypertext markup language. *See* **html.**

ICANN. For *Internet Corporation for Assigned Names and Numbers.* A non-profit corporation that has oversight responsibility for the **domain name system.**

injunction. A court order that forbids a party from doing or continuing a particular action.

intellectual property. Creations of the mind such as literary and artistic works and inventions. Intellectual property is protected by copyright, trademark, patent, trade secret, and similar laws. Often abbreviated to *ip.*

Internet Corporation for Assigned Names and Numbers. *See* **ICANN.**

internet protocol address. A unique series of numbers associated with each computer. To avoid having to remember the numerical ip address for each website we want to visit, we use the **domain name system.** The internet protocol address is expressed as four groups of numbers separated by periods—such as 123.45.78.90. Often abbreviated to *ip address.*

ISP. For *internet service provider.* A company that provides internet connectivity to its customers.

Lanham Act. The federal law that governs trademark law. Each state has parallel laws that mirror the Lanham Act. Also called the *Trademark Act of 1946.*

LISTSERV. A registered trademark owned by the founder of L-Soft, a distributor of discussion forum software. Some people incorrectly use LISTSERV as a general term to refer to any discussion forum.

metatag. A keyword encoded into the **html** of a webpage and used by **search engines** for categorizing and indexing web pages.

non-exclusive. When used in the context of licensing, non-exclusive means that the rights owner may grant the same rights to multiple people.

office action. In the context of trademark registration and patent applications, a letter issued by the examiner indicating that there are questions or problems with the application that the applicant must answer or correct before processing of the application can continue.

peer-to-peer network. A computer infrastructure that enables sharing of computer files by making them available for other users to access and **download** onto their own computers.

performing rights organizations. In the music industry, the associations or organizations that issue and administer public performance music licenses. The performing rights organizations in the United States for songs are ASCAP, BMI, and SESAC. SoundExchange is a United States performing rights organization for sound recordings. Also called *performing rights societies* or *PROs*.

phonorecord. Any material object onto which sound can be recorded such as an audiocassette, a compact disc or a vinyl record.

prior art. In the context of patents, all information publicly available before a given date that may be relevant to a particular invention.

registrars. In the context of the **domain name system**, the intermediaries between the **registry** and those who register domain names. Registrars distribute domain names to registrants, maintain **WHOIS Database** information, and make changes to the registry on behalf of the registrants.

registry. The administrator of one or more **top level domains**. Also used as a reference to the actual listing of all the domain names that are registered and included within a top level domain.

search engine. A website that indexes information from other websites and that can be queried to locate information on the internet. Popular search engines include Google and Yahoo.

secondary meaning. In the context of trademark law, consumers' recognition of a trademark as the source identifier of a specific good or service.

server. A centralized computer that provides services for other computers connected to it via a network. For example, when you want to visit a particular website, your computer connects to the server hosting the website (called a **web server**) and requests the server to route pages from the website to your computer.

service mark. A trademark that identifies the source of a service as contrasted with a trademark that identifies the source of a good. The term trademark is often used as a reference to both trademarks (for goods) and service marks.

specimen. In the context of trademark registration, a real-world example of how a trademark is used on goods or in connection with the offering of services.

spider. A computer program that accesses websites, reads their information, and catalogs the information for **search engine** indexes and other applications.

statutory damages. In the context of a civil lawsuit, monetary damages determined by a formula or schedule in the law.

summary judgment. A court's determination in a lawsuit made without a trial (or at least without a full trial) and based solely on statements and evidence provided by the parties involved in the lawsuit.

TLD. *See* **top level domain**.

thread. A conversation comprised of multiple messages on a particular topic with the conversation taking place on a discussion forum, chat room, email, or other form of electronic conversation.

top level domain. The names at the top of the **domain name system** hierarchy. Top level domains include generic top level domains (gTLDs) like "com" and "net" and country code top level domains (ccTLDs) like "uk" for United Kingdom and "ca" for Canada. Often abbreviated to *TLD*.

uniform resource locator. The location for a website or other internet resource. As an example, www.thiswebsite.com is the uniform resource locator for a website. Also called *universal resource locator*. Abbreviated to *url*.

upload. Transferring a file from your computer to another computer. A cyber citizen who operates a website must upload his web pages to a **web server**. Uploading does not actually *transfer* the same file. Instead, the upload process produces a copy of the file and that copy is placed on the server. *Contrast* **download**.

url. *See* **uniform resource locator**.

web browser. A computer software program used to view pages on the **world wide web**. Internet Explorer and Firefox are popular web browsers. Some **ISP**s provide their own proprietary web browsers. To reach a specific website, you type the internet address or the **uniform resource locator** for that website into your web browser.

web host. A company that rents space on its **web server** to people who want to set up websites without maintaining their own web server.

web server. A type of **server** that hosts websites, serving pages to viewers upon request. Cyber citizens with websites can maintain their own web server or use the services of a **web host**.

WHOIS Database. A centrally maintained and publicly accessible database of contact information for all domain name registrants.

work made for hire. In the context of copyright law, a work prepared by an employee as part of his job or a work prepared by a freelancer under certain conditions. Copyright law views the employer or the person commissioning the work as the author of a work made for hire.

world wide web. A collection of interconnected documents accessible through the internet.

INDEX

ABOUT THE AUTHOR

Joy R. Butler is a transactional business lawyer. Her legal expertise includes copyrights, trademarks, commercial licensing, entertainment law, private equity financing, and mergers and acquisitions.

Ms. Butler is also the author of *The Permission Seeker's Guide Through the Legal Jungle: Clearing Copyrights, Trademarks and Other Rights for Entertainment and Media Productions*. She has a law degree from Harvard Law School and a B.A. degree in economics from Harvard College. Ms. Butler can be contacted through the website: www.joybutler.com